John M. Ashley, Thomas Aquinas

Cogitationes Concionales

being 216 short sermon reflections on the dominical Gospels of the Church's year -

founded upon selected readings from the Summa Theologica of S. Thomas Aquinas

John M. Ashley, Thomas Aquinas

Cogitationes Concionales
being 216 short sermon reflections on the dominical Gospels of the Church's year - founded upon selected readings from the Summa Theologica of S. Thomas Aquinas

ISBN/EAN: 9783337264628

Printed in Europe, USA, Canada, Australia, Japan

Cover: Foto ©Lupo / pixelio.de

More available books at **www.hansebooks.com**

THE CATHOLIC STANDARD LIBRARY.

A series of Standard Works, consisting of Foreign Translations, Original Works, and Reprints. Printed in the best style of the typographic art, demy 8vo, of from 450 to 500 pages, and issued at short intervals, price 12s. each volume, *post free to any part of the world;* twelve volumes may be selected for five guineas.

The Great Commentary on the Gospels of CORNELIUS À LAPIDE. Translated and Edited by the Rev. T. W. MOSSMAN, B.A., D.D., assisted by various Scholars.
  SS. Matthew and Mark's Gospels. 3 Vols. Fifth Edition.
  S. John's Gospel and Three Epistles. 2 Vols. Fourth Edition.
  S. Luke's Gospel. 1 Vol. Third Edition.
  The Six Vols. half calf, £5 5s.; or in whole calf extra, £6 6s.

Henry VIII. and the English Monasteries. An attempt to illustrate the History of their Suppression, with an Appendix and Maps showing the situation of the religious houses at the time of their dissolution. By FRANCIS AIDAN GASQUET, D.D., O.S.B. 2 Vols. *Fifth Edition.*

A Commentary on the Holy Gospels. By JOHN MALDONATUS, S.J. Translated and Edited from the original Latin by GEORGE J. DAVIE, M.A., Exeter College, Oxford, one of the Translators of the Library of the Fathers (*Vols. I. and II. St. Matthew's Gospel*).

Picinio (Bernardine à). Exposition of St. Paul's Epistles. Translated and Edited by A. H. PRICHARD, B.A., Merton College, Oxford. 3 Vols.

The History and Fate of Sacrilege. By Sir HENRY SPELMAN, Kt. Edited, in part from two MSS., revised and corrected. With a Continuation, large Additions, and an Introductory Essay. By Two Priests of the Church of England. Fourth Edition, with Additional Notes by Rev. S. J. EALES, D.C.L.

The Dark Ages: A Series of Essays illustrating the State of Religion and Literature in the Ninth, Tenth, Eleventh and Twelfth Centuries. By the late Dr. MAITLAND, Keeper of the MSS. at Lambeth. Fifth Edition, with an Introduction by FREDERICK STOKES, M.A.

Historical Portraits of the Tudor Dynasty, and the Reformation Period. By S. HUBERT BURKE. 4 Vols., demy 8vo. *Second Edition.*

Edward VI. and the Book of Common Prayer. Its origin illustrated by hitherto unpublished documents. With four facsimile pages of the MS. By FRANCIS AIDAN GASQUET, O.S.B., and EDMUND BISHOP. Third thousand.

History of the Popes, from the Close of the Middle Ages. By Professor Dr. L. PASTOR. Translated from the German. Edited by FREDERICK ANTROBUS of the London Oratory. *Vols. I. and II.*

The Relations of the Church to Society: A Series of Essays by EDMUND J. O'REILLY, S.J. Edited by the Rev. MATTHEW RUSSELL.

The Hierurgia; or, the Holy Sacrifice of the Mass. With Notes and Dissertations elucidating its doctrines and ceremonies. By Dr. DANIEL ROCK. 2 Vols. A new and thoroughly revised edition, with many new Illustrations. Edited, with a Preface, by W. H. JAMES WEALE.

The Complete Works of St. Bernard, Abbot of Clairvaux. Translated into English from the Edition of DOM. JOANNES MABILLON, of the Benedictine Congregation of St. Maur (Paris: 1690), and Edited by SAMUEL J. EALES, D.C.L., sometime Principal of St. Boniface College, Warminster. Vols. I. and II., the letters of St. Bernard. *Vol. III. in the Press.*

JOHN HODGES, BEDFORD STREET, STRAND, LONDON.

CATHOLIC STANDARD LIBRARY.

The following important Works are preparing, and will be published at short intervals during the coming season.

The Great Commentary of À LAPIDE. The Acts of the Apostles to Revelations, completing the New Testament. 4 Vols.

The Reformation in England: A Series of Essays, by the late Dr. MAITLAND, Keeper of the MSS. at Lambeth, Author of the "Dark Ages," etc.

This Vol. is being published at the special request of many renders of the "Dark Ages," to which work it is an admirable Supplement.

A History of the Somerset Carthusians. By MARGARET E. THOMPSON, of Frome and the Record Office.

This Vol. has 16 page Illustrations of Hinton Charter House, Witham Friary, &c., by the author's sister Miss L. B. THOMPSON, and will prove an interesting work to antiquarians, especially of Somersetshire and the West of England generally. *In the Press.*

The Complete Works of St. Bernard, Abbot of Clairvaux. Translated into English from the Edition of DOM. JOANNES MABILLON, of the Benedictine Congregation of St. Maur (Paris, 1690), and Edited by SAMUEL J. EALES, D.C.L., Vicar of Stalisfield. *Vol. III, containing with other Sermons a Course for the Christian Year, in the Press.*

A Complete Manual of Canon Law. Edited by OSWALD J. REICHEL, M.A., B.C.L., F.S.A., &c., sometime Vice-principal of Cuddesdon College. *In the Press.*

The Life of St. Jerome. By Fr. JOSEPHS of Siquenza. Translated from the Spanish by MARIANA MONTEIRO, Author of "Basque Legends," "Life of Columbus," "History of Portugal," etc.

The Benedictine Calendar. By DOM. EGIDIUS RANBECK, O.S.B. This remarkable work was first published in 1677, at the cost of the great Bavarian Monastery in Augsburg. The Life of a Benedictine Saint is given for every day in the year. The great merit of the work, however, consists in the beautiful Engravings, which illustrate the lives. In the New Edition these Engravings have been most effectively reproduced by the Meisenbach Process, and the accompanying Lives, which will be adaptations rather than translations of the originals, will be edited by a Father of the English Benedictine Congregation, and translated from the Latin by Professor MOHOLAN, M.A., of Dowside College. 4 Vols. *Vol. I. in the Press.*

The Church of the Fathers, as seen in St. Osmond's rite for the Cathedral of Salisbury a New and Revised Edition. By the Benedictines of Dowside. 4 Vols.

Cogitationes Concionales. Being 216 short Sermon Reflections on the Gospels for the Church's Year, founded upon Selected Readings from the "Summa Theologica" of S. THOMAS AQUINAS. By JOHN M. ASHLEY, B.C.L., Rector of Fewston, author of "The Promptuary for Preachers," &c. &c.

Aurea Legenda: *Alias* Historia Lombardica : being a Collection of Lives of the Saints. By JACOBUS DE VORAGINE, Archbishop of Genoa. Translated and Edited by the Rev. S. J. EALES, D.C.L., Vicar of Stalisfield.

This was one of the earliest works printed by WILLIAM CAXTON. He translated it into English by the Command of William Earl of Arundel. His edition was printed at the Westminster Press in 1483.

Simpson's Life of Edmund Campion. This valuable Book having been out of print many years, has become very scarce, second hand copies when met with realising fancy prices, it is now reprinted from a corrected copy, made by the learned Author for a new edition before his death. *In the Press.*

JOHN HODGES, BEDFORD STREET, STRAND, LONDON.

Catholic Standard Library

COGITATIONES CONCIONALES

BY THE SAME AUTHOR.

A Promptuary for Preachers. Vol. I, Advent to Ascension-day containing 338 Sermons Epitomized from the Latin, 12*s.* Vol. II Ascension-day to Advent, containing 350 Sermons Epitomized from the Latin, 12*s.*

A Year with Great Preachers. Vol. I. Advent to Whitsuntide, 5*s.* Vol. II, Whitsuntide to Advent, 5*s.* Festivals, 6*s.*

Eucharistic Sermons by Great Preachers, 5*s.*

The Homilies of S. Thomas Aquinas. Sunday and Festival. Second Edition, 4*s.* 6*d.*

Commentary of S. Thomas Aquinas upon the Epistle to the EPHESIANS. Part I, 6*d.*

The Relations of Science, 6*s.*

Thirteen Sermons from the Quaresimale of Quirico Rossi, 3*s.*

The Victory of the Spirit, 2*s.*

Holy Counsel. A Meditation upon the very words of Holy Scripture, 4*d.*

S. Augustine the Preacher. FIFTY SHORT SERMON NOTES founded upon Select Passages from his Writings, 5*s.*

Origen the Preacher. FIFTY SHORT SERMON NOTES founded upon Select Passages from his Writings, 6*s.*

The Preparation for Death. From the Italian, with a Preface, 3*s.*

The Spiritual Exercises of S. Ignatius. From the Latin, with a Preface on Meditations, 3*s.*

The Battle of Senlac, and other Poems, 6*s.*

The Pulpit Lectionary. Part I, 5*s.*

Lisa: a POEM, 6*d.*

The Burial of Polynices: a POEM, 6*d.*

COGITATIONES CONCIONALES

BEING

Two Hundred and Sixteen

SHORT SERMON REFLECTIONS ON THE DOMINICAL GOSPELS OF THE CHURCH'S YEAR

FOUNDED UPON SELECTED READINGS FROM THE

SUMMA THEOLOGICA

OF

S. THOMAS AQUINAS

BY

JOHN M. ASHLEY B.C.L.

VICAR OF FEWSTON AND FORMERLY INCUMBENT OF S. PETER'S VERE STREET

Author of "The Promptuary for Preachers"
etc. etc.

JOHN HODGES
BEDFORD STREET STRAND LONDON

MDCCCXCV

DRYDEN PRESS:
J. DAVY AND SONS, 137, LONG ACRE, LONDON.

PREFACE.

—o—

THE Sermon Thoughts contained in the following pages have been put together with a four-fold object :

I. To supply the material upon which may be formed four sermons for each Sunday upon the Holy Gospels of the Church's year. It is believed that an extempore preacher of slight practice, and ordinary ability, could easily commit to memory one entire sermon-subject in about a quarter-of-an-hour ; and that going into the pulpit thus prepared—unhampered by notes, which are a real stumbling-block to anything like effective preaching—he would probably find that on the expiration of his sermon he had not nearly exhausted all the subject-matter with which he was previously furnished. During its delivery, many new thoughts would have suggested themselves to his mind, and the sermon would thus acquire an originality which would stamp it with the individual characteristics of his own mind. The more these outlines are worked out, the easier will they become for him to use ; and the more suggestive, and capable of expansion, will they prove themselves to be.

II. To form the groundwork and foundation of instruction to be given at Bible Classes, whether holden in Guilds or in Sunday Schools. The Concordance will enable the several "Preludes" to be verified by an appeal to Holy Scripture. Of course, when applied to such a use, every proposition and head contained in the notes must be thrown into the form of an interrogation.

III. To become a manual of private devotion, as furnishing many subjects for spiritual meditation which exercise must become a daily habit, if the life of God the Holy Ghost is to be nurtured and fostered in the soul.

IV. To direct the minds of the younger clergy especially, to the earnest and diligent study of the "*Summa*" itself, which is in itself a complete theological library. This stupendous work may at the first glance appear to be somewhat hard and repelling; but the love of it will grow with constant use; and its vast knowledge, depth, spirituality, power and sweetness will become very dear to the student, and its almost infinite treasures unfold themselves to him one by one.

May all that has been collected in the following pages tend, not only to further and to extend the teaching of, and to awaken a fresh interest in this the greatest work of the "Mighty Dominican;" the "Angelical Doctor," of the greatest spiritual thinker of the Middle Ages, but in some degree contribute also to the rebuilding of the Church of Jesus—in this our land of England—in Her old faith, to Her regaining some portion, at least, of Her lost inheritance; to the leading of some of Her sons and daughters back again to "the old paths;" and by so doing humbly, though unworthy, minister by the salvation of souls to "The Greater Glory of God."

INDEX

TO THE REFERENCES TO THE "SUMMA"

which will be found in the following Sermons.

1^a signifies the First Part,
12^e signifies the First Part of the Second Part.
22^e signifies the Second Part of the Second Part.
3^a signifies the Third Part.
The First Figures after the Parts denote the Questions.
The Second Figures after the Parts denote the Articles.
o stands for the whole Article.
c stands for the body of the Article.
The Figures following as 1, 2, 3, &c., represent the Arguments against the Proposition in the Article.
The Figures written 1^m, 2^m, 3^m, &c., signify the Answers to the several Arguments.

EXAMPLES.

Sermon 1. *Summa*, 3^a, 36, 1 c.—explains that the passage is taken from the Third *Part;* the Thirty-sixth *Question;* the First Argument; the body of the Article.

Sermon 137. 22^e, 158, 3, 2^m—which show that the sermon is taken from the Second Part of the Second Part; from the Hundred and Fifty-eighth Question; from the Third Article; from the Answer to the Second Argument.

NOTE.—The Summa Theologica contains 512 Questions; 2,536 Articles.

Allowing only Four Propositions for and against, in each Article (while some contain as many as Nine), the total number of Arguments will amount to 20,443.

BIOGRAPHICAL NOTICE OF S. THOMAS AQUINAS.

A.D.	
1226.	Born at the Castle of Aquin, a small village in the Kingdom of Naples, in the 9th and last year of the Pontificate of Innocent III, and 10th year of the reign of Henry III, of noble Sicilian parents.
1231-36.	Educated in the Monastery on Monte Casino, of which his uncle was Abbot.
1243.	Studied philosophy and letters at Naples, where he joined the order of S. Dominic.
1245.	Went to Paris with the General of his order; thence to Cologne as a pupil to Albert the Great. Being very studious and thoughtful he was so taciturn that his fellow pupils called him "Dumb Ox." Albert, on hearing this, said that "The learned bellowings of this 'Dumb Ox' would resound one day throughout the universe."
1246.	Accompanied Albert the Great to Paris, where he had been appointed "Master of the Sentences."
1248.	Returned to Cologne to teach philosophy, Holy Scripture, "The Sentences."
1257.	Doctor of Philosophy. Joined Albert the Great and S. Bonaventura at Agnani. Clement IV offered him the Archbishopric of Naples, which he refused.
1272.	At Naples with the Chaplain General of his order.
1274.	In company with Gregory Xth was present at the Council of Lyons, and in the same year he died, aged 48, on the 7th of March, of a fever caught in going to Rome, at Terracina, a town on the south side of the Pontine Marshes, being carried into the Monastery of Forsanova to breathe his last.
1313.	Canonized by John XXII.
1570.	Great Roman edition of his works in eighteen folio volumes.

INDEX TO SERMONS.

Advent Sunday.

1. The Unknown Advent.
2. Why the Advent Comes.
3. The Advent of the World's Youth.
4. The Leading to Glory.

Second Sunday in Advent.

5. The Last Judgment.
6. Recording Angels.
7. The Forms of Antichrist.
8. Our Redemption.

Third Sunday in Advent.

9. The Felt Presence.
10. The Law of Christ.
11. Baptismal Teaching.
12. On Dress.

Fourth Sunday in Advent.

13. Alone.
14. Curiosity.
15. Self-knowledge the Parent of Humility.
16. The Bridle of Humility.

Sunday after Christmas-day.

17. The Purity of the Incarnation.
18. The Old made New.
19. The Work of the Incarnation.
20. The World's Sin.

First Sunday after the Epiphany.

21. Ceremonies.
22. The Lord's Day no Sabbath.
23. Obedience to Parents.
24. Experimental Knowledge.

Second Sunday after the Epiphany.

25. The Hour of Jesus.
26. The Phases of Faith.
27. Doing our Best.
28. The Instrumental Soul.

Third Sunday after the Epiphany.

29. Leprosy a Type of Sin.
30. The Adoration of Jesus.
31. The Higher Law.
32. The Worthy Communicant.

Fourth Sunday after the Epiphany.

33. Why the Righteous Suffer.
34. The Agony of Repentance.
35. The Demon of Sin.
36. Restraining Power.

Fifth Sunday after the Epiphany.

37. The Office of Preacher.
38. Open Sinners are to be Shunned.
39. The Servants of God.
40. The Harvest of the Final Judgment.

Sixth Sunday after the Epiphany.

41. The Trials of the Elect.
42. The Critical Moment.
43. The Foundation of Belief.
44. Man and Nature.

Septuagesima Sunday.

45. The Justice of God.
46. The Power of Working.
47. God's Wages.
48. God Glorified in Man's Work.

Sexagesima Sunday.

49. Preaching is Feeding.
50. Preaching is Defence.
51. Preaching the Instrument of Souls.
52. Preaching an Offering of Souls.

Quinquagesima Sunday.

53. The Universal Saviour.
54. The Abundant Love of Jesus Christ.
55. The Greater Love of Jesus Christ.
56. The Perfect Love of Jesus Christ.

First Sunday in Lent.

57. Jesus Tempted our Help.
58. Jesus Tempted our Caution.
59. Jesus Tempted our Example.
60. Jesus Tempted our Confidence.

Second Sunday in Lent.

61. Perseverance.
62. The Power of Mercy.
63. Prayer for Temporal Blessings.
64. The Greater Faith.

Third Sunday in Lent.

65. Jesus a Thought-reader.
66. Concord.
67. The Strong Man of Sin.
68. My House.

Fourth Sunday in Lent.

69. God's Proving.
70. The Christian Passover.
71. Benevolence.
72. Use of Means.

Fifth Sunday in Lent.

73. The Good Conscience.
74. Vain Glory.
75. The River of Sin.
76. The Faithful Preacher.

Sunday next before Easter.

77. The Tribunal of the Cross.
78. The Lord's Last Lesson.
79. The Power of the Cross.
80. From Death to Life.

Easter Day.

81. The Love of the Risen Lord.
82. The Law of Mediation.
83. The Power of the Resurrection.
84. The Need of the Resurrection.

First Sunday after Easter.

85. The Blessing of Peace.
86. The Penalties of Sin.
87. Reality.
88. The Record of Patience.

Second Sunday after Easter.

89. The Good Shepherd the Door of His Church.
90. Jesus the Shepherd of the Blessed.
91. Jesus the Shepherd of those Without.
92. Jesus the Shepherd of those Loving.

Third Sunday after Easter.

93. Preachers and Hearers.
94. Inward Joy.
95. The Sorrow of the World.
96. The Vision of Jesus.

Fourth Sunday after Easter.

97. Loss and Gain.
98. Needful Truth.
99. The Invisible Mission.
100. The Visible Mission.

Fifth Sunday after Easter.

101. The Power of Prayer.
102. Unanswered Prayer.
103. The Union of Love.
104. Intercessory Prayer.

Sunday after the Ascension.

105. The Obscured Soul.
106. Not Knowing,
107. The Doors of Knowledge.
108. The Eternity of Memory.

Whitsunday.

109. Obedience the Foundation of Love.
110. The Holy Ghost the Giver of Gifts.
111. The Holy Ghost-Wind.
112. The Holy Ghost-Love.

Trinity Sunday.

113. The Baptism of Infants.
114. The Miracles of Jesus.
115. The Procession of the Sacred Three.
116. Assimilation with God.

First Sunday after Trinity.

117. Mental Vision.
118. The Guardian Angel.
119. The Ministry of Angels.
120. Death a Foretaste.

Second Sunday after Trinity.

121. The Catholic Church.
122. The Anger of God.
123. The Passion of Jesus, the Supper of the Lord.
124. Blessedness.

Third Sunday after Trinity.

125. Use and Abuse.
126. The Love of Jesus for Sinners.
127. Lost Innocence.
128. Joy over the Penitent.

Fourth Sunday after Trinity.

129. Liberality.
130. Money.
131. Lost Power.
132. The Grounds of Mercy.

Fifth Sunday after Trinity.

133. Reverence.
134. The Seat of Faith.
135. Industry.
136. Affected Ignorance.

Sixth Sunday after Trinity.

137. Unholy Anger.
138. To Do Good.
139. Declining from Evil.
140. The New Law.

Seventh Sunday after Trinity.

141. Obedience.
142. Abstinence.
143. Fortitude.
144. The Needs of the Body.

Eighth Sunday after Trinity.

145. Ordination.
146. Association with Nonconformists.
147. False Prophets, Ravening Wolves.
148. False Prophets and Holy Scripture.

Ninth Sunday after Trinity.

149. Worldly Prudence.
150. Possessions.
151. Holding one's own.
152. Why one begs and another abounds.

Tenth Sunday after Trinity.

153. The Teaching of Jesus.
154. The Power of Ceremony.
155. The Desolation of the Lost.
156. The House of Prayer.

Eleventh Sunday after Trinity.

157. Presuming upon God.
158. Presumptuous Speech.
159. Self-Presumption.
160. The Higher Rule.

Twelfth Sunday after Trinity.

161. The Church a Witness to the Truth.
162. Sacraments, the Mediation of the Body.
163. Modesty.
164. The Recompense of Gratitude.

Thirteenth Sunday after Trinity.

165. Love is Expansive.
166. The Passions of the Sinless Man.
167. The Sin of the First Man.
168. The Wounds of Sin.

Fourteenth Sunday after Trinity.

169. Jesus, a Name Old and New.
170. Bodily Adoration.
171. Priestly Absolution.
172. Baptism into Death.

Fifteenth Sunday after Trinity.

173. Hatred of God.
174. Our Master an ultimate End.
175. Solicitude.
176. The Need of Prayer.

Sixteenth Sunday after Trinity.

177. God's Punishment.
178. Sympathy.
179. The Soul after Death.
180. Perfection.

Seventeenth Sunday after Trinity.

181. The Outward Christian Life.
182. Four Fruits of Pride.
183. Ambition.
184. The Way of Humility.

Eighteenth Sunday after Trinity.

185. Controversy.
186. Love the First and Great Commandment.
187. The Love of God.
188. Dissimilation.

Nineteenth Sunday after Trinity.

189. The Lessons of the Body.
190. What we can do for God.
191. What Jesus Knows.
192. Contrition.

Twentieth Sunday after Trinity.

193. The Glorification of Life.
194. The Act of Conscience.
195. The Freedom of the Will.
196. Ingratitude.

Twenty-first Sunday after Trinity.

197. Actual Sin.
198. God's Ordering.
199. Miracles.
200. Faith in the Incarnation.

Twenty-second Sunday after Trinity.

201. The Liability of Eternal Death.
202. The Compassion of God.
203. The Burden of Sin.
204. The Sinner Suffers Alone.

Twenty-third Sunday after Trinity.

205. Truth in Life.
206. Hypocrisy.
207. Religion.
208. Obedience to Rulers.

Twenty-fourth Sunday after Trinity.

209. Knowledge the Parent of Desire.
210. Four-fold Salvation.
211. Death the Fruit of Rebellion.
212. The Light of Faith.

Twenty-fifth Sunday after Trinity.

213. Increase.
214. Prayer a Consecration.
215. The Holy Eucharist, Spiritual Food.
216. The Holy Eucharist, Jesus Wholly.

Advent Sunday.

SERMON 1.
THE UNKNOWN ADVENT.
(Holy Gospel, Ser. 1).

(1). S. Matt. xxi. 5 : "Behold, thy King cometh unto thee."
(2). S. John i. 26 : "There standeth one among you whom ye know not."

Summa, 3^a, 36, 1 c. : Had His first Advent been known (1) "That human redemption, which was wrought out upon the cross, would have been hindered; for 'had they known it' &c. (1. Cor. ii. 8). (2) The merit of the faith by which He had come to justify men, would have been diminished; 'the righteousness of faith by Jesus' (Rom. iii. 22). (3) The truth of His human nature would have come into doubt."

Prelude 1. The Prophet Zechariah's words (ix. 9) applied by S. Matt.; were ill understood by the people. Their cry of Hosannah was but an impulse.

—— 2. To the world at large his advent was practically unknown.

—— 3. Yet this was the world's greatest event; it was heaven come down to earth.

—— 4. It changed the condition of the world for evermore.

—— 5. Greatest discoveries, &c., often unknown at the time.

—— 6. Reasons why the Advent should be unknown, given above.

—— 7. The coming of the King to the soul, is after a like manner; hidden as to the

I. TIME, when it comes; in youth, maturity, or old age.
II. How, the manner of its coming. In sacrament, prayer, sorrow, &c.
III. WHERE, in church, at home, abroad, in daily life.
IV. WHAT, it was like, when it came, as an inspiration or a conviction.

Epil.—May its effects slowly perceived, bring forth much fruit unto righteousness

Advent Sunday.
SERMON 2.
WHY THE ADVENT COMES.
(*Holy Gospel, Ser.* 2).

(1). S. Matt. xxi. 5 : "Behold, thy King cometh unto thee."
(2). 1. Tim. i. 15 : "Christ Jesus came into the world to save sinners."

Summa, 3ª, 36, 1, 3ᵐ. " His First Advent was for the salvation of all men, which is by faith ; which is concerned indeed with things not seen (Heb. xi. 1). 'God sent not His Son into the world to condemn the world' (S. John iii. 23). 'Therefore at His First Advent He remits sins ; for if He had not so done all would have perished and come short of the glory of God' (Rom. iii. 23)."

Prelude 1. Pardon, and hope, sound the key-note of Advent tide.

—— 2. The order is inverted, the King comes to us instead of our going to Him.

—— 3. We never could have gone to Him, had He not first come to us.

—— 4. His outward advent in the flesh, is a pledge and a prophecy of His inward coming to us in the Spirit.

—— 5. Jesus comes to us with a pardon which is full, free, and perfect ; in the act of

I. REPENTANCE, penitence draws Jesus to the soul by sympathy.

II. PRAYER, a drawing nigh to Him, in which He reveals Himself to us.

III. WORSHIP and adoration, in which we spiritually fall down before Him.

IV. SACRAMENT, "He was known to them in breaking of bread" (S. Luke xxiv. 35).

Epil.—May this Advent be a time of refreshing from the presence of the Lord ; a feast as well as a fast to the souls; our preparation with pure hearts to welcome our King when He comes to us on Christmas Day.

Advent Sunday.

SERMON 3.

THE ADVENT OF THE WORLD'S YOUTH.
(Holy Gospel, Ser. 3).

(1). S. Matt. xxi. 5: "Behold, thy King cometh unto thee."
(2). Habakkuk iii. 2: "O Lord, revive Thy work in the midst of the years."

Summa, 3^a, 1, 6, 1^m. Augustine says (Retract lib. 1. c. 26) That the time of the First Advent, or the Incarnation, can be compared to the youth of the human race, on account of its vigour and its fervour of faith; which faith works by love (Gal. v. 6) and to the old age of the world, in which "He appeared to put away sin by the sacrifice of Himself" (Heb. ix. 26). Though the body cannot at the same time be both old and young, yet these two states can co-exist in the mind, the former, by its alacrity; the latter, by its gravity.

Prelude 1. The Advent came in the world's youth, a state too young for it to recognize its full value.

────── 2. But not in an age too old to profit by its grace.

────── 3. In the world's youth was His First Advent made in the season of

I. STRENGTH and energy, when powers are as yet fresh and vigorous.

II. TENDERNESS, when the soul is open to receive first and lasting impressions.

III. OPPORTUNITY, before the days come in which things spiritual have lost the savour of their action on the heart.

IV. LONGING, for a better, brighter, holier, and happier future.

Epil.— Dedicate your spring-tide to the Lord, to reap in time the Spirit's fruits.

Advent Sunday.

SERMON 4.

THE LEADING TO GLORY.
(*Holy Gospel, Ser.* 4).

(1). S. Matt. XXI. 9 : " The multitudes that went before and that followed after cried."
(2). Heb. II. 10 : " Bringing many sons unto Glory."
Summa, 3ª, 45, 3 c. : " Men are led by Christ to the glory of eternal beatitude ; not only those who were after Him, but those also who went before Him. Whence, He hastening to His passion, the multitudes who were following, as well as those who were preceding him, shouted ' Hosanna ' to Him as if seeking salvation from Him."
Prelude 1. Under both dispensations all are led to glory by Him.
——— 2. There is a divine power in the presence of Jesus whether in the flesh or in the spirit. He drew men to Him when on earth, and afterwards for as He said " And I if I be lifted up," &c.
——— 3. The end of the means of grace is to draw souls to Jesus and to unite them to Himself in His body, which is the Church.
——— 4. We, the children of the Church, follow after, to enter into the Glory of his finished work. We must follow Him through
I. TRIAL, "after ye have suffered awhile make you perfect," &c.
II. FAITH, realizing the mysteries of grace by their outward signs and symbols.
III. PATIENCE, " Let patience have her perfect work," &c.
IV. SIN and SORROW, "after much tribulation enter into," &c.
Epil.—Follow then O Christian soul in the footsteps of thy Holy Lord, and He will lead thee into the green pastures beside the water of Life.

Second Sunday in Advent.

SERMON 5.
THE LAST JUDGMENT.
(Holy Gospel, Ser. 1).

(1). S. Luke XXI. 27: "They shall see the Son of man coming in a cloud with power," &c.

(2). Heb. IX. 27: "It is appointed unto men once to die, but after this the judgment."

Summa, 3^a, 59, 5 c.: "The judgment upon anything mutable cannot be given till its consummation; so upon any action as to itself and its effects; for many actions seem to be useful which prove to be harmful by their effects. So it is with regard to man, no judgment can be perfectly given until his life is ended; since he may, before this event happen, be changed from good to bad, or conversely so."

Prelude 1. Man is ever changing or liable to change during life.

—— 2. Man can only be perfectly judged in his fixed and eternal state.

—— 3. Time and life often lead to repentance and amendment.

—— 4. In mercy and love the judgment is delayed till the end of time.

—— 5. At the last day, when man will be perfectly judged, this judgment will be,

I. ONE and only one, expressing the sum of life's thoughts, words and deeds.

II. FINAL, its decree working through all eternity.

III. PERFECT, founded upon a perfect knowledge of the whole life.

IV. JUST, because the Judge is holy, just, and true, and knows all things.

Epil.—Prepare for this last Judgment by a life of holiness. Judge yourselves now that ye be not judged of the Lord. Never forget that an account of your life must be rendered.

Second Sunday in Advent.
SERMON 6.
RECORDING ANGELS.
(Holy Gospel, Ser. 2).

(1). S. Luke XXI. 27: "They shall see the Son of man coming with great glory," &c.
(2). S. Matt. XIII. 49: "The angels shall come forth and sever the wicked from among the just.
Summa, 1ª, 113, 7, 4'''.: "The angels are led into the judgment for the sins of men; not as being themselves guilty, but as witnesses for convicting men of their sloth."
Prelude 1. The Lord elsewhere (S. Luke ix. 26) tells us that this glory is His own, is His Father's and that of the Holy Angels.
—— 2. The Holy Angels will witness for, or against man at the judgment.
—— 3. "Now, they are our helpers, then, they will be our excusers, or accusers."
—— 4. S. Greg. Nyss. Orat. ii: "The angels are the spectators of our lives." Theophyl. "The observers of our actions."
—— 5. Theophyl. in Matt. xviii: "Angels are the commissioners of men."
Conceive of one who cannot forget, never leaving us, recording our daily,
I. THOUGHTS, which we foolishly imagine to be known only to ourselves, our daily longings, imaginings, our most secret hopes and fears.
II. WORDS, often spoken in the temper, haste, unkindness, and untruth, words which our reflective and better nature would never suffer us to utter.
III. DEEDS, committed in thoughtlessness, petulance, and indolence.
IV. EVENTS, the combined action of all three, as operating for only one day; extend the thought of their combined operation during life.
Epil.—All these, are beyond our recall; O Lord," set a watch, &c.

Second Sunday in Advent.

SERMON 7.

THE FORMS OF ANTICHRIST.
(*Holy Gospel*, Ser. 3).

(1). S. Luke XXI. 25, 26: "Upon the earth distress of nations," &c.

(2). II. Thess. II. 3: "That man of sin; the son of perdition."

Summa, 3^a, 8, 8, c.: "As in Christ dwelt all the fulness of divinity, so in Antichrist dwelt all the fulness of evil; not that the humanity of it was assumed by the devil in unity of person, as the humanity of Christ was assumed by the Son of God, but because the devil by suggesting, insinuated into Antichrist his evil, more eminently than into others. All the wicked who preceded him were figures of Antichrist."

Prelude 1. S. Paul teaches that Antichrist (II Thess. ii. 1-13) shall precede the second coming of the Lord; and will have full power for a time.

——— 2. Antichrist is a parody, a mockery of Christ.

——— 3. Antichrist will be the cause of the earth's distress and perplexity.

——— 4. Antichrist, the mystery of iniquity doth already work (II Thess. ii. 7), but his power is for the present checked or hindered. Some of the forms of antichrist are,

I. HERESY, choosing some portions of the faith and rejecting others. Heresies are the touchstones of the church. They manifest the truth.

II. SCHISM, the dividing of, and separation from the one Catholic Church.

III. SPIRITUAL PRIDE, by which sin the angels fell.

IV. WILFUL IGNORANCE, which engenders willing sin.

Epil.—Seek safety and protection in the Ark of the Church.

Second Sunday in Advent.

SERMON 8.

OUR REDEMPTION.

(*Holy Gospel, Ser.* 4).

(1). S. Luke XXI. 28 : " Your redemption draweth nigh."

(2). Ephes. IV. 30 : " Sealed unto the day of redemption."

Summa, 3^a, 48, 5, c. : " Redemption, implies an act of redemption, together with the price paid for it. The price of our redemption is the blood of Christ, which He Himself paid when He gave up His own life for the redemption of all."

Prelude 1. Theophyl. in loco : " Out of the terror of signs in the sun, &c., distress, perplexity, failing hearts and the glory of the Second Advent ' your redemption ' is the consummation of your freedom, both of mind and body."

——— 2. Euseb. Emissenus : "As the First Advent of the Lord was for the reformation of our souls : so the Second Advent will be for the reformation of our bodies."

——— 3. In life's hour of darkness, temptation and sin, the application of Christ's redemption—pardon through the Precious Blood, delivers the soul on its,

I. AWAKENING, from the lethargy of sin, the soul needs some reviving power. In its very weakness it is insufficient for itself.

II. CONTRITION, in sorrow and agony for an irrevocable past, not to be condoned but by a mighty redemption.

III. FEARS, deep and intense of a coming death and judgment.

IV. DESPAIR, of obtaining mercy at the last great day.

Epil.—The power of redeeming love pours oil on the troubled waters of the soul.

Third Sunday in Advent.

SERMON 9.

THE FELT PRESENCE.

(*Holy Gospel, Ser.* 1).

(1). S. Matt. XI. 3: "Art thou He that should come?"
(2). I. Cor. XIV. 25: "He will worship God and report that God is in you."
Summa, 22^e, 2, 7, 2^m.: "John the Baptist did not question the Advent of Christ in the flesh as if he was ignorant of it. He expressedly confessed it saying: 'I saw and bare record that this is the Son of God' (S. John i. 34). He foretold also His immolation as an event about to happen. 'Behold the Lamb of God' (S. John i. 29)."

Prelude 1. For the sake of His disciples John sent and asked the question: "Art thou He?"

——— 2. John ever bore a noble testimony to the divinity of the Lord.

——— 3. John knew the Lord, not by knowledge only, or by faith only, but by a kind of feeling or intuition, which also taught him the immeasurable distance which separated him from the Lord.

——— 4. This feeling in spiritual things is a kind of inspiration.

——— 5. It is magnetic drawing the soul by a tie which is beyond analysis.

——— 6. All the saints have acknowledged this felt presence, which brings spiritual persons and things before the soul, and makes them to it,

I. NEAR, as forming a part of our higher spiritual nature.
II. CLEAR, dispelling all the clouds of error, doubt and unreality.
III. REAL, not as abstract truths, but as factors in a new life.
IV. DEAR, forming an integral part of our better and higher selves.

Epil.—The Holy Eucharist nourishes this felt, this sacramental presence.

Third Sunday in Advent.

SERMON 10.

THE LAW OF CHRIST.
(*Holy Gospel, Ser.* 2).

(1). S. Matt. XI. 9: "A prophet? yea, I say unto you, and more than a prophet."

(2). Gal. VI. 2: "Fulfil the law of Christ."

Summa, 3^a, 38, 1, 2^m.: "For he [John] was the end of the Law and the beginning of the Gospel; and therefore it the more pertained to him to lead men both by word and deed to the law of Christ rather than to the observance of the old law."

Prelude 1. "The law of Christ;" its code is in the Gospels; its illustration in Himself.

—— 2. It is our guide to glory: He said "I am the way."

—— 3. It is our help upon earth, both by precept and promise.

—— 4. It is our great teacher. "He taught as one having authority." This law of Christ is a law which is,

I. SPIRITUAL, reaching to the depths of our inner life and nature, placing the inward man of the heart, before the outward man of the body.

II. LIVING, it embodies the life of Jesus as it is embodied in His Church, bringing forth living fruits for life everlasting.

III. QUICKENING, making others partakers of its life, so that the life of Christ may be manifested in our mortal bodies.

IV. SATISFYING, ministering fully to the soul's needs.

V. LOVING, "Love one another, all are members of one body: Bear ye one another's burdens and so fufil the law of Christ" (Gal. VI. 2).

Epil.—Follow this 'Law of Christ' obediently, humbly, faithfully.

Third Sunday in Advent.

SERMON II.

BAPTISMAL TEACHING.
(*Holy Gospel, Ser.* 3).

(1). S. Matt. XI. 10: "I send my messenger which shall prepare thy way."

(2). I. S. Pet. III. 21: "Baptism doth also now save us."

Summa, 3^a, 38, 3, c.: "The baptism of John did not confer grace, but only in a threefold manner prepared men for the reception of grace. By teaching it led men to the faith of Christ; it accustomed them to the rite of baptism; it prepared them by repentance to receive the baptism of Christ."

Prelude 1. The keynote of S. John's teaching was penitence and baptism. Acts ii. 38: "Repent and be baptized." S. Matt. iii. 11: "I baptize with water unto repentance."

—— 2. The initial sacrament of baptism disposed the soul to the reception of all sacramental grace.

—— 3. The sacraments and grace work together for salvation.

—— 4. From the lesser we rise to the higher sacramental teaching.

—— 5. S. John by holy baptism opened the door of the kingdom of heaven. S. John by his baptizings,

I. TAUGHT, the need of baptism and the benefits thereof.

II. ACCUSTOMED, men to its use. So we become used to the Holy Communion.

III. PREPARED, men by penitence for its reception.

IV. INDUCED, or led men to it by his practice, which is before precept.

Epil.—Penitence; reception of spiritual truth; right faith and morals all concentrate themselves around the sacraments of the church.

Third Sunday in Advent.

SERMON 12.
ON DRESS.
(Holy Gospel, Ser. 4).

(1). S. Matt. xi. 8 : "A man clothed in soft raiment."

(2). 1. S. Pet. iii. 3 : "Whose adorning let it not be the putting on of apparel."

Summa, 22^e, 169, 2, c, 3^m, 4^m. : "The adornments of women for pleasing their husbands may be used without sin (1. Cor. vii. 33), but they should be such as belong to the condition of the person using them; their comeliness agreeing with their state; but when they are used for vanity, they are not devoid of sin."

Prelude 1. A neatly dressed man or woman, is a pleasant, comely sight.

——— 2. It denotes a due care for the opinion of others, and a certain amount of self-respect. Finery is one thing, neatness in dress is another.

——— 3. Slovenly dress points usually to a slovenly mind.

——— 4. The "simplex munditiis elegantly neat" of the Poet contains the true theory of dress. Our dress should therefore be,

I. SUITABLE, to the wearer's means and condition of life, so that dress like speech and manners may indicate the rank of the wearer.

II. ADAPTED, to the wearer's use, figure, requirements as to seasons, occupation or pursuit at a particular time. The Church has her sacred vestments.

III. COMELY, since God made our bodies comely in proportion and form.

IV. MODEST, so as not, as the heathen dressed, to lead to temptation and sin.

Epil.—In dress as in other things we can study God's glory, the pleasure of others, and our own comfort.

Fourth Sunday in Advent.
SERMON 13.
ALONE.
(Holy Gospel, Ser. 1).

(1). S. John I. 23: "I am the voice of one crying in the wilderness."

(2). S. John VI. 15: "He departed into a mountain Himself alone."

Summa, 22^e, 188, 8, c, 5^m.: "Solitude agrees with one musing who has already come to perfection. John the Baptist partook of it as of a divine gift and he who was filled with the Holy Ghost from his boyhood was nourished by it (S. Luke i. 80). Solitude is of two kinds, that of the one whose evil soul renders him unable to bear human society; that of the other, who wholly cleaves to divine things, and this kind of solitude is above man. The Philosopher says (Arist. Polit.) that he who does not associate with others is either a beast or a God, *i.e.* a divine man."

Prelude 1. S. John Baptist was a solitary, in boyhood, manhood and in death.

——— 2. His was solitude of body, the higher solitude that of mind. "My God! My God why hast Thou forsaken Me?" S. Paul: "I have no man like minded."

——— 3. Scipio Africanus said: "Nor less alone than when alone" (Cio. De Off. iii. 1).

——— 4. John was austere, active, humble, truthful and prophetic. Alone in his,

I. LIFE, in the desert, coming only at intervals to the haunts of men.

II. STANDING, at the end of the law, and at the beginning of the Gospel.

III. MISSION, as a forerunner to the mightier One coming after himself.

IV. DEATH, in prison, which he suffered for righteousness sake.

Epil.—Many are alone, yet is God's spirit ever with them.

Fourth Sunday in Advent.

SERMON 14.
CURIOSITY.
(*Holy Gospel, Ser.* 2).

(1). S. John I. 19: "The Jews sent priests and Levites from Jerusalem to ask Him."

(2). Coloss. II. 18: "Intruding into those things which he hath not seen."

Summa, 22', 168, 2, 3'".: "To look at or to enquire into the deeds of others with a good mind, in order that a man may either be incited to the better by the good deeds of a neighbour; or, for his own profit, that he may be corrected if he has acted ill, such curiosity is praiseworthy according to the rule of charity as expressed in Heb. x. 24. "Let us consider (observe) one another to provoke," &c.

Prelude 1. There is a good as well as an evil curiosity.

—— 2. This curiosity of the Jews concerning John was to be praised.

—— 3. Bad and idle curiosity about the affairs of others, is common enough.

—— 4. Curiosity about sacred matters is much needed, we have too little of it.

—— 5. Curiosity with a good desire, about good things, is a blessing from God.

—— 6. The sluggish, unthinking, boorish mind is curious about nothing. The exercise of a good curiosity implies a man which is,

I. THOUGHTFUL, neither sleepy nor foolish, not self-satisfied.
II. WISHFULL, to gain more light, knowledge and grace.
III. ACTIVE, in allowing no opportunity of improvement to escape it.
IV. HUMBLE, as feeling what a great unknown lies before it.

Epil.—Never be ashamed to ask and to learn. "Seek after knowledge and your soul shall live."

Fourth Sunday in Advent.

SERMON 15.

SELF-KNOWLEDGE THE PARENT OF HUMILITY.

(*Holy Gospel, Ser.* 3).

(1). S. John I. 27 : "Whose shoe's latchet I am not worthy to unloose."
(2). Philipp. III. 12 : "Not as though I had already attained."
Summa, 22^e, 161, 2, c. : "The knowledge of one's own deficiency belongs to humility, as a certain directive rule of the affections. But humility itself consists essentially in the affection itself, which is foundedupon our own self-knowledge."

Prelude 1. S. John Baptist knew great and wonderful things about himself — about his miraculous birth, powers, mission, &c. Therefore he was made humble by this very knowledge.

—— 2. The ignorant and unthinking are unhumble, self-opinionated, and exactly so in proportion to their ignorance.

—— 3. True knowledge humbles us by showing to us, at least partially, our own ignorance.

—— 4. In proportion as our knowledge is clear and extended, so is our humility.

I. SINCERE, existing in true feeling, not in mere profession.
II. DEEP, lying stored away in the heart's secret recesses.
III. WISE, for he is truly wise, who truly knows himself.
IV. BLESSED, since he who humbleth himself shall be exalted.

Epil.—Pray for S. John's self-knowledge, so to partake of his humility.

Fourth Sunday in Advent.

SERMON 16.

THE BRIDLE OF HUMILITY.

(*Holy Gospel, Ser.* 4).

(1). S. John I. 27 : "Whose shoes latchet I am not worthy to unloose."

(2). 1. S. Peter v. 5 : "Be clothed with humility."

Summa, 22ᵉ, 161, 1, c. and 2 c.: "A virtue is necessary, in regard to the desire of something high and arduous, which may moderate and bridle the mind lest it may tend immoderately to high things; and this restraining power belongs to the virtue of humility. It pertains particularly to humility, that anyone may restrain himself lest he be carried away to those things which are above him."

Prelude 1. Humility is the great check to undisciplined life and thought.

—— 2. Pride bids us estimate ourselves and our doings too highly.

—— 3. It often makes us undertake things too hard for us.

—— 4. To compare ourselves, with others less favoured, which is unwise. Humility steps in and bridles our,

I. THOUGHTS, when they are too lofty, arrogant and vain; curbing many too lofty imaginations, and bringing them into subjection.

II. WISHES, limiting their range; restoring us to contentment.

III. EXPECTIONS, founded upon exaggerated notions of merit.

IV. ATTEMPTS, founded upon insufficient powers and means.

Epil.—This bridle is needed that the soul may become even as a weaned child (Ps. cxxxi. 2) feeling its helplessness. Thus taking the example "Learn of Me for I am meek," &c.

Sunday after Christmas Day.

SERMON 17.

THE PURITY OF THE INCARNATION.

(*Holy Gospel, Ser.* 1).

(1). S. Matt. i. 18: "She was found with Child of the Holy Ghost."
(2). 1. S. Tim. v. 22: "Keep thyself pure."

Summa, 3ª, 28, 3, c.: "Lest we should derogate either from the perfection of Christ, or from the sanctity of His mother; or we should bring in injury to the Holy Ghost; or impute the highest presumption to Joseph himself; it is to be confessed that the mother of God conceived and brought forth as virgin, so that after the birth, she remained ever a virgin."

Prelude 1. Holiness and purity are two attributes of Jesus.
—— 2. The stainless birth produced the sinless offspring.
—— 3. Since the fall, the order of nature is sinful, the order of grace alone is sinless.
—— 4. Purity maintained in the union of the human with the divine nature. Consider the holiness, or purity of the Incarnation in relation to,

I. JESUS CHRIST HIMSELF, our sinless Saviour; as to His divinity "the only begotten of the Father;" so for perfection the only begotten of His mother as to humanity.

II. HOLY GHOST, that the sacrarium in which He formed the flesh of it, should not be violated.

III. MARY, lest her former miraculous purity be invaded.

IV. JOSEPH, the highest presumption if he placed himself on a level with divinity.

Epil.—Purity of body is one of the many lessons of the Incarnation.

Sunday after Christmas Day.

SERMON 18.

THE OLD MADE NEW.
(*Holy Gospel, Ser.* 2).

(1). S. Matt. I. 21: "Thou shalt call His name Jesus."
(2). Isaiah LXII. 2: "Thou shalt be called by a new name."
Summa, 3^a, 37, 2, 2$'''$ and 3$'''$.: "The name of Jesus was not a new name, but it had been imposed upon very many persons in the Old Testament; and rightly so, since they wrought out some particular and temporal salvation; but this name is proper to Christ on account of His spiritual and universal salvation, and as applied to Him it is said to be a new name."

Prelude 1. Jesus said "Behold I make all things new" (Rev. xxi. 5). As it was with His name, so was it also with all other things.

—— 2. It is a greater miracle to make the old new, than to create.

—— 3. Jesus became incarnate to renew our race.

—— 4. He comes by His spirit into our souls to renew them, to make them young again by purity, and by a new faith which is full of joy. He gives to us a new,

I. SALVATION, universal, free and perfect, such as was never known before.

II. NATURE, the new birth of the spirit, "a name better than that of sons," &c.

III. HOPE, of better things to come: to be in us the hope of glory.

IV. LIFE, beginning in baptism. "Because I live ye shall live also."

Epil.—May you be renewed in the spirit of your minds: and so become new in Him.

Sunday after Christmas Day.

SERMON 19.

THE WORK OF THE INCARNATION.

(*Holy Gospel, Ser.* 3).

(1). S. Matt. I. 21 : " She shall bring forth a son."
(2). I. Tim. II. 5 : " The man Christ Jesus."

Summa, 3^a, 1, 2, c. : " God was able out of the infinity of His divine power to restore the human race, by another work than that of the Incarnation; but as man, more easily, and better, He wrought out His salvation; so it was the more necessary that His Word should become flesh. No other way, says Augustine, would have been so suitable for the healing of our misery."

Prelude 1. The fall began with man, so the restoration was by a man.

—— 2. Our humanity corrupted by a sinful man, was made holy by a sinless man.

—— 3. The fall and restoration were both effected by a person.

—— 4. At the Incarnation, Jesus became our personal Saviour. The work of the Incarnation of the Word promotes our,

I. Faith, there is trust or confidence in God Himself speaking (S. August.) that man might walk more trustingly to the truth, the Son of God, Himself the Truth, having become man, founded our faith.

II. Hope, for the Incarnation, showing God's love to us, awakened hope.

III. Charity (S. August.) "If it was irksome to love, at least to love mutually may not vex us."

IV. Participation, in the divine nature, which is the blessedness and end of life.

Epil.—Let not this work be wrought in vain (Heb. ii. 3).

Sunday after Christmas Day.

SERMON 20.
THE WORLD'S SIN.
(Holy Gospel, Ser. 4).

(1). S. Matt. i. 21 : " He shall save His people from their sins."

(2). Rom. v. 17 : " For if by man's offence death reigned by one," &c.

Summa, 3ª, 1, 4, c. 2ᵐ. : " Since Christ came into this world to blot out all sins, He came chiefly rather to take away original than actual sin; for that sin by which the whole human race is polluted is more evil than that which is the particular sin of a single person. 'Original sin' says Bede 'is called the sin of the world as being common to the whole world.' The penalties which we sensibly suffer, in this life, as hunger, thirst, death, &c., flow from original sin. Therefore Christ, that He might make full satisfaction for original sin willed to suffer sensible pain, that He might consume in Himself death, and other things of this kind."

Prelude 1. Baptism is a death unto original sin as well as a new life unto holiness.

We note of original sin that it is,

I. LONGSTANDING, it dates from Adam; it is destroyed by Christ.

II. UNIVERSAL, since "all have sinned," &c. No escape from it by nature.

III. THE SOURCE, and cause of actual sin : " If the root be holy so the branches," and the opposite.

IV. IMMENSE, in " its body of sin," and the multitude of sinners it has produced.

Epil.—It was to deliver us from original sin that, as at this time Jesus was born in Bethlehem. Rejoice in this deliverance.

First Sunday after the Epiphany.

SERMON 21.
CEREMONIES.
(Holy Gospel, Ser. 1).

(1). S. Luke II. 42: "The Custom of the Feast."
(2). I. Cor. XIV. 40: "Let all things be done decently, and in order."

Summa, 12^e, 103, 4, c.: "All ceremonies are protestations of the faith, in which consists the interior worship of God; by these man is able to bear witness to his interior faith by his deeds as well as by words" (id, 12^e, 99, 3, c^m.) "Man was ordained by God not only for interior acts of the mind, such as to believe, hope and love; but also for certain exterior works by which he confesses his divine servitude. These actions are said to pertain to the worship of God, and they are called ceremonies."

Prelude 1. Ceremonies, the outward acts and customs of worship, are not sacraments, but aids to their due administration.

—— 2. There are ceremonies under the new, as under the old law.

—— 3. The church has always had her ceremonies; some from her foundation; others for centuries.

—— 4. With ceremonies, worship is august and reverential; without them, the reverse.

Ceremonies duly observed cause worship to be,

I. REVERENTIAL, to God, as implying order, care and thought.
II. UNITED, all observing the same forms of worship.
III. HEARTY, as expressing a full desire to honour God's worship.
IV. POWERFUL, to influence the thoughtless and unbelieving.

Epil.—As a safeguard against carelessness and irreverence, observe ceremonies.

First Sunday after the Epiphany.

SERMON 22.

THE LORD'S DAY NO SABBATH.

(Holy Gospel, Ser. 2).

(1). S. Luke II. 42 : "The Custom of the Feast."
(2). S. Matt. XII. 1 : "Jesus went on the Sabbath day through the corn" (S. Luke vi. 1).

Summa, 22ᶜ, 122, 4, 4ᵐ. : "The observance of the 'Lord's Day' in the new law, succeeded the observance of the sabbath not by force of a precept of the law, but from the constitution of the church, and the habit of christian people, nor is its observance figurative, like that of the sabbath under the old law; therefore the prohibition against working is not so strict as to the Lord's Day as it was in respect to the sabbath, but certain works are allowed on the Lord's Day which were prohibited on the sabbath."

Prelude 1. The Lord taught that : "The sabbath was made for man," &c. (S. Mark ii. 27), therefore He healed on the sabbath.

—— 2. S. Paul taught : "Let no man judge you in respect of the sabbath" (Coloss. ii. 16), S. Chrysost. on this verse : "Why make yourselves accountable for these petty matters?"

—— 3. Sabbatarians and Judaizers, the pests of the early church. *See* Ignatian Epistles.

The Christian Sunday is the day of,

I. THE LORD, to be spent as He spent it, in worship and in doing good, and taking recreation.
II. HOLINESS, to be kept free from sin, rioting and sensuality.
III. FESTIVAL, not of fast "we will rejoice and be glad in it."
IV. REST, but idleness is not rest, but the worst kind of fatigue.

Epil.—So may our Sundays be holy and happy, foretastes of an eternal festival.

First Sunday after the Epiphany.

SERMON 23.

OBEDIENCE TO PARENTS.

(*Holy Gospel, Ser.* 3).

---

(1). S. Luke II. 51 : " He was subject unto them."

(2). Eph. VI. 1 : " Children obey your parents in the Lord " (Coloss. iii. 20).

Summa, 22^c, 104, 4, 2^m. : " Bodies are subject to their masters, but the mind indeed to its own law. In those things which belong to the interior motion of the will, man is not bound to obey man but God only. But in those things which pertain to the disposition of acts, and of human affairs, the subject ought to obey his superior, by reason of his superiority ; the son to obey the father in those things which pertain to the discipline of life, to domestic care, and so of other things."

Prelude 1. Outward and inward obedience are due to God.

—— 2. Outward obedience in all things lawful is due to parents.

—— 3. True and real obedience must rest upon affection and respect. When mutual love exists children yield to parents an obedience which is,

I. FULL, no grudging element in it ; as perfect as possible.

II. READY, not of compulsion, by that of a ready mind.

III. UNSELFISH, for the parents' sake and good not for their own.

IV. GRATEFUL, as some small return for all the parents have done for them.

Epil.—Such was the obedience which the Lord rendered to His earthly parents. Let the young take Him as their holy example.

First Sunday after the Epiphany.

SERMON 24.

EXPERIMENTAL KNOWLEDGE.

(*Holy Gospel, Ser.* 4).

(1). S. Luke II. 52 : "Jesus increased in wisdom."

(2). Coloss. II. 3 : "In whom are hid all the treasures of wisdom and knowledge."

Summa, 3ª, 12, 3, 2 and 3ᵐ. : "As to experimental knowledge, Christ increased in it; for He did not know all things from the beginning, but He received knowledge from sensible or outward things. The Lord did nothing but what was suitable to His age; therefore He listened to the discourses of teaching for the time in which He was able to have touched such a grade of knowledge by the way of experience."

Prelude 1. As Son of God Jesus knew all things (Coloss. ii. 3), on which S. Chrysost. "He alone knows all things:" Hid "from the angels, not from you only."

—— 2. Two kinds of knowledge; inherent and experimental.

—— 3. As Son of man, Jesus had to learn by experience the sharp lessons of His earthly life of toil, disappointment, sorrow and suffering.

—— 4. Experience is the best teacher; it really teaches; its knowledge is,

I. ADAPTIVE, as suffering, sorrowing, &c., He consoles sufferers, mourners, &c.

II. DISCIPLINAL, "not My will but Thine;" it bends man's stubborn will.

III. PROGRESSIVE, each succeeding day develops a higher and deeper experience.

IV. TEMPORAL, in the eternal state we shall gain knowledge not by experience, but by intuition, when we shall know as we are known.

Epil.—Day by day may we grow in wisdom and knowledge, going on to perfection.

Second Sunday after the Epiphany.

SERMON 25.
THE HOUR OF JESUS.
(Holy Gospel, Ser. 1).

(1). S. John II. 4 : " Mine hour is not yet come."
(2). Eccles. III. 1 : " To everything there is a season, and a time to every purpose."

Summa, 3", 43, 2, c. : "The miracles of Christ were wrought for the confirmation of His teaching, so He did not work any until He began to teach, nor did He begin to teach till He was of full age. His miracles were also wrought to show forth the divine power in Him, that from His deity, men might believe in the truth of His humanity. Therefore Chrysostome says, that He did not work miracles in His early life, for had He done so, men might have considered His incarnation to be unreal."

Prelude 1. A time, season and place for everything.
—— 2. S. Chrysostome defines the hour of Jesus as the season of man's need.
—— 3. Deeds cannot be performed, before, or after, but in their hour.
—— 4. God gives to each, an hour, or season, or an opportunity.
—— 5. This "hour" must be right, seized and well used since it is,

I. FITTING, the best and most opportune time that can be used.
II. APPOINTED, not by ourselves, but by God's providence who ordereth for us.
III. BLESSED, if seized upon, made the most of, and accepted when received.
IV. ONLY ONE, so that if passed by may never again return.

Epil.—May we use our "hour" to God's glory and our own salvation.

Second Sunday after the Epiphany.
SERMON 26.
THE PHASES OF FAITH.
(*Holy Gospel, Ser.* 2).

(1). S. John II. 11: "His disciples believed on Him."
(2). S. Mark IX. 24: "Lord I believe; help Thou mine unbelief."

Summa, 3^a, 43, 3, 3^m.: "Not because then at first they had believed, but because at that time they believed more lovingly and more perfectly. Or, as Augustine says: 'He calls them disciples who were about to become His disciples.'"

Prelude 1. A kind of doubtful following first; a confirmed and believing following after this, His first miracle had been wrought.

—— 2. Faith like a mighty river, often dates its origin from a small beginning.—The soul can hardly tell when and how its germ was planted.

—— 3. To the very last the faith of the disciples was not fully confirmed.

—— 4. The light of faith resembles the light of day in its phases. We note the,

I. DAWN, a gleam of fresh light breaking in upon a dark and ignorant soul. But a ray or two here and there within, containing a hope and a promise.

II. TWILIGHT, a half vision and belief, a seeing of "men as trees walking," the gaining, but still imperfectly, a new spiritual sense and power.

III. DAYLIGHT, now clear, then cloudy, but with light enough for men to walk in, and work out their own salvation in it.

IV. FULL AND PERFECT DAY, not on earth, but in heaven; through grace, in glory.

Epil.—Our prayer: "Lord increase our faith;" walking by faith, not by sight.

Second Sunday after the Epiphany.

SERMON 27.
DOING OUR BEST.
(Holy Gospel, Ser. 3).

(1). S. John II. 10: "Thou hast kept the good wine until now."

(2). S. Mark XIV. 8: "She hath done what she could."

Summa, 3ª, 44, 3, 2ᵐ.: "It is to be considered concerning the miracles of Christ, that commonly He used, as in the case of the 'good wine,' to make His works most perfect as Chrysostome says: 'Such are the miracles of Christ,' that chiefly in those which were wrought on account of nature, they might become more beautiful and more useful."

Prelude 1. Perfection of nature produces perfection of work."

—— 2. The perfect Jesus could do no imperfect work. "He hath done all things well."

—— 3. "We cannot be perfect as He is," but we can all try to do our best.

—— 4. Our best in thought, word, deed and life.

—— 5. A great satisfaction in the best that it lies in our power to do. To do our best implies,

I. EARNESTNESS, in purpose "ye did run well, who did hinder you?"

II. THOUGHT AND CARE, that no carelessness shall injure or hinder our work.

III. ENDEAVOUR, leaving no means unemployed, no power unused.

IV. PERSEVERANCE, that at least a portion of our imperfection may be atoned for, this makes up for ability and advantages.

Epil.—The saints did their best to become holy. All the great deeds and works in the world are the results of their author's best work.

Second Sunday after the Epiphany.

SERMON 28.
THE INSTRUMENTAL SOUL.
(Holy Gospel, Ser. 4).

(1). S. John II. 9 : "The water that was made wine."
(2). Rom. VI. 13 : "Yield your members as instruments of righteousness."

Summa, 3^a, 13, 2, c. : "The soul of Christ can be considered either as to its proper nature and virtue, natural or graced ; or, as the instrument of the World of God united personally to himself. In this sense, the soul of Christ had great instrumental power for performing all miraculous changes, which are ordained to the end of the Incarnation, which is, to restore all things whether in heaven, or on earth. Whatsoever changes can be wrought, are wrought by the soul of Christ, according as it is the instrument of the Word."

Prelude 1. Miracles imply a change in the order of grace, or nature.

—— 2. To change a soul with its passions, desires, &c., is a greater work than to change any body ; as water into wine ; a sightless to a seeing eye.

—— 3. Jesus does change a poor weak soul, which represents water ; into a soul strong in repentance, grace and heavenly joy, which represents wine.

—— 4. Such a change is for eternity and not for time only. Jesus changes the soul from,

I. SIN, to holiness, making it new ; the heart of stone is turned to flesh.

II. SORROW, to happiness ; "your sorrow shall be changed into joy."

III. DESPONDENCY, into "hope, as an anchor of the soul, sure and stedfast."

IV. DEATH, into life : "Because I live, ye shall live also."

Epil.—May this mighty, instrumental soul of Christ, exert its power on us all.

Third Sunday after the Epiphany.
SERMON 29.
LEPROSY A TYPE OF HERESY.
(Holy Gospel, Ser. 1).

(1). S. Matt. VIII. 2 : "Behold there came a leper and worshipped Him."

(2). Gal. v. 19-20 : "The works of the flesh are manifest, which are these......seditions, heresies," &c.

Summa, 12^c, 102, 5, 4^m. : "Worship is twofold ; spiritual, consisting of devotion of the mind to God ; and bodily, consisting of oblations, &c. Sin hinders the former, and under the old law bodily impurity [such as leprosy] the other. Figuratively the uncleanness of leprosy signifies the uncleanness of heretical doctrine ; both because heretical doctrine is contagious like leprosy, and because there is no heretical doctrine which does not mingle things true, with things false ; as, on the surface of the body of the leper, there appears a certain distinction of spots which marks a difference from the other flesh which is sound (Lev. xiii. 38)."

Prelude 1. God has given to us, in the Catholic Church, one pure body of orthodox truth, the quod semper ; quod ubique ; quod omnibus is believed.

—— 2. Heresy defiles this body of truth by omissions, additions and distortions.

—— 3. Heresies often attract from their novelty ; and the spiritual pride they breed.

—— 4. They may endure even for centuries ; at last they die out. Heresy is,

I. CONTAGIOUS, like leprosy it spreads and multiplies very quickly.

II. DECEITFUL, introducing what is false into the truth, to deceive.

III. IMPURE, defiling the pure body of Catholic truth.

IV. MARKED, by its effects as with the spots of Satan and of sin.

Epil.—Be ye clean ; separate, come out from it ; no concord between Christ and Belial.

Third Sunday after the Epiphany.

SERMON 30.

THE ADORATION OF JESUS.

(*Holy Gospel, Ser.* 2).

(1). S. Mark VIII. 2 : "Behold there came a leper and worshipped Him."

(2). 1. Cor. XIV. 25 : "Falling down on his face he will worship God."

Summa, 3ª, 25, 1, c. : "There is one adoration of Christ, and of the two natures in Him, and many causes of the one adoration. So great in Christ is the one person of the divine and human natures, that there is one adoration and one honour on the part of Him who is adored, but on the part of the cause for which he is honoured, there can be said to be many adorations."

Prelude 1. Adoration is one of the children of feeling.

—— 2. Adoration is heart worship in its highest form.

—— 3. As feeling varies, so arises many adorations of Jesus.

—— 4. The one divine Person is many sided, so the adoration to Him takes, though essentially one in itself, many forms. We adore the Lord for His infinite,

I. LOVE, so great and intense towards us; creative and redeeming love.

II. WISDOM, in whom are all treasures of wisdom, so made unto ourselves.

III. POWER, manifest over creation, the spirit world, and men's souls.

IV. GOODNESS, by which He outpours His blessed gifts upon ourselves.

Epil.—Adore Him in sacrament, worship, prayer and in holiness alike of life and conversation.

Third Sunday after the Epiphany.

SERMON 31.
THE HIGHER LAW.
(*Holy Gospel, Ser.* 3).

(1). S. Matt. VIII. 3: "Jesus put forth His hand and touched him."

(2). Rom. VIII. 2: "The law of the spirit of life, hath made me free from the law of sin and death."

Summa, 12^c, 107, 2, 3^m.: "In the old law it was prohibited to touch a man who was a leper (Levi. v. 2—xiii. 14), since by this a man was incurring a certain uncleanness or irregularity, just as in the case of one touching a dead body. But because He was the cleanser of leprosy He was not able to contract any such uncleanness. For the new law as compared with the old; was, as the perfect compared with the imperfect."

Prelude 1. The Lord came to give us a higher law for life than was known before.

—— 2. Not lawlessness, but a more spiritual law.

—— 3. To touch sin, as sin even in thought defiles the soul, but to touch sin to root it out, purifies and exalts.

—— 4. The higher law is more sensive and therefore more exalting than the lower.

The higher law of Jesus is a law of,

I. GRACE, *i. e.* of favour, pardon and benediction.
II. GOODNESS, taking up and expanding all that is better, and so choking the evil.
III. COMPASSION, founded upon His taking all humanity to Himself for ever.
IV. HELP, where need was, there His law of help came into play.

Epil.—Let us strive to walk after this higher law of life, seeking to gain deeper humility, and more perfect purity in body, soul and spirit.

Third Sunday after the Epiphany.

SERMON 32.
THE WORTHY COMMUNICANT.
(Holy Gospel, Ser. 4).

(1). S. Matt. viii. 8 : "Lord I am not worthy that thou shouldest come under my roof."

(2). 1. Cor. xi. 28 : "Let a man examine himself, and so let him eat," &c.

Summa, 3ª, 80, 10, 3ᵐ. : "The reverence of this sacrament (Holy Eucharist) has fear, that fear of reverence to God which is called filial, joined to love. From love arises the desire of partaking ; from fear the humility of reverencing. Both pertain to the reverence due to this sacrament : neither did that Zacchæus (S. Luke xix. 6) nor this centurion differ between themselves when the one of them joyfully received the Lord, whilst the other said 'Lord I am not worthy,' &c. ; both honouring the Saviour, though not in the same way. Yet love and hope, to which the scriptures ever incite us, are to be preferred to fear. Hence when Peter said 'Depart from me,' &c. (S. Luke v. 8), Jesus answered him 'Fear not.'"

Prelude 1. Man's mingled nature admits of mingled feelings.

—— 2. In this life, no perfect concord of affections in the soul. The worthy communicant approaches the sacrament of the altar in,

   I. FEAR, which is reverential ; trembling at his own unworthiness.

  II. HOPE, of there meeting with and receiving Jesus.

 III. JOY, at the invitation ; and the means of realizing so great a blessing.

 IV. LOVE, to Him who hath prepared such spiritual grace.

Epil.—A diligent preparation makes a worthy communicant.

Fourth Sunday after the Epiphany.

SERMON 33.
WHY THE RIGHTEOUS SUFFER.
(*Holy Gospel, Ser.* 1).

(1). S. Matt. viii. 25 : "Lord, save us : we perish."

(2). ii. Cor. iv. 17 : "Our light affliction, which is but for a moment," &c.

Summa, 1ᵃ, 21, 4, 3ᵐ.: "Many righteous are afflicted in this world; but in this also appears justice and mercy, inasmuch as by afflictions of this kind, some corruptions in them are purged, and they are the more drawn up to God, and away from their affection for earthly things: as Gregory says; 'The ills which press us in this world, compel us to go to God.'"

Prelude 1. Affliction may come either as a judgment for sin, or as a mark of God's favour to prepare the soul for higher gifts.

———— 2. "We perish" the cry of the disciples, not of the unholy or the profane.

———— 3. It is the cry of suffering, bodily or mental, of every holy soul, in every age, for the holy, voyaging in the ship of the Church over the stormy seas of life, meet with more seeming tempests than do the wicked.

———— 4. The Lord often seems to sleep whilst His loved ones are in sore trouble. Affliction,

I. PURIFIES, the soul from some secret sins, or sickness of mind.

II. WEANS, the affections from the world and earthly things.

III. DRAWS, the soul upwards to God and His Kingdom.

IV. PLACES, the soul in rest and peace, fixing it upon the bosom of God.

Epil.—May we kiss the chastening rod, and prepare by discipline for the kingdom.

Fourth Sunday after the Epiphany.

SERMON 34.

THE AGONY OF REPENTANCE.
(Holy Gospel, Ser. 2).

(1). S. Matt. VIII. 31 : "If thou cast us out suffer us to go away," &c.

(2). S. Mark IX. 20 : "The Spirit tare him and he fell on the ground."

Summa, 3ª, 44, 1, 4ᵐ. : "He permitted him whom he had liberated from the demons to be more heavily afflicted for the time ; from which, nevertheless He immediately liberated him, showing by this, as Bede says, that often, when after sins, we endeavour to turn to God, we are driven into new and greater ones by the snares of our ancient enemy, who does this either to stir up a hatred of virtue ; or that he may vindicate the injury of his expulsion. Often the healed man becomes as one dead so that ; as Jerome observes ; 'Ye are dead and your life is hid with Christ in God' (Coloss. iii. 3)."

Prelude 1. Theophylact. "He guarded those possessed with devils, lest they should kill themselves."

—— 2. Repentance is the casting out of the demon of sin.

—— 3. It represents the death throes of our old nature.

—— 4. It brings an army of old sins and evil habits against us.

—— 5. It stirs up spirits still lurking within which hate the new life. The agony of repentance is,

I. STRONG, so many powers of evil are opposed to weak human nature.

II. SHARP, as being an inward crucifixion of much held dear.

III. DEADLY, involving the death either of the old or new nature.

IV. DECISIVE, either for heaven or for hell, for an eternal state.

Epil.—The victory of repentance brings pardon, peace, hope and joy.

Fourth Sunday after the Epiphany.

SERMON 35.
THE DEMON OF SIN.
(*Holy Gospel, Ser.* 3).

(1). S. Matt. VIII. 31 : "Suffer us to go away into the herd of swine."

(2). St. Jam. I. 14: "Every man is tempted when he is drawn away of his own lust."

Summa, 3ª, 44, 1, 4ᵐ. : "Christ permitted, as Chrysostom says, the demons to enter into the herd of swine, not as if He was persuaded by them but to teach us the greatness of the harm of the demons who lie in wait for men.

Prelude 1. Every sinful thought and desire is a demon or evil spirit.

—— 2. These demons hide in the soul and work secretly till the crisis comes.

—— 3. Their purpose is not to kill, but to corrupt men, making them rebels to God and bringing them to eternal damnation.

—— 4. They are the soul's parasites, eating out every good and holy desire.

—— 5. They did not destroy these demons after, they made them solitary and fierce.

—— 6. The craft, cruel, cowardly, covetous demon of sin,

I. EXCITES, and stirs up into action all the evil in the soul.

II. DESTROYS, what it can of all that is good in thought and will.

III. CORRUPTS, such good as it cannot kill.

IV. BETRAYS, at last the too credulous soul to its master the devil, to be led captive by him at his will.

Epil.—Cast out this demon, resist him, give place to him no not for an hour.

Fourth Sunday after the Epiphany.

SERMON 36.

RESTRAINING POWER.

(*Holy Gospel, Ser.* 4).

(1). S. Matt. VIII. 23: "When they came out they went into the herd of swine."
(2). II. Thess. II. 7: "He who now letteth, will let, until he be taken out of the way."

Summa, 3ª, 44, 1, 4ᵐ.: "He permitted the demons to go into the herd of swine, according to Chrysostom, to teach us that more grievous things would be performed by these men than in the swine; unless men were helped by divine providence."

Prelude 1. Theophylact writes: "Showing what bitterness they bear towards men and that if they had power and were not restrained they would afflict us more than they did the swine."

———— 2. The state of life, were God's providence, and the grace of Jesus Christ wholly withdrawn.

———— 3. Man cannot be left to himself; if God forsakes, the devil seizes.

———— 4. Some day Antichrist will bring in a terrible reign of sin when "He witholding" shall be removed (II. Thess. II. 3-13). Jesus now restrains the power of sin by,

I. HIS HOLY ANGELS, who have charge concerning us.
II. THE MEMORIES, suggested by His spirit of a holier and happier past.
III. THE DREAD, wholesome, and awakening, of a future judgment.
IV. THE INFUSION, of better, brighter and holier thoughts into the soul.

Epil.—In mercy may He restrain our unholy wills and desires.

Fifth Sunday after the Epiphany.

SERMON 37.
THE OFFICE OF PREACHER.
(Holy Gospel, Ser. 1).

(1). S. Matt. XIII. 24 : " The Kingdom of heaven is likened unto a man which sowed good seed."

(2). Isai. LII. 7 : " How beautiful are the feet of him that bringeth good tidings."

Summa, 3^a, 41, 3, 1^m. : " No one ought to assume the office of preacher unless he has been first purged, and is perfect in virtue; since it is said Acts i. 1 : 'That Jesus began both to do and teach.' Therefore Christ immediately after His baptism assumed austerity of life, that He might teach, that it behoved others to pass on to the office of preaching after the flesh had been subdued, according to that which the Apostle said, 1. Cor. ix. 27 : 'I keep under my body,' &c."

Prelude 1. Preachers, says S. Bruno, are the feet of Christ to whom the people are deservedly said to be subject.

—— 2. Humbert enumerates the necessary qualifications of the preacher to consist in holiness of life, knowledge, power of speech, aptness at illustration and a good report. 'We are unto God a sweet savour of Christ.' (II. Cor. II. 15).

—— 3. Preachers are sowers of the good seed of the word of life.

—— 4. Preachers were formerly a distinct order in the Church.

—— 5. Life and preaching should agree. The austerity of life in the preacher demands,

I. DISCIPLINE, of self and strict watchfulness in converse with others.

II. PIETY, unaffected and deep, both in the outward and inward life.

III. SERIOUSNESS, and solemnity of word and manner.

IV. EARNEST SADNESS, rather than carelessness and joy of heart.

Epil.—Honour the preacher for his Master's sake and the holiness of his calling.

Fifth Sunday after the Epiphany.

SERMON 38.
OPEN SINNERS ARE TO BE SHUNNED.
(Holy Gospel, Ser. 2).

(1). S. Matt. XIII. 29: "Nay; lest while ye gather up the tares ye root up also the wheat."

(2). I. Cor. v. 13: "Put away from among yourselves that wicked person."

Summa, 22ᵉ, 64, 2, 1ᵐ.: "The Lord commanded the abstaining from the rooting up of the tares in order to spare the wheat that is the good (id. 22ᵉ, 108, 1, c.) If the intention of him punishing tends to some good which is to be gained by the punishing of him sinning, as to his correction or to his restraint, or to the quietude of others, to the preservation of righteousness, and to the honour of God, then it will be lawful."

Prelude 1. *Remigius in Rom. c. 6*: "As one sinner can corrupt a whole congregation by his evil example, if they who can punish him, do not do so, they ought to be punished as the sinner himself."

—— 2. "To deliver such an one to Satan" (I. Cor. v. 5).

—— 3. The good in no case are to be injured; hence tares and wheat grow together.

—— 4. Where separation can be made, it ought to be carried out.

—— 5. Notorious sinners are to be shunned.

—— 6. Excommunication formed a part of the discipline of the early church. Sinners ought to be shunned since they corrupt the good by their,

   I. INFLUENCE, even when unconsciously exerted.
   II. EXAMPLE, which like an infection, soon affects others.
   III. PERSECUTION, of the good, jeering, ridicule and malice.
   IV. TEMPTATIONS, and solicitations, to sin, by their trials to corrupt others.

Epil.—Avoid the hardened sinner; touch not the unclean thing.

Fifth Sunday after the Epiphany.
SERMON 39.
THE SERVANTS OF GOD.
(*Holy Gospel, Ser.* 3).

(1). S. Matt. XIII. 27: "The servants of the householder came and said unto him."

(2). Rom. VI. 22: "Made free from sin, and become servants to God."

Summa, 22^c, 104, 4, 2^m, and 5, 2^m.: "God can command nothing which is contrary to virtue, because in this fact chiefly consists the virtue and the rectitude of the human will; that it is conformed to the will of God and follows its commands. Man is placed in subjection to God simply in relation to all things both inward and outward and so he is bound to obey Him in all things."

Prelude 1. *Sedulius, in Rom.* "To serve in the spirit is more than to adore in the spirit; the former binds the affections, the latter can be rendered without them."

—— 2. Conformation to God's will is the highest form of obedience.

—— 3. Its lower form is a meagre following of His commands.

—— 4. God's servants must seek first to learn and then to follow God's will.

—— 5. God's servants must be willing to serve Him; God has given free will to men.

Man's service to God must be,

I. CONFORMABLE, to His nature and attributes; He cannot deny Himself.

II. VITAL, or living; of the spirit not of the dead letter.

III. INCREASING, growing in constancy and energy with man's love and knowledge.

IV. Willing, as a joy of heart, not rendered with any hope of gain.

Epil.—May our service to God daily increase in strength, consistency and devotion; developing in life and action all that is true, just and holy.

Fifth Sunday after the Epiphany.

SERMON 40.
THE HARVEST OF THE FINAL JUDGMENT.
(*Holy Gospel, Ser.* 4).

(1). S. Matt. XIII. 30: "Until the harvest."

(2). S. John XII. 48: "The word that I have spoken shall judge him at the last day."

Summa, 3ª, 59, 5, 1ᵐ.: "After death in respect to the things of the soul, man obtains an unchangeable state; and therefore in relation to the reward of the soul, the judgment need not be delayed; but because there are other things pertaining to man which will be wrought out in the course of time, all these things will be brought into judgment, and they will have to be estimated at the final judgment at the last day."

Prelude 1. *Radulph, Flav. in Levit. lib.* 16. *c.* 3: "The general harvest will be at the consummation of the world, when, after the reparation of human bodies in the land of the living, there will a congregation of all the blessed."

—— 2. The work and probation of the soul ends with life.

—— 3. Death brings the soul to a changeless state, as to happiness or misery.

—— 4. Vast multitudes are dead, vaster multitudes are living; still vaster multitudes have yet to live and die.

—— 5. A mystical number to be completed before the final end. "Other things," the tares and wheat, wrought out in time as it goes on, are ever,

  I. INCREASING, in number and magnitude and significance.
  II. GROWING, in strength and maturity; till fully grown.
  III. RIPENING, into God's eternal purposes.
  IV. CHANGING, as time goes, on according as the influences are good or evil.

Epil.—Pray, repent, struggle and wait.

Sixth Sunday after the Epiphany.
SERMON 41.
THE TRIALS OF THE ELECT.
(*Holy Gospel*, Ser. 1).

(1). S. Matt. xxiv. 24: "If it were possible they shall deceive the very elect."

(2). ii. Thess. ii. 2: "Be not soon shaken in mind or be troubled."

Summa, 1ª, 23, 4, c.: "The predestination of some to eternal life, presupposes that God wills their salvation, to which belongs election and love. All the predestinated are elect and beloved" (*id.* 24, 2, 3ᵐ.) "It is not said that anyone is elected to the life of grace, except so far as the life of grace is ordained to glory."

Prelude 1. *Sedulius, in Ephes. c. 1*: "Predestination is the preparation of grace."

—— 2. All the children of the church are God's predestinated or elect.

—— 3. As creatures of free will it is for the predestinated to make their calling and election sure.

—— 4. The elect are often deceived, and fall like S. Peter; but they arise (Prov. xxiv. 16).

—— 5. The elect will be tried at the last day; no exception will be made.

—— 6. God's baptized children, elected into the body of His church, are ever being tried in this life, by trials which are often,

   I. SEVERE, both as to body and mind in order to be thoroughly tested.

  II. UNEXPECTED, interrupting the calm and even flow of the Christian life.

 III. UNDESERVED, as far as their desires and actions are concerned.

 IV. SEEMINGLY, without purpose, but really sent in order that the greater victory, may win a brighter crown.

Epil.—"Blessed is he that overcometh."

Sixth Sunday after the Epiphany.

SERMON 42.

THE CRITICAL MOMENT.
(*Holy Gospel, Ser.* 2).

(1). S. Matt. XXIV. 27 : "As the lightning cometh out of the East," &c.

(2). I. Cor. XV. 52 : "In a moment, in the twinkling of an eye."

Summa, 1ª, 42, 2, 4ᵐ. : "In time there is something which is indivisible, that is, to say, instant."

Prelude 1. S. Chrysost : "Truly He will not need a herald or a nuncio; but in a moment of time He will appear to all ; so therefore His advent will be seen to shine everywhere and immediately."

—— 2. A moment will change the face of the world for ever.

—— 3. A moment only between life and death, often between riches and poverty; between health and sickness.

—— 4. The destiny of time and eternity hangs upon a moment.

—— 5. The moment in itself is almost nothing, in effect it causes infinite and great results. A moment,

I. CHANGES, our condition, life and being.

II. SEPARATES, the old life from the new.

III. SETTLES, the changed state ; it affixes a seal which cannot be broken.

IV. OPENS up a new and different life for time and for eternity the death of another; the passing of an examination ; the seemingly chance meeting with a friend, and a thousand other circumstances.

Epil.— Prepare for the critical moment, use every moment well.

Sixth Sunday after the Epiphany.
SERMON 43.
THE FOUNDATION OF BELIEF.
(Holy Gospel, Ser. 3).

(1). S. Matt. xxiv. 26 : "Believe it not."
(2). Heb. x. 39 : "We are of them that believe to the saving of the soul."
Summa, 22^e, 2, 1, c : "To believe, is to think with assent ; and it implies the consideration of the intellect, with some inquisition and consent of the will. It is an interior act of faith."
Prelude 1. *Titus Bostrensis, in Luke c. 14* : "To believe is free to everyone, but this gift is not obtained from God without prayers, which bringeth other endowments, of which to believe is the chief."
—— 2. To believe is easy to say, but it is hard to do.
—— 3. To believe is an outcome of faith, which faith is a gift of God through grace.
—— 4. To believe is higher than to know ; faith transcends knowledge.
—— 5. We believe by faith, but not of sight, either of eye or mind.
—— 6. To believe in the unseen is an act of grace and discipline. To believe rightly, the understanding and the will must be united,

I. FREELY, not of necessity, nor by compulsion, but by the free action of the will.
II. STRONGLY, so as not to be severed by any doubt or seeming inconsistency.
III. THANKFULLY, as finding in the union a secure rest and peace in the soul.
IV. HUMBLY, feeling how high are the mysteries of grace, as compared with any human understanding.

Epil.—Use this gift of believing by accepting God's appointed channels of grace through which it comes to us : Holy Scripture, the foundation, flows from the church which has delivered to us the canon of scripture.

Sixth Sunday after the Epiphany.

SERMON 44.
MAN AND NATURE.
(*Holy Gospel, Ser.* 4).

(1). S. Matt. xxiv. 29: "After the tribulation shall the sun be darkened."

(2). Psalm cxxxix. 14: "Marvellous are Thy works."

Summa, 3^a, 20, 1. 2^m.: "Although it cannot be properly said that nature is either a mistress or a servant, yet it can be said that a certain substance (hypostasis) or person is either a mistress or a servant according to this or that nature."

Prelude 1. *S. Ephrem Rhyt. 48*: "Nature was an instructress to us in everything, and every man according to his ability learns in proportion to his pains." *S. Anast. Sinai;* "Nature is that which exist only in truth."

—— 2. Here, as at the Crucifixion and elsewhere in Holy Scripture, nature is said to serve the Lord, or to help Him to fulfil His purposes.

—— 3. The books of nature and of God go hand in hand; same author; like difficulties in both books.

—— 4. A certain soul in nature. "The Spirit within nourishes heaven and earths and the watery plains. Mind infused through the members agitates the whole mass" (Verg. lib. vi. 725).

—— 5. Wonderful relationship between mind and matter.

—— 6. Lord becoming incarnate, consecrated the outward nature which He loved.   Nature,

I. FEEDS, not the body only by food, but the mind also by its scenery and effects.

II. DEVELOPES, and draws out fear, wonder, admiration, &c.

III. TEACHES, many lessons, of obedience to law, patient waiting (S. James v. 7).

IV. ADMINISTERS to many of our higher needs of Life.

Epil.—Learn to love and reverence nature, God's handiwork, a parable of grace.

Septuagesima Sunday.
SERMON 45.
THE JUSTICE OF GOD.
(Holy Gospel, Ser. 1).

(1). S. Matt. xx. 2: "He had agreed with the labourers for a penny a day."
(2). Rev. xv. 3: "Just and true are Thy ways thou King of saints."

Summa, 1ª, 21, 1, 3ᵐ.: "The justice of God has regard to what is seemly for Himself. He recompences Himself by what is due to Himself. There is also a debt which is due to every created thing so that it may obtain that which was ordained for itself; as to man, hands, &c. God works justice when He gives to each one that which is due to its nature or condition, which was ordained to be given by Himself by the order of divine wisdom. Though so, God allows a debt to some one, He is no debtor. Justice is sometimes the condescension of God's goodness; at others it is His retribution for our deserts."

Prelude 1. *S. Ephrem. Ryth. 3 on Faith*: "He [God] gat Him a name as being just. The eye looked upon His justice, His goodness seized upon it. Betwixt His goodness and His justice, the mind is amazed and astonished."

——— 2. All we are and have belongs to God; we can make Him no return.

——— 3. Man can only stand in His judgment through Jesus Christ. God's justice is,

I. CONSISTENT, with God's own attributes.
II. RETRIBUTIVE, as in the cases of Adam; the flood; cities of the plain; overthrow of angels.
III. STRICT, as in cause and effect in the natural and moral worlds.
IV. PERSONAL, adaptive to each one's estate; either of condescension or retribution.

Epil.—Place ourselves in God's hands who tempers mercy with justice.

Septuagesima Sunday.

SERMON 46.
THE POWER OF WORKING.
(Holy Gospel, Ser. 2).

(1). S. Matt. xx. 4: "Go ye also into the vineyard."

(2). 1. Thess. iv. 11: "Study to work with your own hands."

Summa, 12ᵃ, 114, 1, c: "Man can have no merit with God except on the presupposition of divine ordination; so that man obtains it from God, by his operation, as if wages; to which end God has assigned to him the power of working (virtutem operandi)."

Prelude 1. *Aëlredus. Ser.* 12. *in Isai. c.* 13: "In every good work three points are to be observed; the virtue of discretion; purity of intention; a foundation of humility." Theophyl. in loco: "Each one is hired to work in the vineyard of his soul."

—— 2. The vineyard of the Lord has many divisions; many works are to be done for God, for the soul; and for life in this world.

—— 3. True and holy work produces fruit for this and the next world.

—— 4. God ever provides the means to fulfil His commands.

—— 5. The power of working is a great gift of God; it implies.

I. BEING, endowed with certain faculties and powers.

II. GRACE, without which any really good work is vain.

III. OPPORTUNITY, occasion comes when the means are ripe.

IV. WILL, wanting which all other means are useless.

Epil.—The due exercise of our power of working brings not only profit but pleasure with it. In heaven there will be the fulness of work and energy combined with perfect rest.

Septuagesima Sunday.

SERMON 47.
GOD'S WAGES.
(Holy Gospel, Ser. 3).

(1). S. Matt. xx. 4 : " Whatsoever is right I will give you."
(2). S. Matt. xvi. 27 : " He shall reward every man according to his works."

Summa, 12ᵉ, 114, 1, c. : " Man is not able to merit anything from God according to the absolute reason of justice, but according to a certain presupposition of the divine ordination; according as truly it is, as if man obtained wages for his work. That which recompenses anyone, as repayment for work or labour is called wages, as if there was a certain price for it, the payment for which is an act of justice."

Prelude 1. *S. Clem. Epist.* ii. 9 : " The Lord Christ who saved us, being first indeed in spirit 'was made flesh' and so He called us: so also we in this flesh shall receive wages."

—— 2. No holy thought, word or deed will ever be lost.

—— 3. Our wages will not depend so much on results, as upon our means, endeavours and desires.

—— 4. God pays us wages in this world, as well as in the next.

—— 5. He rewards not from our but from His point of view. His wages are,

I. JUST, as having been worked for: after all " we are unprofitable servants."

II. LIBERAL, beyond all our deserts or even expectations.

III. SUITABLE, He giving not what men may want, but that which is best for them.

IV. SURE, though they may be given soon, they may be long delayed.

Epil.—Seek to serve God wholly, earnestly, actively; He is the very best Master possible; as the devil is the very worst.

Septuagesima Sunday.

SERMON 48.
GOD GLORIFIED IN MAN'S WORK.
(*Holy Gospel*, Ser. 4).

(1). S. Matt. xx. 6 : " Why stand ye here all the day idle ? "

(2). I. Pet. IV. 11 : " That God in all things may be glorified by Jesus Christ."

Summa, 12ᵗ, 114, 1 2ᵐ. : " God does not seek utility from our good works, but glory ; that is, the manifestation of His goodness. We deserve something from God, not as if anything can accrue from them to Him, but inasmuch as we work for His glory.

Prelude 1. *Theod. on I. Cor. x. 31* : " Rightly He comprehended all things, sitting, walking, talking, showing mercy and teaching ; regarding the one end of all things, the Glory of God."

—— 2. God invites all in their several capacities to work for His glory.

—— 3. God is often glorified by a small work ; as by the cup of cold water.

—— 4. This thought should consecrate our common daily life.

—— 5. All honest work tends to God's glory according to the given means. We work in God's vineyard when we glorify Him in lives which are,

I. GODLY, as being lives which profess godliness.

II. CONSISTENT, profession and practice ; faith and morals, go hand in hand.

III. INDUSTRIOUS, as knowing how short is man's day of life.

IV. PURE, as being defiled by no wilful, or allowed sin.

Epil.—So may divine grace enable us to live ; that out of sins, sorrows, &c., God may indeed be glorified.

Sexagesima Sunday.

SERMON 49.

PREACHING IS FEEDING.

(*Holy Gospel, Ser.* 1).

(1). S. Luke VIII. 5 : "A sower went out to sow his seed."
(2). 1. Pet. v. 2 : "Feed the flock of God."
Summa, 22^e, 188, 4, 1, and 3^m. : "To preach is to feed or to teach others. It is not permitted that anyone indifferently should be allowed to preach."
Prelude 1. *Arnulphus Lexov*. "Three things are required in the preacher; holiness of conversation, fulness of knowledge, and a fertile vein of eloquence."
—— 2. Preaching an important function in the church.
—— 3. *Summa, id.* 5 : "Besides bishops and parochial presbyters no person is permitted to preach."
—— 4. Preaching as supplemental to sacrament, a great power for good.
—— 5. The Church, both by education tested by examination, as well as by her grace of orders, prepares her clergy to feed or teach her members.
—— 6. The 'order of preachers' formed a distinct body in the mediæval church. The preacher is bound to provide for his hearers food which is,

I. WINNING, or attractive. "He that winneth souls is wise."
II. WHOLESOME, good and sound, nourishing the soul.
III. SUFFICIENT, lest souls be sent away from church hungry.
IV. SUITABLE, such as the mind can digest and by which the soul is nurtured.

Epil.—In every sermon something to be learned. If it be needful to preachers, 'Take heed how ye preach;' it is no less needful to hearers 'Take heed how ye hear.'

Sexagesima Sunday.

SERMON 50.

PREACHING A DEFENCE.

(*Holy Gospel, Ser.* 2).

(1). S. Luke VIII. 5 : "A sower went out to sow his seed."
(2). II Tim. III. 17 : " That the man of God may be perfect, thoroughly furnished."

Summa, 22ᵉ, 188, 4, c : "It is a greater thing, as Gregory says, to defend the faithful by spiritual arms, than to defend a faithful people with bodily arms."

Prelude 1. *S. Laur. Justin. De Inst. Præl. c. 8*: " Preaching is for the faithful people, that they may learn what to believe ; what to do ; whither they ought to tend, lest they fail, being wearied in the journey of this life, and wander through the bye paths of vices and fall into hostile hands which rob, slay and destroy."

—— 2. Many, cruel, and varied are the enemies of souls.

—— 3. The faithful preacher arms his people against these enemies.

—— 4. Warnings, admonitions and instructions tend to this end.

—— 5. The preacher is not ignorant of Satan's devices, these he exposes. The true and faithful preacher defends his people against,

I. IGNORANCE, of the faith ; of the origin and constitution of the church.
II. ERROR, of doctrine, which is the offspring of ignorance.
III. INDIFFERENCE, or spiritual lukewarmness, arousing and exciting
IV. TEMPTATION, which is varied and coming in many forms.
V. SUPERSTITION, or false religions, which are modern and unscriptural.

Epil.—May you, listening to the voice of the preacher, be armed with the whole armour of God; and so be enabled to fight for and win a victory for the faith.

Sexagesima Sunday.

SERMON 51.
PREACHING THE INSTRUMENT OF SOULS.
(*Holy Gospel, Ser.* 3).

(1). S. Luke VIII. 5 : "A sower went out to sow his seed."
(2). Philipp. II. 5 : "Let this mind be in you which was also," &c.
Summa, 22^c, 188, 4, 1^m. : "He who works upon the virtue [or heart] of another, does this after the manner of an instrument. The minister or preacher is a certain instrument of souls" (Instrumentum animarum).

Prelude 1. *S. Laur. Justin. De Discipl. c. 9:* "Before all things they (preachers) should study, the natures, habits so as diligently to know the desires of each one committed to them; that they may be able to apply antidotes to each one. For all bodies are not healed by one kind of medicine, neither are all souls purged, &c. by a like treatment."

―― 2. The sinful, unawaked soul is ugly and ungainly.

―― 3. The preacher takes in hand such souls; fitting them for the master's use.

―― 4. As the soldier his arms, as the mechanic his tools, so the preacher must keep his tools bright and sharp; his knowledge, his keenness of thought, his devoutness of soul, &c. By this instrument of souls the preacher,

I. FORMS, moulds souls: "Let this mind be in you which also," &c. (Philipp. ii. 5).
II. PURIFIES, souls: "Purifying their hearts by faith" (Acts xxi. 26).
III. DISCIPLINES, souls; subduing unholy wills and desires.
IV. DIRECTS, souls, to walk in the right way: "This is the way." (Isai. xxx. 21).

Epil.—So may your souls and life be conformed to Jesus Christ.

Sexagesima Sunday.

SERMON 52.

PREACHING AN OFFERING OF SOULS.

(*Holy Gospel*, Ser. 4).

(1). S. Luke VIII. 5: "A sower went out to sow his seed."

(2). Prov. XI. 30: "He that winneth souls is wise."

Summa, 22ᵉ, 182, 2, 3ᵐ.: "There is no sacrifice which is more acceptable to God than a zeal for souls. The merit of an active life is not to be preferred to the merit of a contemplative life; but it is more meritorious if anyone offers to God his own soul and the souls of others, rather than any other exterior gifts how great soever they be."

Prelude 1. *S. Laur. Justin. De Obed. c. 15:* "Of how great efficacy with God is the sacrifice of a man, knowing his own sin; confessing his wickedness and supplicating with a sincere soul, pardon from the Lord."

—— 2. A man can offer no greater offering to God than his own soul.

—— 3. He cannot do a greater work than to offer the souls of others.

—— 4. The faithful preacher is ever offering to God this sacrifice of souls, which is a sacrifice which is,

I. Living, and therefore capable of action, growth and expansion.

II. Infinite, in its capacities alike for good and evil.

III. Eternal, both in nature and duration.

IV. Redeemed, at so great a cost (1. Pet. i. 18).

Epil.—May this sacrifice be offered alike by preacher and hearer.

Quinquagesima Sunday.

SERMON 53.
THE UNIVERSAL SAVIOUR.
(*Holy Gospel, Ser.* 1).

(1). S. Luke XVIII. 31 : "All the things that are written concerning the son of man," &c.

(2). I. Tim. II. 3-4 : "God our Saviour; who will have all men to be saved."

Summa, 3ª, 44, 3, c : "The things which are ordained to an end ought to be proportionate to that end. But Christ for this end, came into and taught in the world, that He might save men (S. John iii. 17); therefore it was fitting that He by miraculously healing men, might show especially that He was the universal and spiritual Saviour of men."

Prelude 1. *De S. Polyc. Mart, c. 17:* "Neither at any time are we able to forsake Christ who suffered for the salvation of the whole world of those being saved."

——— 2. "Saviour" is a history in a word, of infinite import and comfort.

——— 3. His name Jesus, Saviour; saving from ruin, misery and hell.

——— 4. "Spiritual;" of the soul which is the greater; of the body which is the lesser. Jesus is a "universal Saviour" as His salvation is limited neither by,

I. TIMES OR SEASONS, He saved before the law, under it, after it.

II. PLACE, He is everywhere present in power and spirit.

III. NUMBER, the saved will be a multitude that no man can number.

IV. RACE, or condition. He reduces all nations to one in Himself.

Epil.—How shall we escape eternal death if we neglect so great salvation?

Quinquagesima Sunday.

SERMON 54.

THE ABUNDANT LOVE OF JESUS CHRIST.

(*Holy Gospel, Ser.* 2).

(1). S. Luke VIII. 33 : " They shall put Him to death."
(2). S. John XV. 13 : " Greater love hath no man than this," &c.

Summa, 3^a, 47, 4, 1^m. : " Christ for the purpose of showing the abundance of His love; by which He suffered; when placed upon the cross, prayed for the pardon of His persecutors; that so the fruit of this petition might come to both Jews and Gentiles, for he willed to suffer for them both."

Prelude 1. *S. Chrysost. T. ix.* 515. A. : " If one would not readily die for a virtuous man, think of the love of your Master; since He, not for the virtuous, but for sinners and enemies, is shown as crucified."

—— 2. Love like other human affections has different degrees of strength.

—— 3. The love of Jesus far exceeds the highest love of any mortal.

—— 4. Fulness and perfection of nature, implies fulness and perfection in love. This love of Jesus without stint or measure flowed from the strength of His,

I. POWER, which is almighty in action, feeling, and in wisdom.

II. COMPASSION, so well knew He our lost and helpless state.

III. ADAPTATION, of mind to our unsatisfied yearnings.

IV. WILL, to carry out any scheme of redemption however stupendous.

Epil.—May you all be partakers of His abundant love, receiving from Him " grace for grace."

Quinquagesima Sunday.

SERMON 55.

THE GREATER LOVE OF JESUS CHRIST.

(Holy Gospel, Ser. 3).

(1). S. Luke XVIII. 34: "They understood none of these things."

(2). S. Luke XXIII. 34: "Father forgive them; for they know not what they do."

Summa, 3^a, 49, 4, 2 and 2^m.: "The passion of Christ was fulfilled by the men who slew Him; who by this act heavily offended God. But the love of Christ suffering, was greater than the iniquity of those slaying; so His passion availed more for the reconciling of God to the whole human race, than to the provoking Him to anger."

Prelude 1. *Ludolp. Vita Christi, Pt. ii. c. lxiii. fol. 492*: "With what sweetness of mind; with what devotion of spirit; in what fulness of love, He exclaimed 'Father forgive them!'"

——— 2. This "greater love" is wholly a divine gift.

——— 3. It is seen the love of parents for unworthy children whose misdeeds, deepen it by the pity and compassion with which it is accompanied.

——— 4. The greater love and pardon of Jesus is evoked by man's greater sin. A love,

I. THE STRONGEST, being founded upon an infinite pity.

II. MOST UNSELFISH, seeking for no possible return.

III. PURIFYING, the soul from every particle of dross.

IV. DIVINE, being a faint reflection of the love of the Lord.

Epil.—Seek to love not for self but for others.

Quinquagesima Sunday.

SERMON 56.

THE PERFECT LOVE OF JESUS CHRIST.
(Holy Gospel, Ser. 4).

(1). S. Luke XVIII. 32 : "He shall be delivered unto the Gentiles."

(2). 1. S. John IV. 18 : "Perfect love casteth out fear."

Summa, 1ª, 27, 5, 3ᵐ. : "God understands all things by one single act; and He similarly wills all things : whence in Him there is not able to be any procession or going out of love; but there is in Him alone one perfect love, and in this, is manifested His perfect fecundity."

Prelude 1. *S. Ignat. ad Ephes. c. 14* : "Perfectly may you have faith and love in Jesus Christ; which are the beginning and the end of life. Faith, indeed the beginning; but love the end."

—— 2. "Perfect love," unknown on earth, yet how often sighed for.

—— 3. Imperfect love even, is one of the great motive powers of the world.

—— 4. In heaven, perfect love has infinite power and sway.

—— 5. Perfect love can only exist in a perfect nature.

Perfect love casts out all,

I. FEAR, for it unites the loving and the loved one in one being.

II. DOUBT, such a full recognition and understanding, the one of the other.

III. LONGING, it is sufficient in itself to fill the heart's deepest longings.

IV. SELF, which is lost and absorbed in the object of its love.

Epil.—Strive after that love of God which hereafter can be perfected.

First Sunday in Lent.

SERMON 57.
JESUS TEMPTED—OUR HELP.
(*Holy Gospel*, Ser. 1).

(1). S. Matt. IV. 1 : "Then was Jesus led up of the Spirit to be tempted."

(2). Heb. II. 8 : "Being tempted He is able to succour them that are tempted."

Summa, 3^a, 41, 1, c : "Christ willed to be tempted indeed, that He might bear help to us against our temptations."

Prelude 1. S. Greg. Mag. Hom. 16. In Evan. : "It was not unworthy of our Redeemer that He willed to be tempted, who had come to be slain. It was therefore just, that so He might overcome our temptations by his own; since He came to overcome death by His death."

—— 2. All need help, all are at times very helpless and weak.

—— 3. The devil is very strong, crafty and cruel.

—— 4. Some can, yet will not help us; others will, but cannot help.

—— 5. Jesus is both willing and able to help in temptation.

—— 6. The temptations, trials and dangers of the soul are far more subtle and dangerous than those of the body. The help of Jesus is,

I. STRONG, He is mighty to save and deliver: Holiness is stronger than sin.

II. READY, for those, who, seeking His help, also strive to help themselves.

III. SYMPATHETIC, as fully entering into their struggles and difficulties.

IV. REWARDING, as marking His approval of personal effort.

Epil.—As no one, with His help, need be overcome by sin and Satan, let all seek it on worthy grounds. If men fall it is their own fault.

First Sunday in Lent.

SERMON 58.
JESUS TEMPTED—OUR CAUTION.
(Holy Gospel, Ser. 2).

(1). S. Matt. IV. 1 : " Then was Jesus led up . . . to be tempted of the devil."

(2). 1. Cor. X. 12 : " Let him that thinketh he standeth take heed lest he fall."

Summa, 3^a, 41, 1, 2^m. : " Christ willed to be tempted for our caution (cautela), that no one however great a saint might deem himself to be secure and exempt from temptation."

Prelude 1. *S. Hil. Op. p, 473, A* : " The Lord indicating by His temptation that the trials (or temptations) of the devil are chiefly to attack the holy amongst us ; for a victory over the saints is greater to him and more to be desired." Again (*Op. p, 910*), *A* : " The care to the devil and his ministers is to take away all the glory from a faithful man, and not to suffer him to be of the portion of God."

—— 2. We are often in the greatest danger, when feeling more secure.

—— 3. Satan tries to lull the soul into a false security, that it may fall.

—— 4. Satan never slumbers, no one is secure from his attack.

—— 5. The temptations of the devil are infinite as to the,

I. Variety, of sins, agreeing with every variation and condition of life.

II. Range, of sins, from the smallest venial to the greatest mortal sin.

III. Adaptation, of sins to the particular and peculiar weakness of each soul.

IV. Degrees, of sin which is needful to cause a soul to fall from grace.

Epil.—" Be sober, be vigilant for your adversary the devil," &c. : let not the devil overreach you by craft and malice.

First Sunday in Lent.

SERMON 59.
JESUS TEMPTED—OUR EXAMPLE.
(Holy Gospel, Ser. 3).

(1). S. 'Matt. IV. 1 : " Then was Jesus led up of the Spirit," &c.

(2). I. Pet. II. 21 : " Christ also leaving us an example," &c.

Summa, 3ª, 41, 1, 3ᵐ. : " Christ willed to be tempted, that He might instruct us how we may overcome the temptations of the devil."

Prelude 1. *S. August. de Trin. lib. iv. c. 13* : " Christ offered Himself to the devil to be tempted, that He might be our mediator in overcoming temptations not only as a helper, but also as an example." *Theophy. in loco* : " For our sakes Christ did and showed all things."

—— 2. Infinite value of having an example or pattern of holiness, trial, action, life and work, the Christian has His footsteps to follow.

—— 3. Example is better by far than precept; it is easier to follow.

—— 4. Example sets before us an ideal; a something to imitate.

—— 5. This ideal or example is a stimulus to holiness, or to exertion. How can the temptations of sin be resisted? We learn from Him by,

I. PREPARATION, the Lord prepared Himself by fasting and prayer.

II. WAITING, He did not attack the devil; He waited for the attack.

III. ARMING, His armour was Holy Scripture, so ours " the armour of God."

IV. ENDURING, the devil exhausted his resources, then came the angels.

Epil.—Place the life of Jesus, our great example, ever before the eye of the mind.

First Sunday in Lent.

SERMON 60.

JESUS TEMPTED—OUR CONFIDENCE.

(*Holy Gospel, Ser.* 4).

(1). S. Matt. IV. 1 : "Then was Jesus led up," &c.

(2). Heb. IV. 15 : "In all points tempted like as we are."

Summa, 3ª, 41, 1, 4ᵐ.: "Jesus was tempted that he might increase our confidence (fiducia) by His compassion."

Prelude 1. *Guarric Abb.*: "By confidence the remedies for spiritual healing are obtained; sins are driven back; fears are despised; the world is overcome; all things are possible to him that believeth."

—— 2. The consciousness of compassion, gives much confidence.

—— 3. If the compassion be united with strength, the confidence is increased.

—— 4. The ever living and ever compassionating Lord has passed through all that we are enduring now: Shall we fail?

—— 5. The ground of confidence must be in a pure heart and a true faith. Our confidence in temptation is founded upon the assurance of our Lord's,

I. SYMPATHY, He feels our every throe; all our agony.

II. WATCHFULNESS, over us whilst the conflict is going on.

III. PRESENCE, with us by His Spirit "I will never leave thee."

IV. SUPPORT, His strength is made perfect in our weakness.

Epil.—So can we endure to fight manfully the good fight of holiness against sin; for Jesus against Satan.

Second Sunday in Lent.

SERMON 61.
PERSEVERANCE.
(*Holy Gospel, Ser.* 1).

(1). S. Matt. xv. 27: "Truth Lord: yet the dogs eat of the crumbs," &c.

(2). S. Matt. x. 22: "He that endureth to the end shall be saved."

Summa, 12^a, 109, 10, c: "Perseverance signifies the habit of mind by which a man stands firmly lest he should be removed from that which is according to virtue, by griefs rushing in upon him; which habit holds itself equally in respect to sorrows and joys."

Prelude 1. *Pet. de Blois, Ep.* 22: "All the other graces run, perseverance alone is crowned," *Ep.* 36: "Humility does not profit unless it finally perseveres; nor does the glory of good conversation profit in the beginning unless it has a glorious end."

—— 2. The woman of Canaan persevered and so gained her request from the Lord.

—— 3. Perseverance is opposed to instability which is a sign of weakness.

—— 4. It is the secret of success in this life; and the due preparation for the life to come.

—— 5. Persevering signifies the adhering firmly to anything. We must persevere in,

I. THE FAITH, once delivered to the saints; hold on to it; forsake it not,

II. MORALS, in spite of all temptation; persuasion; solicitation, &c.

III. PURPOSE, Turning aside neither to the right nor to the left.

IV. ACTION, doing what is right, as being right regardless of consequence.

Epil.—Pray for grace to fail not. "He that hath begun a good work," &c.

Second Sunday in Lent.

SERMON 62.

THE POWER OF MERCY.
(Holy Gospel, Ser. 2).

(1). S. Matt. xv. 22 : " Have mercy on me O Lord."
(2). S. Matt. v. 7 : " Blessed are the merciful for they shall obtain mercy."

Summa, 1ª, 21, 3, c : " Anyone is said to be merciful, as if having a heart affected to sadness by the misery of another, as if it were its own : and from this, it follows as an effect of mercy that it seeks to expel the misery of another as if it were its own."

Prelude 1. *S. Aug. De Civ. Dei*, IX. 5 : " Mercy is the compassion of our heart for the misery of another ; by which therefore, if we are able, we are compelled to render help" (S. Greg. Nyssa, Orat. 5) " Mercy is the father of benevolence ; the pledge of charity ; the bond of loving affection."

—— 2. Whole earthly life of Jesus was one long act of mercy.

—— 3. Holy souls so feel their infirmities that they cannot but have mercy on others.

—— 4. Mercy as an affection draws out and expands the soul.

—— 5. Mercy is a great power ; and as such it is,

I. LOVING, in intention ; it longs to remove all grief and suffering.

II. UNLIMITED, in application ; the deeper the sorrow, the deeper the mercy.

III. FRUITFUL, in good and blessed results ; as to souls and bodies.

IV. DIVINE, in origin and example. God tempers judgment with mercy. " I will sing of mercy " first and afterwards of judgment.

Epil.— The power of mercy, well exercised, obtains mercy, likens to the Lord.

Second Sunday in Lent.

SERMON 63.
PRAYER FOR TEMPORAL BLESSINGS.
(Holy Gospel, Ser. 3).

(1). S. Matt. xv. 22: "My daughter is grievously vexed," &c.
(2). Philipp. iv. 19: "My God shall supply all your need."
Summa, 22^e, 83, 6, c.: "It is lawful to pray for temporal things, and Augustine said to Probus (Epist. 121, c. 6), 'that not unbecomingly he desires a sufficiency for life whosoever may wish it; and not more than a sufficiency.' Such things are not desired on account of themselves, but for the safety of the body, or according to habit of the person asking. When such things are not possessed it is meet that they should be prayed for."

Prelude 1. *M. Aurelius*: "When necessity, the mother of crimes, is taken away; the desire of sinning is removed;" or lessened.

——— 2. The body and life have pressing claims whilst on earth.

——— 3. Claims appointed by God's providence, to be brought before God.

——— 4. Temporal things are needful for us, health and sufficiency, &c.

——— 5. Not the highest objects for prayer but they cannot be neglected. Prayer for temporal blessings teaches,

I. DEPENDANCE, upon God; an acknowledgment that all come from Him.

II. SUBMISSION, to God's will whether granted or withheld.

III. RIGHT USE, of all God's creatures, if viewed as His gifts.

IV. THANKFULNESS, to Him for every temporal blessing bestowed by Him.

Epil.—Ask and ye shall receive; in receiving your joy shall be full.

Second Sunday in Lent.

SERMON 64.
THE GREATER FAITH.
(*Holy Gospel*, Ser. 4).

(1). S. Matt. xv. 28 : "O woman, great is thy faith."

(2). S. Luke xvii. 5 : "Lord increase our faith."

Summa, 22^e, 5, 4, c : "Wheresoever is found the small and great, there is also found the greater and the less; so in faith likewise there is found the small and the great; since the Lord said to Peter 'O thou of little faith;' and to the woman 'great is thy faith.'"

Prelude 1. *Theophy. in loco*: "When her faith was manifested He praised it, 'great,' &c." The greater faith is shown by word and deed.

—— 2. The smaller faith may become greater; "as the bird breaks through the egg to the nest, and perfected, flies in the air" (S. Ephrem.)

—— 3. Faith is the great need of the world.

—— 4. A little faith is better than none; as a little sight than blindness.

—— 5. "Greater faith" implies the larger understanding of divine things. This greater faith gained the Lord's,

I. ATTENTION, so many in the world with weak and failing faith,

II. HEART, it appealed to the fulness of His love and compassion,

III. PRAISE, He seldom praised; here too, not the woman but her faith,

IV. BLESSING, as if great, it could remove mountains, of which all things are possible.

Epil.—Treasure up and mature thy faith; that if small at first it may pass into the greater faith to help in time of need.

Third Sunday in Lent.

SERMON 65.
JESUS A THOUGHT-READER.
(Holy Gospel, Ser. 1).

(1). S. Luke XI. 17 : " He knowing their thoughts said," &c.
(2). Psalms XLIV. 21 : " He knoweth the secrets of the heart."
Summa, 3^a, 10, 2, c : " He, because He is the Son of Man is constituted the Judge of all men, and therefore, the mind of Christ in the Word, knows all existing things in all time and what is thought of by man; for " He knew all men, and needed not," &c., for he knew what was in man (S. John ii. 24-25)."

Prelude 1. *S. Cyril Alex.* (*Hom.* 80 *in Luc.*) : " He proved Himself to be God for He knew their thoughts : it is an act which belongs wholly to God to be able to know that which is in the mind."

—— 2. This thought-reading is not granted to any angel (Haymo).

—— 3. The knowledge that the very secrets of the heart are read by God must strike a certain awe into all ; terror in sinners ; watchfulness in the holy.

—— 4. As He reads our hearts, so He remembers ; He registers the thought for ever.

—— 5. As He registers, so will He judge. Jesus reads our thoughts,

I. INSTANTLY, before we know them ourselves ; when half formed.

II. TRULY, man's introspection often errs ; God's inspection never.

III. WHOLLY, not leaving any thought undiscovered " all things," &c. (Heb. iv. 13)

IV. LOVINGLY, with a gentle spirit ; to correct in love not in anger.

Epil.—(Prov. iv. 23) : " Keep thy heart with all diligence," &c., by prayer, confession of sin, continual watchfulness.

Third Sunday in Lent.

SERMON 66.
CONCORD.
(Holy Gospel, Ser. 2).

(1). S. Luke xi. 17: "A house divided against a house falleth."

(2). S. James iii. 16: "Where strife is, there is confusion and every evil work."

Summa, 22ᵃᵉ, 37, 2, 3ᵐ.: "By concord small things increase, and by discord the greatest things waste away; for virtue by how much the more it is united, by so much the more is it stronger, whilst by separation it is diminished. Discord, by which each one inordinately follows his own concerns, receding from that which is another's, is the daughter of vain-glory and pride."

Prelude 1. *S. Ign. ad Eph. c. 4*: "In your concord and harmonious love Jesus Christ is sung." *John of Salis, Ep. 81*: "All things stand fast by mutual help; heavy things are tempered by light things; universally the spirit of unanimity within, nurtures so great concord of differing things, and so great difference of things agreeing."

—— 2. Concord is a note of the church as strife is of heresy.

—— 3. Concord is,

I. STRONG, the threefold cord not quickly broken.

II. PROSPEROUS, it gathers and increases, whilst discord disintegrates.

III. PLEASANT, "Behold how good and pleasant it is for brethren," &c. (Ps. cxxxiii. 1).

IV. PROPHETICAL, of the heavenly state and life in which the mind of one is the mind of all.

Epil.—Preserve concord in the body, health; in the church, the faith; in the world, prosperity, and kindly feeling towards all.

Third Sunday in Lent.

SERMON 67.

THE STRONG MAN OF SIN
(*Holy Gospel, Ser.* 3)

(1). S. Luke xi. 22 : "When a strong man armed," &c.
(2). 1 S. John iii. 8 : "The Son of God was manifested that He might destroy," &c.

Summa, 3^a, 49, 2, 3^m. : "God permits the devil to deceive men in certain persons, times and places; for a hidden reason of His judgments. Yet ever by the passion of Christ is a remedy prepared for men, by which they can defend themselves against the wickedness of evil spirits. But if any neglect to use this remedy, such neglect destroys nothing of the efficacy of the passion of Christ."

Prelude 1. *S. Cyril. Alex. in loco.* : "After the word of the most high God, the Giver of all strength and the Lord of virtues was made man, He invaded him, and took away all his arms."

—— 2. The passion of Christ effects our liberation from the power and machinations of the devil; it strips him of his armour; it despoils him of his goods or souls.

Jesus stripped Satan of,

I. REBELLION, and disobedience by His obedience unto death (Philipp. ii. 8).

II. CRAFTINESS, by His simplicity, "who did no sin," &c. (1 Pet. ii. 22).

III. HATE, by His infinite love "more than conquerors through Him," &c. (Rom. viii. 37).

IV. DEATH, by His resurrection from the dead, "Who by His death," &c. (Heb. ii. 14).

Epil.—We as partakers of the death and passion of Jesus, can despoil the strong man of sin and lead captivity captive.

Third Sunday in Lent.

SERMON 68.
MY HOUSE.
(*Holy Gospel, Ser.* 4).

(1). S. Luke xi. 24 : " I will return unto my house."

(2). Eph. iv. 27 : " Neither give place to the devil."

Summa, 1ª, 114, 5, c : " The demon when overcome, ceases from the temptation of the same man ; not for ever, but for a time. The devil, says Chrysostom, does not tempt man as long as he is willing to do so, but only for so long a time as God permits ; and if He suffers him to tempt man for a little while, He then drives him away on account of the weakness of our nature."

Prelude 1. *Ven. Bede in loco*: " Iti s to be feared, lest the sin which we thought was extinct within us, may again subdue us through our negligence."

——— 2. God drives the devil away, but he tries to leave his representative sins behind him, in the soul, which he then still calls his house.

——— 3 Every form of sin must be thoroughly cast out of the soul.

——— 4. One sin left behind therein, is ready to open the door for Satan. Such sins, evil spirits, left behind in the soul are,

  I. TRUE, to their absent master ; ready to deliver up to him the soul.

 II. WATCHFUL, to act when the master of the house is off his guard.

III. CUNNING, keeping in the background till the opportunity comes.

IV. DISCONTENTED, with their present state of subjection.

Epil.—" Make me a clean heart O God," &c. (Ps. li. 10).

Fourth Sunday in Lent.

SERMON 69.

GOD'S PROVING.
(Holy Gospel, Ser. 1*).*

(1). S. John vi. 6: "This He said to prove him."
(2). S. James i. 12: "Blessed is the man that endureth temptation."

Summa, 22ʳ, 97, 2, c: "To tempt is to make an experiment, which no one does concerning a thing of which he is certain; so that all temptation proceeds either from ignorance or doubt. Some try or tempt for their own sakes; others to make something manifest to others. It is for this latter purpose that God is said to tempt us; not because He does not know, but that He may show something to others," and to ourselves.

Prelude 1. *Smaragdus, Abbas*: "By so much the more it behoves to rejoice in temptations, by how much it appears more certain, that God often lays a greater weight of temptations upon those whom He loves, that by the exercise of temptations they may be proved perfect in the faith."

—— 2. God tempts or proves man that he may know himself.

—— 3. Proving, trial and temptation, purify the soul, and awaken its energy.

—— 4. God's proving is in mercy and love, not in anger for punishment. He proves us that we may test,

I. Ourselves, so learning all our weakness and our strength.
II. Our Faith, how far it is capable of supporting us under trial.
III. Our Endurance, so as to win a crown or more or less glory.
IV. His Power and Will, to help us, leading to greater trust in Him.

Epil.—Not merely bear, but learn to glory in temptations.

Fourth Sunday in Lent.
SERMON 70.
THE CHRISTIAN PASSOVER.
(*Holy Gospel, Ser.* 2).

(1). S. John vi. 4 : " The Passover a feast of the Jews was nigh."

(2). 1 Cor. v. 7 : " Christ our Passover is sacrificed for us."

Summa, 12ᶜ, 102, 5, 2ᵐ. : " The figurative meaning is manifest, for by the immolation of the Paschal Lamb is signified the immolation of Christ. The blood of the Lamb sprinkled upon the lintels and side posts of the houses (Ex. xii. 23), liberating from the destroyer, is the faith of the passion of Christ, by which we are liberated from sin; in the mouths and hearts of the faithful (1 Pet. i. 18-19). The flesh eaten is the eating of the body of Christ in the sacrament : ' Roast with fire ' is the love of Christ; the unleavened bread the conversation of the faithful partaking of the body of Christ (1 Cor. v. 7). Let us keep the feast not with old leaven; yet with the loins girded with the girdle of chastity. It was commanded that the Paschal Lamb should be eaten in 'one house,' that is, in the church of catholics not in the conventicles of heretics."

Prelude 1. *S. Cyril. Jerus. Lec. xii. 1* : " Let us who are accounted worthy to partake of the flesh of the Spiritual Lamb, partake of the head, His Godhead; of the feet, His Manhood." *S. Ephr. Ryth.* v : " That Paschal Lamb who handed down and made present the Passover of the Son."

—— 2. Refreshment Sunday, or Easter Day Communion, being the Christian Passover, brings before the Christian soul, the

I. Sacrifice on Calvary, its love and pardon.
II. Feast upon that Sacrifice, our Eucharist.
III. Chastity, needful for communicants.
IV. Unity of the Church, one house of the Passover.

Epil.—All these things uniting in our passover, make our communion a eucharist indeed.

Fourth Sunday in Lent.

SERMON 71.
BENEVOLENCE.
(*Holy Gospel, Ser.* 3).

(1). S. John VI. 5: "Jesus saw a great company come unto Him."

(2). Titus III. 4: "After the love of God our Saviour towards man appeared," *i.e. benevolence or philanthropy.*

Summa, 22ᶜ, 27, 2, c: "Benevolence is an act of the will by which we wish good to another. Sometimes it arises suddenly which love does not. It is not like love existent in the sensitive or the intellectual appetite; neither does it imply any union by affection of the loving for the loved one, since the loving deems the loved one to be in a certain way one with himself, or else belonging to him; it is act of the will wishing good to others."

Prelude 1. S. *Greg. Naz. Orat. xvi. T.* 1, *p.* 240. B: "Benevolence, or philanthropy, is a beautiful thing, and Jesus Himself is a witness, who not only created man for good works, but for our sakes became man."

—— 2. The Lord had compassion and benevolence, for the "great company."

—— 3. It is fruitful in general good, as in founding hospitals, schools, &c.

—— 4. Though not love, it is the outcome of the highest form of love.

—— 5. Benevolence softens life and breeds sympathy in the heart. Benevolence, or philanthropy, is,

I. COMPREHENSIVE, embracing large schemes for the general good.

II. UNSELFISH, looking for no return, ministering to no passion.

III. IMPERSONAL, in the sense of being large and kind hearted to all men.

IV. ACTIVE, strong in action. Lord's benevolence led Him to feed the multitude.

Epil.—So feel kindly towards all men and benevolently seek to do them good.

Fourth Sunday in Lent.
SERMON 72.
THE USE OF MEANS.
(Holy Gospel, Ser. 4).

(1). S. John VI. 11 : "Jesus took the loaves."
(2). 1 Cor. VII. 30 : "They that buy, as though they possessed not."

Summa, 3ᵃ. 44, 4, 4‴. : "The multiplication of the loaves was not made after the manner of creation, but by the addition of extraneous matter turned into loaves. As Augustine says 'He multiplied the crops from a few grains;' thence in His hands He multiplied the five loaves."

Prelude 1. *Remigius Bp. in i. Cor. vii.* 30 : "Many buy temporal goods and prepare them for their own use and for that of others, which things are necessary in this world, but 'as though they possessed not;' so cleaving to earthly as not to lose things eternal, providing beforehand for the sake of those whom they leave."

——— 2. "All things were made by Him:" He had the power of creating.

——— 3. Yet He used the loaves, the means which were at hand.

——— 4. He taught us to make the most of our means, of those at hand.

——— 5. We are bound to use all the means that God gives us for eternity and for time. These means we must use,

I. PRAYERFULLY, asking a blessing upon our work; of what kind it may be.

II. DILIGENTLY, husbanding resources, and turning small means to their best account.

III. HOPEFULLY, believing in God's blessing, and help to prosper the work of our hands.

IV. PATIENTLY, leaving the issue in God's hands; "The husbandman waiteth," &c.

Epil.—Mark those who make much of a very little, for imitation, and those who waste means and great opportunities, so as to avoid their loss.

# Fifth Sunday in Lent.

SERMON 73.
THE GOOD CONSCIENCE.
(Holy Gospel, Ser. 1).

(1). S. John viii. 46: " Which of you convinceth Me of sin."
(2). Acts xxiv. 16: " A conscience void of offence towards God and men."

Summa, 22", 132, 1, c: "That anyone may know and approve of his good quality is not sin (1. Cor. ii. 12), likewise it is not sin if anyone desires his good works to be approved by others (S. Matt. v. 16). He does not name as anything that is faulty the desire of glory as touching self."

Prelude 1. *Smargdus Abb.*: "The 'good conscience' is far from doubt; it has no accusation of sins; nor does the blame of sin bite it; nor a load of crimes accuse it; it hates none; detracts from none; harms none; envies none; is sweet, meek, peaceful and benign to all."

—— 2. The Lord could throw down this challenge without contradiction.

—— 3. All sin, but the "good conscience" repents of and is sorry for sin.

—— 4. The "good conscience," judging others by itself, makes allowance for all. The "good conscience" implies.

I. SELF-RESPECT, which respects others, and is itself respected.
II. SATISFACTION, feeling that inward grace which preserves from sin.
III. ENDEAVOUR, to be more worthy of its high Christian calling.
IV. GRATITUDE, to God for His gift of grace which keeps the soul unspotted.

Epil.—How different is all this from the evil conscience of the wicked, that troubled sea, whose waters throw up mire and dirt.

Fifth Sunday in Lent.

SERMON 74.
VAIN-GLORY.
(Holy Gospel, Ser. 2).

(1). S. John VIII. 50: "I seek not mine own glory."

(2). Philipp. II. 3: "Let nothing be done through vain-glory."

Summa, 22', 132, 1, c: "The desire of empty or vain-glory denotes defect, for to seek anything vain is a defect or fault (Ps. iv. 2). Glory can be called 'vain' from the thing out of which anyone seeks glory, being unworthy, fragile or failing; or, from the person from which glory is sought, as from a man whose judgment is uncertain; or lastly, from him who desires glory, but not for its due end, *i.e.* the honour of God and the salvation of his neighbour."

Prelude 1. *S. Nilus. de Inani. Glor. Orat. 7:* "Vain-glory is like the ivy which as it embraces the tree and grows aloft dries up its root. So vain-glory is born with virtues from which it does not depart till it has killed their strength."

—— 2. Vain-glory is a feeble and foolish form of pride.

—— 3. It is the product of an ungraced and undisciplined and weak mind. He is vain-glorious who seeks glory for a bad,

I. OBJECT, as glorying in sin or shame; like the open sinner.

II. SUBJECT, from the unworthy.

III. MEANS, seeking by unworthy acts to deceive others.

IV. END, which is selfish, proud, boastful and utterly useless.

Epil.—The source of all true glory is lowliness of heart; and "before honour is humility."

Fifth Sunday in Lent.

SERMON 75.
THE RIVER OF SIN.
(Holy Gospel, Ser. 3).

(1). S. John VIII. 48: "Say we not well that thou art a Samaritan."

(2). Gal. II. 13: "Barnabas was carried away with their dissimulation."

Summa, 2 2ᶜ, 72, 4, c: "One sin arises from others, yet each sin owns a particular sin to which it chiefly owes its origin, from the sin which usually precedes it on account of its alliance with its end. So contumely or bitter reproach has affinity with the end of anger which is vengeance, for no vengeance is more ready to an angry man than to hurl reproaches at another, so contumely chiefly arises from anger."

—— 2. S. Odo. of Cluny. Moral. in Job. lib. 4: "Sin is perpetrated in the heart by suggestion, delight, consent, and by boldness in defence."

—— 3. In the Lord's case, in this Gospel, the order is anger, contumely and the casting of stones.

—— 4. The chain of sin is formed by the links of many sins hanging the one from the other.

—— 5. Sin begins in thought and ends in action.

—— 6. Sin can be compared to a river, ever flowing, ever increasing. The river of sin has,

I. A HEAD, or spring arising from the recesses of the heart; dropping at first.
II. WIDTH, increasing in width as it flows, adding sin to sin.
III. DEPTH, as sins deepen in number and intensity.
IV. LENGTH, reaching onwards and carrying the entire man, body and soul.

Epil.—Stay the fountain of sin at its source; dam it up; cut it off; let not the dark flood flow on till it reaches the ocean of eternal death.

Fifth Sunday in Lent.

SERMON 76.
THE FAITHFUL PREACHER.
(*Holy Gospel, Ser.* 4).

(1). S. John VIII. 46 : "If I say the truth, why do ye not believe Me?"

(2). II. Tim. IV. 2 : "Preach the word ; be instant in season, out of season."

Summa, 3ª, 42, 2, c : "The salvation of the multitude is to be preferred to the peace of single men, how great soever they may be : Therefore when by their perversity they hinder the salvation of the multitude the offending of them is not to be feared by the preacher. The Scribes, Pharisees, &c. of the Jews were hindering the salvation of the people, for they were opposing the teaching of Christ by which alone they could be saved. This was their offence, but they could not check Him, for He publicly taught the truth which they hated, and reproved their vices. Hence the Lord's reply to His disciples (S. Matt. XV. 12-15)."

Prelude 1. *S. Jerome T. ix.* 3189 : "It is meet willingly to hear ; it is grievous to preach to the unwilling. Censure those sinning ; bear witness lest they sin ; blame those resisting thee."

—— 2. People dislike home truths, like the Scribes, &c. of old.

—— 3. The bitterest medicines are often the most healing.

—— 4. Men like to hear what is pleasing not what is profitable. The faithful preacher is bound to proclaim saving truth,

I. HONESTLY, not reasoning it away, or watering it down to nothing.

II. WHOLLY, repressing nothing : to preach the "truth, the whole truth, and nothing but the truth."

III. FEARLESSLY, as God's faithful servant and exponent of His mind.

IV. EARNESTLY, feeling that the eternal life or death of souls may hang upon his words.

Epil.—Preach or prophecy not smooth but true doctrine.

Sixth Sunday in Lent.

SERMON 77.

THE TRIBUNAL OF THE CROSS.
(*Holy Gospel, Ser.* 1).

(1). S. Matt. XXVII. 38 : " Then were two thieves crucified with Him."
(2). II. Cor. II. 15-16 : " A sweet savour of Christ . . . savour of death unto death."

Summa, 3ª, 46, 11, 2ᵐ. : " Augustine says (*Tract. 31. In Ioan.*) : 'The cross itself, if you study it, was a tribunal, for in the midst of it, the judge being appointed, the one who believed was liberated, the other who derided was condemned.' He now signified what would be done with the living and the dead ; some to be placed at the right hand and others indeed at His left."

Prelude 1. *S. Chrysost. in Luc.:* "The Saviour in the midst of thieves was weighing faith and infidelity in the scales of justice.

—— 2. As the Cross was once a tribunal on Calvary, so is its preaching now. A savour either of life or death ; it judges between the faithful and the unbelieving.

—— 3. The weakness of the Cross showed the power of the crucified one.

—— 4. From the Cross, the tribunal of judgment, came the opening of heaven to the penitent. The Cross and the preaching of the Cross, now in our midst is a tribunal,

I. JUDGING, us even now in our daily life.
II. SEPARATING, as with the thieves, the righteous from the wicked.
III. SEALING, the condemnation of the impenitent.
IV. SECURING, in Paradise the glory and lasting happiness of the righteous.

Epil.— May we stand through life beneath the shadow of the Cross and so live to Jesus as rightly to be fit to pray to Him. " Lord remember me," &c.

Sixth Sunday in Lent.

SERMON 78.
THE LORD'S LAST LESSON.
(*Holy Gospel, Ser.* 2).

(1). S. Matt. xxvii. 50: "Jesus cried again with a loud voice."

(2). Heb. xi. 34: "Who .. out of weakness were made strong."

Summa, 3ª, 47, 1, 2'''.: "Augustine said that they who were suspended on the cross, were crucified by a lingering death; but this did not happen in the case of Christ; for when He had 'cried with a loud voice' &c. 'So Pilate marvelled if He were already dead' (S. Mark xv. 44), and the Centurion also acknowledged His divinity. (Id. v. 39) By His will He preserved His natural body, in its vigour till the last, and when He willed it, it ceased to be, being taken away by a sudden applied energy."

Prelude 1. *Theophy. in loco:* "With a loud voice, that we may know that to be true which He said 'I have power,' &c., for He had power to lay down His life."

—— 2. As His last lesson, Jesus taught the true discipline of self.

—— 3. He taught the power of the mind or will over the body.

—— 4. The mind can either subdue or bring on bodily suffering.

—— 5. In case of great mental excitement, no sense of bodily pain remains. The power of the mind over the body is,

I. STRONG, in its action; it overcomes weakness and fear.

II. COMPLETE, in itself; it does not leave its work half done.

III. WISE, in purpose; given to enable us to endure.

IV. LOVING, in rule, so as not to tax the body beyond its powers.

Epil.—Learn we to place the flesh in subjection to the spirit.

Sixth Sunday in Lent.

SERMON 79.
THE POWER OF THE CROSS.
(Holy Gospel, Ser. 3).

(1). S. Matt. xxvii. 51 : "The earth did quake and the rocks rent."

(2). Ezek. xxxvi. 26 : "I will take away the stony heart and give you a heart of flesh."

Summa, 3ᵃ, 44, 4, 3ᵐ. : "Showing that the stony hearts of men were to be softened by His passion; and the whole world to be by it changed for the better."

Prelude 1. *Gloss. Ordin.* : "'The rocks' the hearts of the gentiles; of the earthly ones; were changed by the Passion of Christ; the Judaic hardnesses were softened."

S. Hilary Poict.: "The rocks were rent, the Word of God penetrating all things mighty and strong; the power of eternal virtue had broken them."

—— 2. The hard and sinful heart must be broken if it is to be saved.

—— 3. The heart must be led to the Cross at any cost.

—— 4. No price is too great to be paid for the breaking up of our sinful souls.

—— 5. The harder the rock, or heart, the greater the force needed to rend it.

—— 6. The broken rock tells of power; the broken heart of power and love combined. The powers or forces of the Cross are,

I. SUFFERING, contrition, remorse, humiliation, and fear.

II. PATIENCE, wait and the breaking will come, first the death, then the rending.

III. TENDERNESS, even as the drops of water hollow out the hard rock.

IV. LOVE, a divine love stronger than all the powers of nature.

Epil.—So may these "powers of the cross" break up and soften the soil of the heart, that it before barren may bring forth much fruit into life eternal.

Sixth Sunday in Lent.
SERMON 80.
FROM DEATH TO LIFE.
(*Holy Gospel, Ser.* 4).

(1). S. Matt. xxvii. 6: "The graves were opened."
(2). Rom. vi. 11: "Dead indeed unto sin, but alive unto God through Jesus Christ."

Summa, 3^a, 44, 4, 3^m.: "To show that by His death, life is given to the dead."

Prelude 1. *S. Jerome in loco*: "As Lazarus when dead rose again, so many bodies of the saints had arisen that they might show the Lord rising again, yet when the graves were opened they did not rise before the Lord that He might be the first-begotten of the resurrection from the dead." "These rose again immortal and they ascended with the Lord ascending."

—— 2. Life out of death is after the order of nature, which is a parable of grace.

—— 3. So is it in the spiritual world, we die with Christ through Him to rise.

—— 4. Out of our dead and dying selves a better and immortal life can spring.

—— 5. The Lord did not create a new race of immortal beings, but He brought life to those existing, as dead in trespasses and sins.

—— 6. The passage is made by means of the sacraments of the new law. The life out of death which Jesus gives is,

I. PURE, a newness of life, in Him, purified by a death unto sin.

II. HAPPY, because a spring and source of eternal happiness is opened by it.

III. ETERNAL, begun in time to be continued and perfected in eternity.

IV. BEFITTING, those preparing for a higher and more glorious state of being.

Epil.—So pass ye onwards and upwards as time goes by, casting away the works of darkness so as to become light in the Lord.

Easter Day.
SERMON 81.
THE LOVE OF THE RISEN LORD.
(Holy Gospel, Ser. 1).

(1). S. John xx. 1 : " The first day of the week cometh Mary Magdalen," &c.
(2). S. John xx. 15 : " Woman why weepest thou ? "

Summa, 3ᵃ, 55, 1 and 3ᵐ. : " The glory of the Resurrection is as Augustine says the reward of the humility of the passion ; and therefore He first appeared to the women ; that woman who first brought the tidings of death to the man, might also first announce the life of Christ rising in glory; whence, as Cyril says, woman who formerly was the minister of death, first perceived and told of the mystery of the Resurrection to be venerated. Also in relation to the state of glory, the female sex should suffer no loss; if they burned with a greater love, they should receive a greater glory from the divine vision."

Prelude 1. *Dionysius Carth. on v. 16:* " How affectionately and sweetly Jesus said to her 'Mary,' and immediately the Master being known, the name being heard, all her bowels were changed, and her heart also melted when her Loved one spoke."

—— 2. The love of Jesus shone through the Resurrection, itself an act of love.

—— 3. Suffering often engenders a deeper love.

—— 4. Glory ensures the perfection of love. The Resurrection love of Jesus was,

I. THOUGHTFUL, for Mary Magdalene; and for us, our justification.
II. SYMPATHETIC, why weepest thou ? He felt as before for our humanity.
III. HUMBLE, as to its first object (S. Luke viii. 2) out of whom He cast seven devils.
IV. INTENSE, as of an intense nature, now glorified.

Epil.—Draw we nigh more closely to our Risen Lord in full assurance of faith.

Easter Day.
SERMON 82.
THE LAW OF MEDITATION.
(*Holy Gospel*, Ser. 2).

(1). S. John xx. 2: "She runneth and cometh to Simon Peter."
(2). ii. Cor. v. 18: "God hath given unto us the ministry of reconciliation."

Summa, 3^a, 55, 1, 1^m. and 2^m.: "The passion of Christ had a natural suffering which by a common law is known to all, and therefore it was immediately manifested to all people; but the Resurrection was by 'the glory of the father' (Rom. vi. 4), therefore it was not known to all, but only to some persons, by the testimony of whom it was carried to all men (Acts x. 40). As the Resurrection of Christ was for the salvation of all, so it came to the knowledge of all; not indeed that directly it was manifested to all; but to certain persons by whose testimony it was carried to all."

Prelude 1. *Pet. de Blois. Ser.* 61: "See ye brethren your vocation, the eminence and dignity of your order to whom the dispensation of the body and blood of the Lord has been committed."

—— 2. Peter and John were the first priests or mediators between the risen Jesus and His Church.

—— 3. Moses the mediator under the law—Gabriel a mediator or annunciator.

—— 4. In the Christian Church the Priesthood carried on the work of mediation, to whom is committed the powers of

I. PREACHING the ministry of reconciliation (Malc. ii, 7), God's "Messenger."
II. INTERCESSION, as conducting the offices of prayer.
III. ABSOLUTION, general and public, private, and particular of confession.
IV. CONSECRATION, which by the epiclesis or invocation becomes no longer common bread, etc.

Epil.—Use this mediation, that all the graces of the Holy Ghost may become yours.

Easter Day.
SERMON 83.
THE POWER OF THE RESURRECTION.
(Holy Gospel, Ser. 3).

(1). S. John xx. 8: "He saw and believed."
(2). II Cor. xiii. 4: "He was crucified through weakness, yet He liveth by the power of God."

Summa, 3ª, 51, 3, 3ᵐ.: "Christ rose from the sepulchre by a divine power, which was restrained by no limits; and that He did this, was a sufficient argument that men were to be raised again by the divine power, not only from sepulchres, but from every kind of ashes."

Prelude 1. *S. Ign. ad Smyr. c.* 2: "He also truly raised up Himself." *S. Fug. de Incar. et Gratia, c.* 19. "Christ the son of God, dead in the flesh, rose again; because dead in the flesh, He did not lose the immortality of His divinity."

—— 2. The Resurrection is a great miracle of the power of God.

—— 3. A mighty contrast to the weakness and death of man caused by sin.

—— 4. The exercise of this power by Jesus on Himself is an earnest of a like exercise of it in and upon ourselves.

—— 5. In the body even, we can now rise, since He rose, never again to come to nothing.

—— 6. Our Easter Festival is a prophecy of our resurrection in the body. This "Resurrection Power" is to us one of

I. CERTAINTY, "Christ is risen, we are risen." As He truly arose, so with ourselves.

II. JOY AND COMFORT: The victory and sting of our enemy death is destroyed.

III. GRATITUDE infinite and deep: for us He died, for us He rose again.

IV. ETERNAL BEING, full, perfect and eternal, both in body and soul.

Epil.—By faith says S. Chrysostom, this Resurrection power can be felt.

Easter Day.
SERMON 84.
THE NEED OF THE RESURRECTION.
(Holy Gospel, Ser. 4).

(1). S. John xx. 1 : " Mary Magdalene seeth the stone taken away."

(2). S. Luke xxiv. 46 : " It behoveth Christ to suffer, and to rise from the dead."

Summa, 3ª, 53 1, c. : " It was needful that Christ should rise from the dead, not only for the commendation of the divine justice, for the instruction of our faith, and for the erection of our hope, but truly also for the information or conception of the life of the faithful, and for the consummation (or completion) of our salvation."

Prelude 1. *S. Ignat. ad Trall, c.* 9 : " Who was also truly raised from the dead by His Father, who after the same manner, His Father will so also raise us, believing in Jesus Christ, without Whom we have no true life."

—— 2. In the order of grace or of nature, God never acts without need or purpose.

—— 3. This purpose of God is wise, loving, just and consistent with Himself.

—— 4. The Resurrection, a most needful link in the plan of redemption.

Following the guidance of S. Thomas, we note that Jesus rose for the

I. COMMENDATION OF THE DIVINE JUSTICE. Those humbled for God will be exalted (S. Luke i. 52).

II. INSTRUCTION OF OUR FAITH, which was confirmed by it. " We are weak," etc. (2 Cor. xiii. 4).

III. LIFTING UP OF OUR HOPE. We hope to rise ; our Head rose (1 Cor. xv. 12).

IV. FORMATION OF THE LIFE OF THE FAITHFUL. " We should walk," etc. (Rom. vi. 4, 5).

V. CONSUMMATION OF OUR SALVATION ; rising gloriously He promised blessings (Rom. vi. 25).

Epil.—Rise we with Him in spirit, in spirit now, hereafter in spirit and body too, we shall in and with Him rise to the life immortal.

First Sunday after Easter.

SERMON 85.
THE BLESSING OF PEACE.
(*Holy Gospel, Ser.* 1).

(1). S. John xx. 19 : " Praise be unto you."
(2). Gal. v, 22 : " The fruit of the spirit is peace."

Summa, 22', 29, 1, c : " Peace includes concord, but concord does not include peace. Concord signifies the meeting of the wills in different hearts, in one consent; but the heart of each one varies according as the sensitive or rational appetite prevails; but peace besides the union of concord implies the union of the appetites of each one desiring. The union of the appetitive motions is the ground of peace. Man has no peaceful heart as long as he has not what he wishes for."

Prelude 1. *S. Ignat. ad Ephes. c.* 13 : " Nothing is better than peace." S. Cyril Alex. Acts, Ephes. " If anyone is a partaker of that peace which is given by God, he is in want of nothing which is good."

—— 2. Peace is the union of the desires of the many in one.

—— 3. Peace is inward and can only exist in the heart.

—— 4. It can be experienced only in part in this life.

The state of peace implies

I. REST of soul; no disturbing element being left. " Thou wilt," etc. (Isai xxvi. 3).

II. SATISFACTION or completion; nothing remaining to be wished for.

III. RELIEF from all strife, of flesh and spirit, or with those without.

IV. CONFIDENCE. It casts out all dread and fear.

Epil.—" Seek peace and ensue it " ; seek Jesus who is our true peace.

First Sunday after Easter.
SERMON 86.
THE PENALTIES OF SIN.
(Holy Gospel, Ser. 2).

(1). S. John xx. 20: "He showed unto them His hands and His side."

(2). Heb. ii. 2: "Disobedience received a just recompense of reward."

Summa, 3^a, 14, 1 c.: "The Son of God having assumed flesh, came into the world that He might make satisfaction for the sin of the human race. But one makes satisfaction for the sin of another, when he receives in himself the punishment which is due for the sin of another. Bodily defects, such as death, hunger, etc., were introduced into the world by Adam (Rom. v. 12), so it was fitting to the end of the Incarnation that He for our sakes should receive these penalties (or sufferings) for our sakes (Is. liii. 4).

Prelude 1. *S. Chrysost. Hom. vi, ad Pop. Antioch:* "Sin is an ulcer, its penalty is an iron surgery." *S. Clem. Alex. Strom.* 7, *p.* 762: "God chastises for man's profit, both in common and in private, those who are subject to the penalty."

—— 2. Every sin is subject to a penal retribution. "It will find you out."

—— 3. The Lord carried the signs of His vicarious sin-bearing that He might show to all how severe are the penalties of sin.

—— 4. The marks on the Lord are our warnings. The penalties of sin are,

I. VOLUNTARY, we are not under sin but under grace: so we need not sin.

II. HEAVY in proportion to means and opportunities. Few and many stripes.

III. LONG ENDURED, like the marks of fire on a restored building.

IV. SOLITARY or single, each sinner bears his own particular penalty.

Epil.—Avoid the penalties; avoid the sins. "Purge me with hyssop," etc.

First Sunday after Easter.
SERMON 87.
REALITY.
(Holy Gospel, Ser. 3).

(1). S. John xx. 20: "He showed unto them His hands," etc.
(2). Gal. vi. 3: "If a man think himself to be something when he is nothing," etc.

Summa, 3ᵃ, 14, 1, c: "The Lord showed these marks on account of the faith in the Incarnation which was to be confirmed, for His human nature, unless He had subjected it to these defects, would not have been known to men; He would have been thought not to be a real man, or to have had real flesh, but phantom flesh, as the Manichæans stated Him to have." Whence (Philipp. ii. 7, 8), "He made Himself," etc. S. Thomas was recalled to the faith by the sight of His wounds (S. John xx. 28).

Prelude 1. *S. Ignat. ad. Trall. c.* 9.: "Jesus Christ . . . Who was of the race of David; Who was of Mary; Who was truly born, ate and drank; truly suffered persecution under Pontius Pilate; truly was crucified and died, heavenly and earthly, and infernal powers beholding, Who truly rose," etc.

—— 2. The Lord was intensely real; inferior natures are unreal.

—— 3. Reality is a test of power, purity, and sincerity and truth.

—— 4. Reality brings with it a sense of conviction and homage. Jesus was real in His

I. Person, hence He is the "pattern man" in all that is good and glorious.

II. Purpose formed in the glory of His Father, and worked out to a full end.

III. Word, inasmuch as He is the truth and His words are truth and life.

IV. Action, which completed the full harmony of His earthly life.

Epil.—In all things strive after "Reality," rest not in shams, shadows and empty outward appearances.

First Sunday after Easter.
SERMON 88.
THE RECORD OF PATIENCE.
(Holy Gospel, Ser. 4).

(1). S. John xx. 20 : " He showed unto them His hands."
(2). Rev. I. 9. : " The patience of Jesus Christ."
Summa, 3ª, 14, 1, *c.* : " Jesus showed these marks for an example of the patience which He showed for us by so boldly bearing sufferings and defects (Heb. xii. 3)."
Prelude 1. *S. Ignat. ad. Rom.* 10 : " Farewell to the end, in the patience of Jesus Christ." *S. Cyril. Alex. ad. Eph., p.* 266 : " Patience is the patron and conciliatrix to us of all good ; the food of the hope of the coming ages." *S. Chryst., Ep. xvi. ad. Olymp. :* " It is the queen of good things, it. is the coronet of crowns." *Id. Hom. xiv. ad. Rom. :* " It is the name of sweats and of much endurance." *Plaut. Capt. II.* 1, 1 : " It behoves to suffer with a calm mind ; if you do this, the labour will be lightened." *Hor. Od.,* 1, 24, 19 : " It is hard, but whatever it is unlawful to correct, is made lighter by patience.

—— 2. The Lord with infinite and perfect patience carried His spiritual cross all through His lifetime, and in many forms.

—— 3. Some forms of patience are very trying from the vexations being small.

—— 4. The Lord might ask, " Have I suffered ? Was my patience exhausted ? Behold my hands and my side." Jesus afforded us an example of a patience which was

I. LONG CONTINUED. It was exercised from the circumcision to the Ascension.
II. WISE, for He suffered because He willed it.
III. MEASURELESS, when it is noted Who it was that so endured ; taking into account His first estate ; His perfection of being
IV. LOVING, which love lightened it, it was the expression of His infinite longing to save mankind.

Epil.—In patience possess ye your souls, in submission and contentment.

Second Sunday after Easter.

SERMON 89.

THE GOOD SHEPHERD THE DOOR OF HIS CHURCH.
(*Holy Gospel, Ser.* 1).

(1). S. John x. 2, 7 : "I am the Good Shepherd, the door of the sheep."

(2). Rev. iv. 1 : "A door was opened in heaven."

Summa, 3ª, 8, 6, 3ᵐ. : " He gave to His members the office of a shepherd ; but no one calls himself a 'door.' He reserved this office to Himself as His own ; for by a door is signified the chief authority, since by it all enter into the house, and it is Christ Himself alone by whom we have access into that grace by which we stand."

Prelude 1. *Amb. Aug. in Apoc. lib.:* " This door which was opened is Christ according to the flesh, Who was born, Who suffered and Who was raised the third day, ' opened ' to the presence of the believing, but closed to the unbelieving."

—— 2. Only one door, Jesus, into the one house of the Church.

—— 3. Entrance into this door is by Holy Baptism.

—— 4. Not as "a," but as "the" Good Shepherd, Jesus is the door of His Church.

—— 5. By the door we enter, by Himself, by the Sacraments of His love and pardon. This door of the fold, of the Church, is

   I. COMMON for all to enter in ; no restriction of race or time.

  II. FREE, enter in "without money, without price;" " Him that cometh unto Me," etc.

 III. WIDE enough to let " the forces of the gentiles " enter in by it.

 IV. EVER OPEN, its gates are never shut either by night or by day (Isaiah lx. 11).

Epil.—See that it be not opened for you in vain ; think of those who are without (Rev. xxii. 15) and tremble.

Second Sunday after Easter.
SERMON 90.
JESUS THE SHEPHERD OF THE BLESSED.
(*Holy Gospel, Ser.* 2).

(1). S. John x. 16.: "There shall be one fold [flock] and one Shepherd."

(2). 1. S. Pet. II. 25: "Ye are now returned unto the shepherd and bishop of your souls."

Summa, 3ª, 8, 3, c.: "There is this difference between the natural body of man and the mystical body of the Church, that the members of the former are altogether, whilst those of the body mystical are not, and they are considered not only by what they are in act, but also according to what they are in power. First and principally, Christ is the head of those who are in act joined to Himself in glory."

Prelude 1. *S. Chrysost. on* 1 *Colos.*, 18: "He Who is above and above all, connected Himself with those below. For everywhere He is first; above, first; in the church first, for He is the Head; in the Resurrection, first."

——— 2. Jesus is the Good Shepherd or Head of the Church Militant, and triumphant, and of the holy angels (Heb: xii. 22-25). *Ammon Presb.*: "He is about to join together both."

——— 3. Sheep are the blessed, the children of the Church, of whom (Rev. vii. 17) of the blessed or sheep, Jesus is the Shepherd or Head, giving to them

I. LIFE, S. John XIV. 19: Life, the world's one great want, supplied by Him who is "the life."

II. POWER, S. John I. 12; 2 Cor. xii. 9: With whom is all power, both in heaven and earth.

III. GRACE, S. John I. 16, *Gk. Cat.*: "Not communicated, He being the fountain itself, and the root itself of all good things."

IV. GLORY, S. John XVII. 22, *S. Chrysost*: "By my miracles and by my teachings."

Epil.—May He be your Shepherd; you seeing Him with the eye of faith; hearing Him in the Holy Gospels; obeying His commands; rejoicing ever in His guidance.

Second Sunday after Easter.
SERMON 91.
JESUS THE SHEPHERD OF THOSE WITHOUT.
(Holy Gospel, Ser. 3).

(1). S. John x. 16 : There shall be one fold [flock] and one shepherd.
(2). Rom. v. 8: While we were yet sinners Christ died for us.
Summa, 3ª, 8, 3, c: Jesus is the Head or Good Shepherd, "of those who are united to Him only in power (or possibility, potentiâ) ; but which not yet reduced into act, is nevertheless meet to be reduced into act, according to the divine predestination."
Prelude 1. *S. Chrysost. ad Ephes.* III. 8, 10: "It seems indeed, firstly, that He died; secondly, for the ungodly; thirdly, that He reconciled, that He saved, that He justified, that He made them immortal; that He wrought them out to become sons and heirs."
—— 2. Jesus rejects none in whom there remains a power or possibility of salvation ; who are within the range and pale of His divine grace.
—— 3. Infinite is the number of those who have not yet turned their inherent and native power of union with Him, into action.
—— 4. Dreadful state, to want the power or possibility of reformation, of progress, or of using the gifts of grace.
—— 5. Power or possibility is useless unless it be acted upon. This power is
I. PRESENT, an agency of life and grace for the time that now is.
II. SECRET, not as yet developed into manifest holiness ; into a rule of life.
III. INACTIVE, as the leaven before it begins to leaven the whole lump.
IV. TO BE QUICKENED into a new, better and holier life.
Epil.—Each one bears this power and possibility ; use it, excite it, whilst there is yet time and opportunity. Horrible to perish with the seed of grace lying dormant within the soul.

Second Sunday after Easter.
SERMON 92.
JESUS THE SHEPHERD OF THOSE LOVING.
(Holy Gospel, Ser. 4).

(1). S. John x. 16: "There shall be one fold [flock] and one Shepherd."

(2). Ephes. III. 17-19: "Rooted and grounded in love to know the love of Christ."

Summa, 3ª, 8, 3, c.: "Jesus is the Head or Good Shepherd, of those who are joined to Him in act, by charity."

Prelude 1. *S. Jerome:* "The habitation of Christ in the heart, which in the beginning is framed by faith, has its roots and foundation in love, that since we are the husbandry of God (1. Cor. iii. 9) all things grow up and are built in love." *B. Theod. Stud. Ser. Catec.* 12: "Love, O unspeakable gift, out of what, to what has it led? from death to life, from darkness to light, from servitude to freedom, from enmities to true friendship, until it renders us conformed to the image of His Son."

―― 2. Love joins us to the Sinless One, and also covers a multitude of sins.

―― 3. Love forms the strongest heavenly as well as earthly ties.

―― 4. When the soul goes out to Jesus in love, He joins that soul to Himself. The loving soul joined to Jesus as its shepherd, is by Him.

I. GUIDED by the preachers and doctors of the Church into all truth.

II. TENDED by the priests of God's Church, it grows "unto the measure," etc.

III. FED by the Blessed Sacrament of His blessed Body and Blood.

IV. GUARDED by the deposit of doctrine once delivered to the saints.

Epil.―So let the Church as His Body minister to your souls, bringing the Lord to it, and joining Himself as the bishop and shepherd of souls, so to them that girded by His grace, they may hereafter be received into glory.

Third Sunday after Easter.
SERMON 93.
PREACHERS AND HEARERS.
(Holy Gospel, Ser. 1).

(1). S. John xvi. 18 : "We cannot tell what He saith."
(2). S. James i. 19 : "Let everyone be swift to hear."

Summa, 3^a, 42, 3, 2^m : "Whatsoever things of His own wisdom the Lord deemed worthy to deliver to others, He propounded not secretly, but openly, although they might not be understood by all. Hence Augustine says, that the Lord's statement (S. John xviii. 20), 'I spake openly to the world,' was as if He had said, 'Many have heard Me,': and on the contrary it was not 'openly,' for the many did not understand."

Prelude 1. *S. Greg. Mag. in Ezek.*: "When from the mind of the faithful the words of holy preaching flow down, as if from the mind of those believing, rivers of living water flow down." *Eric. Hom. in Joan. vii.*: "The holy preachers are the feet of Christ, the prophet saying, 'How beautiful,'" etc. (Isa. 52, 7). *Euseb. Emiss. Exp. in Matt*: "Whatsoever may be the preacher, if he delivers not his own words, but those of God, the people ought to obey and believe him."

—— 2. Whether the Lord spake "openly," or in "parables," the result was often the same.

—— 3. Many preachers preach in vain. Why so? The language is plain, the matter is good and sound, the delivery of the sermon is good; all is useless, unless the preacher and hearer be united in

I. KNOWLEDGE, so as to understand somewhat of the message delivered.
II. AIM OR DESIRE, the one to teach and move, the other to be taught and guided.
III. EARNESTNESS of thought and feeling for the matter in hand.
IV. SYMPATHY, both preacher and hearer being vitally interested.

Epil.—May divine grace and blessing be sought for alike by preacher and hearer, that the spoken word may not return void, but do God's work.

Third Sunday after Easter.
SERMON 94.
INWARD JOY.
(*Holy Gospel, Ser.* 2).

(1). S. John XIV. 22 : "Your heart shall rejoice."
(2). Rom. XII. 12 : "Rejoicing in hope."
Summa, 22^e, 28, 1, 3^m : "Spiritual joy, which is of God, is when we rejoice in the divine good according as it is participated in by us; and it proceeds from hope, by which we expect the fruition of the divine good."
Prelude 1. S. Ignat. ad Magnes. c. 7 : "One hope in charity, and in joy undefiled."
—— 2. No spiritual blessing can exist alone; it is one of a large family.
—— 3. All are needy, so all are more or less selfish and personal.
—— 4. To desire spiritual blessedness is a holy selfishness.
—— 5. This desire is founded upon the hope of present help and of future glory.
—— 6. When hearts can rejoice in the expectation or hope of the divine good, there is opened in the soul a spring of joy, it may be hidden, but it is ever flowing, ever refreshing and fertilizing the heart. This "inward joy" is
I. HIGH, exalting, lifting up the heart and life above fear and sorrow.
II. PURE, as being founded upon what is altogether pure and holy.
III. SECURE, founded upon a hope, full of immortality, independent of the world.
IV. HELPFUL, as the spring in the desert, enabling the soul both to do and suffer.
Epil.—S. August. in loco T., xi. p. 178, H. : "May our joy be not such as the world has, of which it is said, 'but the world shall rejoice,' but as the Apostle says, 'Rejoicing in hope,' being of good cheer as having overcome the world of sin and sorrow."

Third Sunday after Easter.
SERMON 95.
THE SORROW OF THE WORLD.
(Holy Gospel, Ser. 3).

(1). S. John XVI. 20: "Ye shall be sorrowful."
(2). II. Cor. VII. 10: "The sorrow of the world worketh death."

Summa, 22^c, 35, 1, 3^m : "Sadness pertains to humility, as a man considering his own defects does not exalt himself. But there is another kind of sadness (*acedia*), which belongs rather to ingratitude than to humility, for the good things which a man receives from God he despises, and out of such a contempt, sadness (*acedia*) arises."

Prelude 1. *S. Nilus Orat.* 6 : Sadness (*acedia*) is a weakness of the mind, which neither has natural strength, nor does it strenuously fight against temptations. What food is to a strong and healthy body, trial is to a strong and noble mind. Winds nourish the plants, and trial strengthens the fortitude of the mind. Clouds without water are dissipated by the wind, and the mind void of patience is dissipated by the spirit of sadness."

—— 2. The sorrow or sadness the Lord spoke of, was the Godly sorrow which ends in joy.

—— 3. The larger proportion of sorrow is that of the world (*acedia*), "which worketh death."

—— 4. This inferior worldly sorrow eats out of life, its

I. CONFIDENCE in God's providence, which is ever good for those who fear Him.
II. THANKFULNESS for His infinite mercies, which are renewed day by day.
III. ENERGY of life and action—a sign of weakness, moral and spiritual.
IV. HOPE, either of the present or the future, causing a listless despair.

Epil.—The remedy against this worldly sorrow is to be "Strong in the Lord," etc.

Third Sunday after Easter.
SERMON 96.
THE VISION OF JESUS.
(Holy Gospel, Ser. 4).

(1). S. John XVI. 17: "A little while and ye shall see Me."
(2). I. Cor. IX. 1: "Have I not seen Jesus Christ our Lord?"

Summa, 1ª, 67, 1, c.: "Vision at first signified the action of sensual sight, but on account of the dignity and certainty of this sense, its name was extended according to the use of those speaking, to all the knowledge gained by the other senses; as when men say, 'See how it tastes;' 'see how cold it is.' Lastly, sight is applied to intellectual knowledge, (S. Matt. v. 8) to the sight of God."

Prelude 1. *S. Laur. Justin., de Humil. c.* 22, *p.* 584: "That which is prohibited to be discovered by the sense of the seeing flesh, and by the perceptibility of material light, no one doubts, is possible to be seen by the reasoning spirit of the intellectual light which is more excellent, more delightful, and more useful, since the spiritual act and spiritual light, exceeds that which is bodily and visible."

—— 2. The outward sight of the Lord sustained the disciples; but it was not to last long, but to be replaced by a spiritual vision of the Lord, which will abide in the church till the end of time.

—— 3. The factors of this vision are not eyes, but love, holiness, faith and imitation. This spiritual sight of Jesus

I. SUPPORTS under all the sorrows, trials and sufferings of life; it is full of encouragement.
II. CHEERS, as the beacon light to mariners on a dark and tempestuous sea.
III. INSTRUCTS, the example before the mind ever shows new beauties and glories.
IV. CONFORMS the mind to His mind, by looking and seeing it becomes light.

Epil.—May you ever see Jesus; at the altar; in the offices of the Church; in your daily life; see Him ever blessing you with His blessing of peace.

Fourth Sunday after Easter.

SERMON 97.
LOSS AND GAIN.
(*Holy Gospel, Ser.* 1).

(1). John xvi. 17 : "It is expedient for you that I go away."
(2). Eph. iv. 8 : "He ascended up on high and gave gifts unto men."

Summa, 3ª, 57, 6, c. : "'I go away,' that is, 'I depart from you by the Ascension,' by which He prepared a way for us (S. John xiv. 2, Micah ii. 13). That where the head is the members might be, 'There ye may be also.' So also He led the souls from hell (Ps. lxviii. 13). As high priest under the law, Christ 'entered into heaven itself,' now to appear in the presence of God for us (Heb. ix. 24) to intercede for us. Lastly, that in the seat of the heavens, as constituted God and Lord, He might send down gifts unto men (Eph. iv. 8)," He sent also the Holy Ghost.

Prelude 1. *S. Chrysost. in loco.* : "He seemed to propound two contraries, 'for if we shall see Thee,' they say 'now do you go away'; 'but if you go away, how shall we see Thee?' Moreover, showing that sadness begets joy, and since sadness is short, joy truly is infinite" (*Alcuin*). "All the faithful pressed down by present tears are striving after eternal joys." (Pr. ii.) Loss and gain a part of providence (Pr. iii.) The disciples grieved, the Lord departing, but He went to help them the more. For an eternal and spiritual gain, an earthly loss is one which is

I. NEEDFUL, this world and heaven; this life and the next are opposed spiritually.
II. FLEETING, the loss can at most be but for a few years; the gain is for eternity.
III. DISPROPORTIONATE, the loss so small; the gain beyond conception.
IV. BLESSED in the discipline of the life here, and in the work being carried on elsewhere.

Epil.—Like S. Paul, learn to "count all things but loss," etc. (Philipp. iii. 7, 8).

Fourth Sunday after Easter.

SERMON 98.
NEEDFUL TRUTH.
(Holy Gospel, Ser. 2).

(1) S. John xvi. 13: "The Spirit of Truth will guide you into all truth."

(2) Acts i. 7: "It is not for you to know the times or the seasons," etc.

Summa, 12^c, 106, 4, 2^m: "Christ being glorified in the Resurrection and the Ascension, immediately the Holy Ghost was given, Who taught the holy apostles all the truth concerning these things which belong of necessity to salvation, which are to be believed in and performed; but He did not instruct them as to all future events (Acts i. 7), for this knowledge did not pertain to them."

Prelude 1. *Euthym. Zig.*: "All the truth of the divine dogmas which it is expedient for you to know." (*S. August. in loco*) "He will now teach the faithful as great spiritual things as each is able to receive, and He will kindle in their hearts a greater desire for them." The range of truth is beyond our range of reason.

——— 2. The early Church used and acknowledged "the discipline of the secret;" by the Lord and His apostles religious knowledge was taught with reservations.

——— 3. Many things in Holy Scripture and the faith we cannot understand.

——— 4. In faith we accept the articles of the creed and many precepts of the Gospel. Truth needful for salvation is what all can

I. BELIEVE, as being above, but not contrary to reason.

II. UNDERSTAND in relation to themselves, but not as to the economy of heaven.

III. USE, for the guidance of life as to faith and morals.

IV. ASSIMILATE, take into the soul to nourish it, form part of it, and purify it.

Epil.—Bear in mind the apostolic injunction (Coloss. ii. 18), not vainly "puffed up."

Fourth Sunday after Easter.
SERMON 99.
THE INVISIBLE MISSION.
(Holy Gospel, Ser. 2).

(1). S. John xvi. 7 : " I will send Him unto you."
(2). II. Tim. i. 14 : " The Holy Ghost which dwelleth in us."
Summa, 1ª, 43, 6, 1ᵐ : " To all the participators of grace there is an invisible mission. In him to whom the mission is sent; there are two things to be considered: the inhabitation or indwelling of grace, and a certain innovation or renewal by grace. This invisible mission was made to the fathers of the Old Testament and to the prophets. But when it was said (S. John vii. 39) 'the Holy Ghost was not yet given,' etc., we understand it of that giving with a visible sign which was revealed on the day of Pentecost."
Prelude 1 *Didym. in Joan. xiv.* : " He, the Holy Ghost will teach all things spiritual and intellectual of the truth and the sacraments of wisdom, not as others teach arts by study and industry, but the ' Spirit of truth ' invisibly insinuates into the mind the knowledge of divine things.
—— 2. The faithful besides their guardian angel, carry an invisible presence of the Holy Ghost.
—— 3. Awful if that presence should become visible to bodily eyes. This invisible mission carries with it the
I. INDWELLING of grace, to correct, enlighten, and to comfort.
II. RENEWAL by grace, which repairs day by day the waste caused by sin.
III. REVERENCE for grace, by which our bodies become temples of the Holy Ghost.
IV. RESPONSIBILITY, to make a right use of this heavenly, invisible mission.
Epil.—May this mission, work in each one lovingly, helpfully, savingly.

Fourth Sunday after Easter.
SERMON 100.
THE VISIBLE MISSION.
(*Holy Gospel*, Ser. 4).

(1). S. John XVI. 7 : " I will send Him unto you."
(2). I. Cor. XII. 7 : " The manifestation of the Spirit is given to every man."

Summa, 1^a, 43, 7, 6^m : "A visible mission was made to Christ at His baptism by the fœcund dove, showing the gift of baptismal regeneration ; at the Transfiguration, the light cloud showing the exuberance of His teaching; to the Apostles as wind showing the power of the ministry in the dispensation of the sacraments ; in tongues of fire denoting the office of preaching. The visible mission is also seen in the outward effects of grace (I. Cor. xii. 7), and 'in the gifts of the Holy Ghost' (Heb. ii. 4), as the Son manifested the Father, so the Holy Ghost manifested the Son."

Prelude 1. *Ven. Bede in Joan. xiv.* ; This pertained to the greater gift of the Holy Spirit, that He should be made known by those in whom He dwells," *i.e.*, by the fruits.

—— 2. The life should be a manifestation of the visible mission of the Spirit.

—— 3. There is a visible power of the Holy Ghost in the Church to change the world.

—— 4. This mission is rather to be thought of as in power. This visible mission of God the Holy Ghost in the Church is shown in her,

I. TEACHING and doctrine, the fruits of the spirit of wisdom, truth, etc.

II. SACRAMENTS, the Spirit dwells in the fount, and on the altar to consecrate.

III. POWERS of absolution and consecration.

IV. PREACHING, bringing so many sons and daughters by grace to glory.

Epil.—Love, honour and obey the Church, as carrying on the visible mission of the Holy Ghost in the world.

Fifth Sunday after Easter.

SERMON 101.

THE POWER OF PRAYER.

(*Holy Gospel, Ser.* 1).

(1). S. John XVI. 24 : " Ask and ye shall receive."
(2). S. Jam. I. 5 : " Ask in faith nothing wavering."

Summa, 22^c, 83, 15, c, and 2^m : "Prayer not only inwardly brings spiritual consolation, but it also supplies the power of deserving and obtaining. If truly that which is asked for is useful for the beatitude of a man as pertaining to his salvation, he gains this not by praying alone, but also by doing other good works, and therefore undoubtedly he will gain what he begs for, but he gains it only when he ought to receive it."

Prelude 1. *S. Nilus Ep.* 595 : "Nothing is more forcible than prayer, for it is omnipotent and cannot be overcome."
—— 2. Human nature is weak, ailing, ever needy.
—— 3. There is a treasury, out of which all man's needs can be supplied.
—— 4. There is a power by which all good things can be gained, and all evil things can be turned into blessings.
—— 5. A power provided by God in mercy and love. Prayer is this power, which is

I. PRICELESS, beyond all the value of earthly bliss ; a gift not to be bought.
II. COMMON to the penitent and the holy, to whom the ears of God are ever open.
III. STRONG, nay, omnipotent, as seen by examples in Holy Scripture.
IV. BLESSED in its effects ; a mighty power for good, not for evil.

Epil.—The prayerless life is weak and wretched ; use this power as the one great stay of life.

Fifth Sunday after Easter.

SERMON 102.

UNANSWERED PRAYER.

(*Holy Gospel*, Ser. 2).

(1). S. John XVI. 24: "Ask and ye shall receive."
(2). II. Cor. XII. 8: "For this thing I besought the Lord thrice."

Summa, 22ᶜ, 83, 15, 2ᵐ: "He faithfully supplicating God for the necessities of this life is mercifully heard, and mercifully not heard. What is profitable for the sick man, the Physician knows rather than he who is ill. For this cause, Paul even was not heard when asking for his thorn in the flesh to be taken away."

Prelude 1. *Euseb. Emmiss. in loco.* "Sometimes the holy by not receiving that which they ask for are more heard [and answered] than if they had received it. He who asks what is not good for him, thinking it to be good; receiving what he asks for, is not heard; but not receiving it, is truly heard."

—— 2. Men often ask in prayer, through ignorance, things harmful for them.

—— 3. Few know what is really good for them.

—— 4. Unanswered prayer tries the faith, but gains the blessing.

—— 5. Never think that God does not hear, because He answers not. Unanswered prayer is a sign of God's,

I. LOVE, Who withholds His answer out of compassion.
II. KNOWLEDGE, Who knows perfectly what is best for us.
III. CARE AND THOUGHT, for us men alike in granting and withholding.
IV. WISDOM, Who ordereth all things with an infinite wisdom.

Epil.—Pray and trust, and wait; an answer will come in due time—a different one perhaps from that which was asked for.

Fifth Sunday after Easter.
SERMON 103.
THE UNION OF LOVE.
(Holy Gospel, Ser. 3).

(1). S. John XVI. 27 : " The Father Himself loveth you."
(2). 1. S. John IV. 16 : " He that dwelleth in love dwelleth in God, and God in him."

Summa, 1ᵃ, 20, 1, 3ᵐ. : " Properly to love anyone is to desire some good for him ; so when anyone loves himself, he desires good for himself ; so love is said to be a unitive power ; it is also called a concretive power because it adds something to itself deeming itself to be related to it as to itself. So divine love is a concretive power, inasmuch as it wills good things for others."

Prelude 1. S. Chrysost. in Ioan. III. 16, " Indicates the great intention of love. Great and infinite is the distance, for He Who is immortal, without beginning, and unlimited in greatness, loved those who were of earth and ashes, those filled with sins. So great was His love, that He sent not servant, nor angel, nor archangel, but He gave His own Son," *i. e.* to join man to Himself, and to the Son, and to the Holy Ghost.

——— 2. The power of love joining, condensing, hardening into one, is one of union.

——— 3. By love God joins Himself to us, and He cements and increases this union.

——— 4. We, loving God, become united to Him as to the source of all blessing.

——— 5. Hate disintegrates ; love unites. This " Union of Love " implies a union of,

I. WILL, the unruly will of man is lost in the will of God.
II. IMITATION, or likeness, which re-fashions the mind to God's likeness.
III. KNOWLEDGE, now in part ; hereafter we shall know as we are known.
IV. POWER, so that we can do all things through Christ. " My strength is made perfect."

Epil.—This union of love should join us to God, and to all that is loving, good and holy.

Fifth Sunday after Easter.

SERMON 104.
INTERCESSORY PRAYER.
(*Holy Gospel, Ser.* 4).

(1). S. John XVI. 26 : "I say not unto you that I will pray the Father for you."

(2). Rom. VIII. 34 : "Christ at the right hand of God, maketh intercession for us."

Summa, 2 2^{ae}, 83, 10, 1^m. : "To pray is an act of the reason, and it is properly a prerogative of the rational creature; but to the divine Persons and to brute animals, it is not suitable to pray; which is the action of one desirous of receiving grace. The Son is said to pray according to His assumed human nature, but not according to His divine nature. The Holy Ghost is said to intercede, Rom. VIII. 27, because He makes us interceders," "demanding that mind and will which are grateful, holy, and acceptable to God. (S. Chrys.)

Prelude 1. *S. Chrysost. T.* IX. p. 597. E. "The Lord being of equal honour with the Father, raising and quickening the dead, the very life and fount of all good things, what need had He of intercession to help us, save that the warmth and ripeness of His love to us might be shown?"

—— 2. To pray acknowledges inferiority; to intercede equality.

—— 3. We pray to God for ourselves and others; we intercede between man and man.

—— 4. The Church, "which is His body" carries on His work of intercession on earth, which is one with the intercession of the Son of God before the Father, and which is,

I. UNCEASING, for the Church, like her glorified Redeemer, can never die.

II. AVAILING, pleading by His person and His all atoning work.

III. PARTICULAR, according to the needs and circumstances of each soul and life.

IV. UNIVERSAL, partaken of by every baptised soul.

Epil.—Ever pray to Him that His intercession may avail for our salvation.

Sunday after the Ascension.

SERMON 105.
THE OBSCURED SOUL.
(*Holy Gospel, Ser.* 1).

(1). S. John XVI. 2: "Will think that he doeth God service."
(2). Rom. I. 21 : " Their foolish heart was darkened."
Summa, 22ᵉ, 5, 1, 2ᵐ. : " In the first condition of man there was no obscurity or darkness, either of sin, or of punishment; yet there was present in the intellect of man a certain natural obscurity, by which every creature was darkness as compared with the immensity of the divine light.
Prelude 1, S. Jer. T. IX. 292. c. Eph. IV. 18. "The understanding darkened by blindness of heart ; obscured by ignorance, and by the solicitude for worldly things, and by mist and darkness." Such, (S. Chrysost. T. IX. 450. D.) compares to travellers on a moonless night who perish by seeking the bodiless in bodies, and the formless in forms.
——— 2. How greatly was this darkness or obscurity of soul increased by the fall.
——— 3. This obscurity of soul is the cause of error and evil deeds.
——— 4. The obscured mind of the Jews thought by killing Jesus to please God.
——— 5. The light of Christ and of Grace is opposed to this obscurity of mind.
——— 6. Holy Baptism removing the obscurity and darkness of original sin, was called by the early Church "the sacrament of illumination." The obscured soul has a sight which is,
 I. DIM, unable to see anything clearly; neither doctrine nor consequences of action.
 II. DISTORTED, so that the forms of truth, etc. become altered.
 III. DECEPTIVE, as hiding realities and substituting shadows for them.
 IV. DIMINISHED, or limited as to range and perceptive power.
Epil.—Seek to be " light in the Lord," with a clear and bright soul and understanding.

Sunday after the Ascension.

SERMON 106.
NOT KNOWING.
(Holy Gospel, Ser. 2).

(1). S. John XVI. 3: " They have not known the Father nor Me."

(2), I. Cor. II. 2: " I determined not to know anything among you save Jesus Christ."

Summa, 12ᵉ, 76, 2, c.: " It is not to be imputed to a man as negligence if he knows not the things which he cannot learn, since the ignorance of such an one is invincible, for it is not able to be overcome by study; wherefore such ignorance, since it is involuntary, is not sin."

Prelude 1. *S. Chrysost. Hom.* 76, *in Matt.*: " It is better to be detained in honest ignorance, [or not knowing] than to be enslaved by false opinion; for he who knows not, is easily led by reason; he truly who believes he knows when he does not know, is not able easily to receive the truth. It is a work of greater labour, as before true things can be inculcated, false things must be cast out of his mind. " The ground which is barren yields more easily to the plough than that which is full of brambles."

——— 2. It is much harder to unlearn than to learn. Knowledge of the false, implies ignorance of the true.

——— 3. A great distinction between wilful ignorance and simple " not knowing."

——— 4. The Jew was not " not knowing," but wilfully ignorant of the true Messiah. The effect of this " not knowing " is to render the mind,

I. SIMPLE, as a virgin soil which is uncultivated; as simple, candid.

II. WEAK, incapable of any mental effort requiring deep thought.

III. NARROW, whose mental horizon is confined to the smallest limit.

IV. DOUBTFUL, as the child who fears the dark; as wanting a guide in life.

Epil.—Get knowledge which purifies, exalts, yet humbles the soul.

Sunday after the Ascension.
SERMON 107.
THE DOORS OF KNOWLEDGE.
(*Holy Gospel, Ser.* 3).

(1). S. John XVI. 3: "They have not known the Father nor Me."

(2). Coloss. III. 10: "Put on the new man which is renewed in knowledge."

Summa, 12^e, 78, 1^m.: "Ignorance is the privation of knowledge (1^a, 101, 2^m). For ignorance shuts out that knowledge by which anyone can learn that what he does is evil: such an one therefore sins through ignorance. In this way knowledge is shut out by passion, and from him who sins by a particular act of wickedness."

Prelude 1. *S. Cyril Alex. in Ioan.* 14: "Although 'we see through a glass darkly' and 'know in part' (1. Cor. XIII. 12), yet adhering to the dogmas of the true Church, and following sincerely the sense of scripture we gain that perfect knowledge which no one is able to obtain unless by the light of the Holy Ghost."

—— 2. As there is a baptism of enlightenment, so "the unenlightened one, is the man baptized in ignorance." (S. Clem. Alex. Ad. ad. Gent. p. 3).

—— 3. Ignorance closes the door by which knowledge can enter into the soul.

—— 4. Sensuality and sin also close their doors likewise against knowledge.

—— 5. God opens for us many doors by which knowledge can enter the heart. The doors of spiritual knowledge are,

I. HOLINESS, "If any man will do," ed. S. John VII. 17.

II. FAITH, and knowledge go hand in hand, leading, and opening the door to the treasury of knowledge.

III. LOVE, is the best teacher of all, for its pupils are humble, obedient, quick to learn.

IV. GRACE, which is itself the illuminator, pours its flood of knowledge into the soul.

Epil.—As we grow in likeness to Him "in whom are hid all the treasures," etc. (Coloss. II. 3), so shall we also increase in the knowledge of God.

Sunday after the Ascension.
SERMON 108.
THE ETERNITY OF MEMORY.
(Holy Gospel, Ser. 4).

(1). S. John XVI. 4 : " Ye may remember that I told you."
(2). I. Cor. XV. 2 : " Ye are saved if ye keep in memory what I preached unto you."

Summa, 1ª, 77, 8, 3 and 4ᵐ. : " The powers of the mind are not corrupted with the corrupt body, but they remain in the separated soul. Memory is a power of the mind. That memory remains in the separated soul, is proved by Abraham's appeal to the rich man in Hades (S. Luke XVI. 23). Remembrance is to be understood in the same sense in which Augustine (De Trin. lib. x. CII.) places it in the mind."

Prelude 1. *S. Greg. Naz. Orat.* 26 : " Memory is the preservation of a thing received ; and the recovery of that which had slipped by, is reminiscence." Plato Phil. 39, a. " Memory coinciding with our sensations works in our souls."

—— 2. Pains of the body end with death.
—— 3. Pains of mind last for ever in eternal memory.
—— 4. Saved from fire and shipwreck, etc., a temporary rest of mind and body.
—— 5. Without a hell, no rest though memory, remains for the wicked.
—— 6. We make a lasting heaven or hell for ourselves by the memory of past life. This eternal memory implies,

I. A GIFT, which is priceless as to its infinite capacities of joy and thankfulness.
II. RESPONSIBILITY, we cannot banish the past if we would.
III. ETERNAL REMORSE, it is the worm that dieth not within the soul.
IV. ETERNAL JOY AND GLADNESS, springing from the memory of past mercies.

Epil.—Use memory as an instrument of grace to preserve you from sin.

Whitsunday.

SERMON 109.
OBEDIENCE THE FOUNDATION OF LOVE.
(Holy Gospel, Ser. 1).

(1). S. John xiv. 21 : " He that hath my commandments," etc.

(2). 1. Tim. i. 5 : " Now the end of the commandment is charity," etc.

Summa, 22^e, 44, 1, c. : " The end of the spiritual life is that man may be united to God, which is by charity ; and to this, as to an end, are all things ordained, which pertain to the spiritual life. An impure heart is drawn away from the love of God, inclining by passion to earthly things. An evil conscience makes a man tremble at the divine justice from the fear of punishment. A feigned faith draws away the affection to a feigned God. Therefore love is the great commandment (S. Matt. xxii. 26)."

Prelude 1. *S. Chrysost. in Ioan.* xiv. : " This is love to obey and believe in him who is loved." Ven. Bede : " Love is to be shown by act lest it be the unfruitful appellation of a name." Euth Zinga : " The sign of love of Me " is the keeping of My commandments."

—— 2. Obedience to God's commands is of a ' pure heart, good conscience,' etc.

—— 3. Out of these three forms of obedience, love springs up in the soul.

—— 4. The unholy cannot love God, practically they hate Him. Obedience leads to a love which begets,

I. SYMPATHY, with God as to being, purpose or aim of life.
II. IMITATION of, or likeness to God—moral, mental and spiritual, after man's degree.
III. SUBMISSION, to His most holy will in all things.
IV. UNION, with God, as being one with Him in thought, action and desire.

Epil.—Seek to know and to do God's will, then God's love will come to you and you will grow to love God more and more until the day of Jesus.

Whitsunday.

SERMON 110.
THE HOLY GHOST THE GIVER OF GIFTS.
(Holy Gospel, Ser. 2).

(1). S. John. XIV. 26 : " The Holy Ghost Whom the Father," etc.

(2). 1. Cor. XII. 4 : " There are diversities of gifts, but the same Spirit."

Summa, 1ª, 38, 2, c. : " A gift is a proper and personal name for the Holy Ghost, for a gift properly signifies an unreturnable giving ; one not given with any thought of retribution, it implies a gratuitous donation, but the ground of this is love, for what we give to another, is of the love by which we will some good to him; whence it is manifest, that love is the cause of the first gift, by which all gratuitous gifts are given. Hence Augustine says: 'by the Gift, which is the Holy Ghost,' many particular gifts are divided to the members of Christ."

Prelude 1. *Theod. in* 1. *Cor.* XII. 4. : " Many and diverse are the gifts given but one is the fount of all." S. Fulgent, Contra. Fab. Frag. 29. : " When we see a spiritual gift, it is called by the name of Spirit."

—— 2. The gifts of the Holy Ghost are the fruits of the Spirit.

—— 3. The highest gifts of the Holy Ghost are regeneration, consecration and absolution. The other 'gifts of the Spirit' are partly spiritual and partly moral. All the gifts of the Holy Ghost are,

I. GOOD, tending to some power of good, for this or the next world.

II. TRUE, for the Spirit is the Spirit of Truth, to lead into all truth.

III. BEAUTIFUL, in the effects of these gifts in glorifying our common life.

IV. HELPFUL, as enabling men to endure and to overcome sin, sorrow, etc.

Epil.—Use these gifts prayerfully, practically, and thankfully.

Whitsunday.
SERMON III.
THE HOLY GHOST—WIND.
(*Holy Gospel*, *Ser.* 3).

(1). S. John xiv. 26 : " The Holy Ghost Whom the Father will send."
(2). Acts ii. 2 : " A rushing mighty wind."   Epist. Whitsunday.

Summa, 1ª, 36, 1, c. : " This name ' Holy Spirit ' is taken from the use of scripture, and it has a proper significance, since the word or name ' Spirit ' seems to signify in relation to bodily things, a certain impulse or motion ; for breath and wind we call spirit."

Prelude 1. *S. Chrysost. Hom.* 20, *Op. Imperf.*: " The earth cannot fructify with showers unless the wind blows over it ; so it is not possible that doctrine alone can correct man unless the Holy Ghost co-operates in the heart. S. Cyril Jeru. Cat. Lec. xvii. 15. : " The mighty wind signifying the presence of Him Who was to grant unto men to seize the Kingdom of God with violence, that their ears might hear the sound."

—— 2. A type of the Holy Ghost coming and going we know not how (S. John iii. 8).

—— 3. A breath or Inspiration of the Almighty.

—— 4. We cannot see but we can feel wind ; we cannot see but we can feel the action of the Holy Ghost breathing upon our souls.   This wind of the Holy Ghost,

I. CLEARS, (Prov. xxv. 23), driving the clouds of sin and doubt out of the soul.

II. COOLS, (Dan. iii. 25), the air of the soul heated by sorrow, toil and care.

III. DRIES UP, (Ex. xiv. 21), all undue confidence and pride.

IV. CARRIES, our prayers to God, making intercession for us (Rom. viii. 26).

Epil.—So may this divine Wind cool, purify and invigorate the soul.

Whitsunday.
SERMON 112.
THE HOLY GHOST—LOVE.
(Holy Gospel, Ser. 4).

(1). S. John xiv. 26 : " The Holy Ghost Whom the Father will send," etc.

(2). Rom. v. 5 : " The love of God is shed abroad in our hearts by the Holy Ghost."

Summa, 1^a, 37, 1, c. and 2^m. : " Love, personally understood, is the particular name of the Holy Ghost. There are two processions in divine things, one by the intellect, the other by the will, which last is the procession of love. Love in us, is something remaining in him loving. When it is said that the Holy Spirit is the Love of the Father for the Son, or for anything else, the passage of one thing passing to another is not signified, but only the habit (habitudo) of love towards the thing loved."

Prelude 1. *S. Chrysost. in Rom. T.* ix. ? 514, *E.* : " Giving the Holy Ghost He showed the warmth of His love, He honoured us not a little nor in a small degree, but He poured upon us a continuous fountain of good things."

—— 2. The Spirit of love is an abiding presence and power in the Christian soul.

—— 3. From a presence it passes into a part of the soul; "filled with the Holy Ghost." This Spirit of Love in the soul,

I. PURIFIES, the fire of His love burning up sin and all unworthiness.
II. CONFORMS it to the image of the Son.
III. CONFIRMS, and strengthens it in all goodness.
IV. COMFORTS, as the loving Comforter, by sympathy and hope.

Epil.—Keep, O keep this blessed loving guest. Quench not the Spirit.

Trinity Sunday.

SERMON 113.
THE BAPTISM OF INFANTS.
(Holy Gospel, Ser. 1*).*

(1). S. John III. 5: "Except a man be born again of water," &c.

(2). 1. Cor. 1. 16: "I baptized also the household of Stephanas."

Summa, 3ª, 68, 9. c.: "Children are to be baptized as being (born) in original sin, and that having been nurtured in the Christian religion, they may the more firmly persevere in it (Rom. v. 18). Being also born in condemnation through Adam, that they also being mortal, may be re-born to obtain salvation by Christ." In the same part, question, and article, S. Thomas uses the arguments cited below.

Prelude 1. *S. Iren. lib.* 11, *c.* 39: "Christ came to save all by Himself; all, that is, who are by Him regenerated to God; infants and little ones (infantes et parvulos) and boys, and youths, and old men. Therefore He went through every age being made an infant for infants."

—— 2. Infant baptism is proved by S. Justin Martyr, Tertullian, Origen, and S. Cyprian.

—— 3. Baptism is the appointed means of entering into the Kingdom of God.

Holy Baptism like the other sacraments demands certain conditions,

I. AUTHORITY, (*a*). The command of the Lord, S. Matt. XXVIII. 19, not restricted to men and women only. (*b*). The example of the apostles. (*c*). The practice of the early Church.

II. INTENTION, "As the child is nourished by the mother before the birth and the existence of reason, so are the unreasoning nourished in the womb of the Church. Mother Church furnishes the maternal mouth to her children." S. August.

III. FAITH, which expressed by the sponsors, operates through the whole church by the Spirit.

IV. ANSWER OF A GOOD CONSCIENCE, towards God I. Pet. III. 21, supplied for infants by their sponsors.

Epil.—Let not the parents delay the baptism of their children, life being uncertain.

Trinity Sunday.
SERMON 114.
THE MIRACLES OF JESUS.
(*Holy Gospel, Ser.* 2).

(1). S. John III. 2 : " No man can do these miracles," etc.
(2). I. Cor. XII. 10 : " To another the working of miracles,"
Summa, 3ᵃ, 43, 4, c. : " Since the miracles of Christ exceed human powers and were wrought by the peculiar power of Christ, they abundantly prove His divinity."

Prelude 1. *Theodot. Ancyr.* : " That is called a miracle which cannot be explained by human reasonings." S. Chrysost. speaks of a miracle as a " manifestation of divine honour or glory; a gift of divine grace; it surpasses our nature."

—— 2. The Lord did not work miracles to astonish and convert the unbelieving, but to confirm the faithful.

—— 3. Our common life and the world in which we live form one continuous miracle of the power and love of God.

—— 4. Ven. Bede : The will and operation of the Father, the Son, and the Holy Ghost is one. Of our Lord's miracles we note the,

I. KIND (id. 42, 4). They exceed all power of created virtue, they could only be performed by divine power; as that on the blind man (S. John IX. 32).

II. MANNER of working them. " By His own power, and not by praying, as others." S. Luke IX. 19 : " There went virtue out of Him." S. Matt. VIII. 16 : " He cast out the spirit."

III. PURPOSE ; not to astonish but to do good. " Mark how great is the multitude of men the Evangelists recount as cured " (S. Chrysost.)

IV. TEACHING confirmed by them ; deduced from them (S. Mark I. 27).

Epil.—Divine grace enables us, through Him, to work miracles on our souls ; repentance, amendment of life, the hope of Heaven, are all miraculous.

Trinity Sunday.
SERMON 115.
THE PROCESSION OF THE SACRED THREE.
(Holy Gospel, Ser. 3).

(1). S. John III. 13 : " He that came down from Heaven, the Son of Man."

(2). Eph. IV. 9 : " That He ascended, what is it but that He also descended first."

Summa 1ᵃ, 27, 1, c. : " Every procession is for some action; if it tends to exterior matter it is a procession to the without; so for the action which remains in the doer himself, the procession is applied to the within. This chiefly is manifest in the intellect, the action of which, *i.e.* to understand, remains in him understanding. But whosoever understands, out of this itself which he understands proceeds some thing within himself which is a conception of the thing understood, and arising from intellectual power and proceeding from the conception of it; which conception the voice signifies and it is called the word of the heart; signified by the word of the voice."

Id. 30, 2, c.: " Paternity, filiation, and procession are called personal properties, as if constituting persons. Paternity is the person of the Father, filiation of the Son, and procession the person of the Holy Ghost proceeding—

—— 2. In the soul of man, the image of God, by spiritual meditation, is formed the procession of an interior word, which the tongue can express.

—— 3. Man's processions want personality and life; the divine processions are living Persons. The Procession of the Sacred Three teaches the Christian soul to

I. MEDITATE deeply and prayerfully upon spiritual things.
II. CONCEIVE by the procession of thought, conceptions of things heavenly.
III. EMBODY these processions in a clear, tangible form.
IV. EXPRESS them in language, for the guiding of self and of others.

Epil.—Realize the power of thought illumined by the grace of the Holy Spirit.

Trinity Sunday.
SERMON 116.
ASSIMILATION WITH GOD.
(Holy Gospel, Ser. 4).

(1). S. John III. 15: "He that came down from heaven, the Son of man."

(2). II. S. Pet. I. 4: "Partakers of the divine nature."

Summa, 1ª, 43, 5, 2ᵐ.: "The mind by grace is conformed to God; whence to this end that some divine Person might be sent to some one by grace; it is needful that there should be an assimilation of him, to the divine Person Who is sent, by some gift of grace. The Son is sent, not for any general perfection of the intellect, but for such instruction of the intellect as may break forth in the affection of love; as it is said (S. John VI. 45), 'Every man therefore,' etc. (Ps. XXXIX. 3), 'While I was musing the fire [of love] burned,' and because the Holy Ghost is love, by the gift of charity the soul becomes assimilated to the Holy Spirit."

Prelude 1. *Theod. in Epist. Gal.* II. 20: "I put away my former life, I have passed over to another life, in this I live, I put on the life of it.

—— 2. Assimilation means likeness, and more than likeness: a joining, a partaking of the nature, life and habits of another. This spiritual assimilation, for which the Son and Holy Ghost came into this world, implies a,

I. LIKENESS, as Jesus was made like unto His brethren, so should we become like Him.
II. UNION, "He that is joined to the Lord," assimilated, "is one spirit," mind and aim.
III. LOSS, of much of the old sinful self and its past desires.
IV. GAIN, of a new and better nature, supplanting the old and consecrating its whole.

Epil.—The Lord came first, and He sent the Holy Ghost afterwards, not only to give a pattern for life, but infuse a new and better life into man by the assimilation which is carried on by the power of God the Holy Ghost.

First Sunday after Trinity.
SERMON 117.
MENTAL VISION.
(*Holy Gospel, Ser.* 1).

(1). S. Luke XVI. 23 : " He seeth Abraham afar off."
(2). Ps. XXXIV. 7 : " The angel of the Lord encampeth round about them that fear Him."

Summa, 1ª, 89, 2, c. : " So the separated souls see both demons and angels, they do not regard phantoms, but the things which they can understand ; whence they understand themselves by themselves. The state of the substance of the separated soul is below the state of angelic substance, but it is equal to the state of other separated substances. It has perfect knowledge of other separated souls, but imperfect and deficient knowledge of the angels"

Prelude 1. *Batholo. Sybill. c.* 3, *q.* 4 : " The souls of the lost, to the day of judgment, will see the souls of the blessed and the glory of them."

—— 2. Abraham, Lazarus and Dives were all separated souls ; as yet no resurrection.

—— 3. Hard to imagine the condition of the soul, without a body, without eyes, etc.

—— 4. The weight of the body hinders the soul from a perfect intelligence.

—— 5. So there is a sight of the eye of the mind, as well as of the body. In the separated state, the soul by itself will have of itself and others a sight which will be,

I. SEARCHING, nothing concealed from it by any imperfection.
II. UNCHANGING, until the resurrection.
III. AGONIZING, to the lost, the beholding the glory of the righteous.
IV. REJOICING, to the righteous a foretaste of the Beatific vision.

Epil.—So live as to gain after death a vision of eternal glory.

First Sunday after Trinity.
SERMON 118.
THE GUARDIAN ANGEL.
(*Holy Gospel, Ser.* 2).

(1). S. Luke xvi. 22: "The beggar died and was carried by the angels."

(2). Ps. xci. 2: "He shall give His angels charge over thee."

Summa 1ª, 113, 4, c.: "In this state of life man is placed as if in a certain way to tend to his country; in which way many dangers, both outward and inward, hang over him. Ps. cxlii. 3: "In the way," etc. So to men walking in an unsafe way are given guards. To man, as long as he is a traveller, is granted a guardian angel. When he shall have come to the end of his way he will not have a guardian angel, but in that kingdom an angel ruling with him." "This guardian angel is given at baptism" (Summa 1ª, 113, 5 c.).

Prelude 1. *S. Chrysost. Hom. v. in Luke*: "Each one of the angels rejoices, willing to bear so great a burden. The angels are laden with many such burdens that they may carry men into the kingdom of heaven."

—— 2. Full of comfort is the thought that man is not left solitary and unaided either in life or at death—that he is ever an object of care to God's ministering spirits.

—— 3. One special angel is appointed to watch over us from the cradle to the grave. He our angel guards us

I. STRONGLY, he bears us up under sorrow, and in temptation and attack.

II. TENDERLY, lest we dash our feet against the stones of stumbling in our path of life.

III. WATCHFULLY, not being ignorant of Satan's devices, vigilance, and strength.

IV. UNCEASINGLY, never leaving us unguarded; often grieved; never turning away.

Epil.—Receive the angel ministry with faith, thankfulness, and courage.

First Sunday after Trinity.
SERMON 119.
THE MINISTRY OF ANGELS.
(Holy Gospel, Ser. 3).

(1). S. Luke xvi. 22 : "The beggar died and was carried by the angels."

(2). Heb. i. 14: "Are they not all ministering spirits?"

Summa 1ª, 112, 1, c. : "The angel is sent from God, and the action which the angel who is sent exercises, proceeds from God, by Whose consent and authority the angels act; and their action is referred to God as to its ultimate end. This is the ground of their ministry and the minister is as an intelligent instrument, which is moved by another and is ordered according to the will of another; whence the actions of the angels are called ministries, and so they are said to be sent for ministry."

Prelude 1. *Pet. de Blois. Ser.* 40 : "The angels minister to our salvation, for our sakes, who in our souls have a like nature to theirs ; for God's sake, whose bowels of mercy they see poured out around us ; for their own sakes, as if by living stones the vision of the coelestial walls of their city may be restored."

—— 2. Lazarus enjoyed the protection of this angel ministry though he knew it not.

—— 3. As at the temptation, the ministration succeeds the suffering and the trial. The ministry of angels is

I. APPOINTED by God Himself, Whose servants they are ; part of the economy of grace.

II. PROVIDENTIAL, so that man may neither faint nor fall under sorrow and temptation.

III. LOVING, one long ministry of love founded upon man's need.

IV. BLESSED in effect, as guiding the soul by grace and carrying it into glory.

Epil.—Realize the position, that with this ministry of angels the Christian soul is master of the situation ; that strength and wisdom are ever present with it, ready to help in time of need.

First Sunday after Trinity.

SERMON 120.
DEATH A FORETASTE.
(*Holy Gospel, Ser.* 4).

(1). S. Luke XVI. 22, 23: "The rich man also died, and in hell," etc.

(2). II. Cor. v. 8: "Absent from the body, and to be present with the Lord."

Summa 3", 59, 5, 1'": "To the Penitent thief the Lord said, 'To-day, etc. in Paradise' (S. Luke XXIII. 43); the Apostle also (II Cor. v. 6, 7, 8): for to be present with the Lord is to 'walk by sight,' is to see God by essence, in which sight is eternal life. S. John XVII. 3: whence it is manifest that [holy] souls separated from the body are in eternal life obtaining after death an unchanging state. In respect therefore to the reward of the soul there is no need for the judgment to be further differed. But because certain other things pertain to man, which are done in the whole course of time, and which are not alien to the divine judgment, it behoves that at the end of times all such things should again be brought into judgment, which things will not alter either man's merits or his demerits."

Prelude 1. *Nic. de Lyra:* "He (the rich man) was the parishioner of the devil, and he was paying back the principal temporal goods which he had badly consumed."

—— 2. The separate soul passed at once to torment; the life is framing the sentence. Death is a foretaste of man's eternal

I. STATE or condition, of his lasting dwelling-place—heaven or hell.

II. LIFE, for the life and dwelling go together; a holy life, and a holy home.

III. REWARD, either from God, of happiness; from Satan, of torment.

IV. GLORY, or of shame and "everlasting contempt." Note the degradation of hell.

Epil.—Let the holy life here, be but one long preparation for a glorious future.

Second Sunday after Trinity.
SERMON 121.
THE CATHOLIC CHURCH.
(Holy Gospel, Ser. 1).

(1). S. Luke XIV. 21 : "Go out quickly into the streets and lanes," etc.

(2). Isaiah LX. 11 : "Thy gates shall be open continually that men may bring unto thee," etc.

Summa, 3ª, 42, 1, 3 and 3ᵐ. : "Christ instructed certain of the Gentiles—as the woman of Samaria (S. John IV.), and the woman of Canaan (S. Matt. XV.)—for it was not right wholly to drive away the Gentiles, lest the hope of salvation should be shut out from them; and on this account some of the Gentiles were admitted on account of the excellency of their faith and devotion."

Prelude 1. *S. Aug. in loco.* : "The nations came from the broad roads and from the streets, and the heretics from the hedges or enclosures. For they who construct hedges seek divisions, they are drawn out from the hedges, they are rooted out from the thorns, but they are unwilling to be forced. ' Let us enter ' they say ' of our own will.' "

——— 2. The Church, as being catholick, receives all within her pale.

——— 3. Multitudes have never been invited to enter the fold, and many refuse to enter when invited. The poor and the outcast obtained the supper rejected by the others.

——— 4. Those who come within the Church will find that they are gainers of those spiritual blessings which are,

I. ETERNAL, which is the nature of all spiritual things.

II. THEIR VERY OWN, graces, promises, powers which become elements in the spiritual life.

III. REAL, in their action on both the heart and life; in the help and hope they give.

IV. PRECIOUS, as true riches, passing current in heaven as on earth.

Epil.—Come then within the Church's fold, as to the supper of our King and High Priest; come hungering and thirsting after righteousness, that ye may be more than filled—satisfied for ever.

Second Sunday after Trinity.

SERMON 122.
THE ANGER OF GOD.
(*Holy Gospel, Ser.* 2).

(1). S. Luke xiv. 21 : " The master of the house being angry."

(2). Ps. lxxvi. 7 : "Who may stand when once Thou art angry ?"

Summa, 1ª, 3, 2, 2ᵐ. : "Anger, joy, and such like passions are joined to the soul, and are attributed to God in scripture according to the similitude of their effects; for as it is the habit of the angry to punish, so God's punishment is metaphorically called anger."

Prelude 1. *Ven. Bede in loco:* "The passion of anger never happens in the divine substance, but such operation which in us arises from anger, is called the anger and indignation of God."

―― 2. God is subject to no passions; He is "without passions."

―― 3. In God, anger is an act of the will to punish, but not of passion.

―― 4. Here in this gospel, the sin of ingratitude aroused the expression of punishment.

―― 5. *Palladas, Epg.* 136 :
" God, a philosopher I deem ;
Not waxing wroth at once with evil men,
Who utter blasphemies against His name ;
Increasing not their punishments just then ;
Reserving retribution for the same."

God's anger against the unrepentant sinner is often,

I. Hidden ; He allows the sinner to go on his own way for a time.

II. Abiding, while the sinner draws sin as with a cart rope.

III. Increasing, as the weight of lead cast upon the mouth of the ephah (Zech. v. 6-8).

IV. Ready, to break forth when the measure of iniquity is fully ripe.

Epil.—" Kiss the Son lest He be angry," etc., and remember, that in judgment as often as in mercy, God delays His chastisement and withholds His hand.

Second Sunday after Trinity.
SERMON 123.
THE PASSION OF JESUS, THE SUPPER OF THE LORD.
(Holy Gospel, Ser. 3).

(1). S. Luke xiv. 16 : " A certain man made a great supper."
(2). 1. Cor. xi. 26 : "As often as ye eat this bread and drink this cup ye do shew the Lord's death."

Summa, 3^a, 49, 5, c. and 4^m. : " We are freed by the Passion of Christ from the sin which is common to our human nature, and from the special sins of each one. They are freed, who communicate in His Passion by faith, love, and the Sacraments of the Church ; and therefore by His Passion is the door of the kingdom of heaven opened to us, He having entered by his own blood into the holy place (Heb. ix. 1, 2). Christ by His Passion gained for us an entrance into the kingdom of heaven, and He removed the impediment."

Prelude 1. *Titus Bost.* : " Supper " in which time Christ endured death for our sakes, and set forth his flesh for our food. S. August. Ser. 33, De Verb. Dom. " The supper is now prepared ; Christ having been sacrificed, it is now commended after the Resurrection of Christ, that the faithful might know the Supper of the Lord."

—— 2. *S. Cyp. Ep.* LXII. 11 : " That Priest truly acts in Christ's stead who imitates that which Christ did ; and he then offers a true and full sacrifice in the church to God the Father."

—— 3. *S. Cyr. Jerus. Lect.* XXIII. 8 : " The Spiritual sacrifice is perfected, the bloodless service upon that sacrifice of propitiation." Partaking of this supper, the sinner is,

I. PARDONED, the Precious Blood was "shed for the remission of sins."—S. Matt. xxvi. 28.
II. SATISFIED, neither hungering nor thirsting any more. S. John vi. 35.
III. STRENGTHENED, for His flesh and blood is "truly meat and drink."—S. John vi. 55.
IV. GLORIFIED, for he hath dwelling in him the principle of eternal life.—S. John vi. 54.

Epil.—The disposition in which the faithful communicate in the Passion of Christ is one embracing thankfulness, faith, humility, and adoring love.

Second Sunday after Trinity.
SERMON 124.
BLESSEDNESS.
(*Holy Gospel, Ser.* 4).

(1). S. Luke xiv. 16 : " A certain man made a great supper."
(2). Rev. xix. 9. : " Blessed are they that do His commandments."

Summa, 12ᵃᵉ, 2, 3, c. and 2ᵐ. : " Beatitude, the perfect good, is the ultimate perfection of man, but inasmuch as it is perfect insomuch it exists in action ; for power without action, is imperfect ; so it behoves blessedness to consist in the ultimate action of man."

Prelude 1. *Honor. Presb.* : " Perfection is the sufficiency of all good without any need," of all goodness in action which is blessedness.

—— 2. "Supper," of eternal beatitude Cai. " This feast is called not a dinner in S. Mathew, but a supper ; after the dinner, is a supper with no after meal ; many are cast out after the dinner, but more from the supper." —*Gloss. Ordin.*

—— 3. Blessedness is a state of action ; not a mere passive existence.

—— 4. Action which is holy, makes life happy ; idleness makes life miserable.

—— 5. Action develops man ; inaction stunts his growth.

—— 6. Action tends to perfection, which is blessedness. Real, or good action, which is blessedness, is,

I. HOLY, tending to God's glory and to man's salvation.
II. CONTINUAL, no mere spasmodic effort, but a continuous course of life.
III. INTENSE, taxing to the uttermost the powers of both body and mind.
IV. EFFICIENT, leading upwards and onwards to all that is great and good.

Epil.—Try somewhat to realize the heavenly life of energy, power, and action.

Third Sunday after Trinity.
SERMON 125.
USE AND ABUSE.
(*Holy Gospel, Ser.* 1).

(1). S. Luke xv. 2 : " This man receiveth sinners and eateth with them."

(2). 1. Tim. iv. 4 : " Every creature of God is good, and nothing to be refused."

Summa, 3ª, 40, 2, c. and 1ᵐ. : " Since it was meet that Christ should converse with men, it plainly behoved Him to order His conversation like other men as to his food and drink, abstinence from which in itself does not pertain to salvation ; " For the kingdom of God is not meat and drink (Rom. xiv. 17).

Prelude 1. *S. T. Aq. on* 1. *Tim. vi.* 2-6 : " He calls these Minichæans ' devils,' who prohibit the use of flesh and wine The Apostle rebukes this error as twofold, as against the intention of God creating food (Gen. ix. 3), and against the condition of the creature. Were not the plants made for the animals, and the animals for man ? "

—— 2. Use of wine and strong drink (Deut. xiv. 26), Lord at Cana (S. John iii., S. Paul i., Tim. v. 23).

—— 3. All God's " creatures " of food or drink can be used well and rightly.

—— 4. All can be abused by lust or excess in their use.

—— 5. Gluttony and drunkenness alike forbidden; suspend drink, then suspend food.

—— 6. " The Son of Man came eating and drinking," etc., " but wisdom," etc. (S. Matt. xi. 19). Showing how both can be used to God's glory. Use God's creatures

I. MODERATELY, with the appetites kept in due subjection.

II. THANKFULLY, as acknowledging that " every good gift is from above."

III. NEEDFULLY, as enabling life, health, and strength to be preserved for action.

IV. AS AN EXAMPLE to others of a holy and right use in which there is no abuse.

Epil.—1. Cor. vii. 31. So may we use this world and the things of it, as not abusing it.

Third Sunday after Trinity.
SERMON 126.
THE LOVE OF JESUS FOR SINNERS.
(Holy Gospel, Ser. 2).

(1). S. Luke xv. 2: "This man receiveth sinners."
(2). Eph. iii. 19: "The love of Christ which passeth knowledge."

Summa, 22^e, 25, 6, c.: "In sinners two things are to be considered, their nature which they have from God capable of blessedness, and their sin, which is opposed to God, and is an hindrance to salvation. We ought then, as being fellow sinners, to love them, because they are men capable of blessedness. This is to love sinners out of charity for God's sake."

Prelude 1. *S. T. Aquinas ad Ephes. c. iii., lect. v.:* "To know the love of Christ is to know all the mysteries of His incarnation, and of our redemption which proceeded out of the immense love of God, which love exceeds every created intellect, and the knowledge of all since it is incomprehensible by thought." S. Peter Chrysos.: "Christ does not receive sins, when He receives sinners."

—— 2. The Lord hated the sin, but He loved the sinner; so also should we.

—— 3. As men the Lord loved them, subjecting Himself to like temptations.

—— 4. He loved sinners as being "capable of blessedness," of higher and better things. The love of Jesus for sinners was at once

  I. Gentle and tender towards those who, like the Magdalen, sought Him in repentance.
  II. Sorrowful over the lost and fallen. "O Jerusalem" (S. Matt. xxiii, 37).
  III. Forgiving: "Neither do I condemn thee," etc. (S. John viii. 2).
  IV. Hopeful as to their restoration and conversion. Hence His commission to His Apostles.

Epil.—Learn to love and pity, and try to rescue sinners for Jesus' sake.

Third Sunday after Trinity.
SERMON 127.
LOST INNOCENCE.
(Holy Gospel, Ser. 3).

(1). S. Luke xv. 16: "I have found my sheep which was lost."
(2). 1 Tim. v. 22: "Keep thyself pure."

Summa, 3ª, 89, 3, c.: "It seems, that by penitence, man cannot be restored to his pristine dignity. Amos (v. 2) says: 'The virgin of Israel is fallen'; the Gloss, adds: 'it is not denied that she can arise, but she cannot arise a virgin of Israel.' Man, by penitence, can return to the principal dignity which he lost by sinning, so that he can become a son of God, but he is not able to regain his lost innocence."

Prelude 1. S. *Greg. Mag. Hom. in loco*: "It is to be noted that He does not say 'Rejoice with the lost sheep,' but 'with me'; for our life is His joy, and we fulfil the solemnity of His delight."

—— 2. S. *John Clim. Scal. Parad. Grad.* 24: "Innocence is the serene tranquility of mind which is far removed from every perverse thought."

—— 3. *Humbt. De Spec. Relig. lib.* 1, c. 7: "If innocence is lost, all good things are lost—the foundation of righteousness and God the giver of it."

—— 4. S. T. *Aq. in* 1 *Tim. v.* Firstly he exhorts him to purity, and from this he represses his immoderate abstinence."

—— 5. Innocence is the great gift of Jesus at Baptism, and on the cross. Innocence once lost remains as a,

I. Loss, much is restored by grace, but not the past consciousness of purity.
II. Mark of the former fire, though the house of the soul may be rebuilt.
III. Shame, still lurking in the soul as a sting of conscience; as a humbling memory.
IV. Warning against temptation; as a still small voice not to be stilled.

Epil.—Cherish innocence as God's greatest gift; seek for pardon for every sin.

Third Sunday after Trinity.
SERMON 128.
JOY OVER THE PENITENT.
(Holy Gospel, Ser. 4).

(1). S. Luke xv. 7: "Joy shall be in heaven over one sinner that repenteth."

(2). II. S. Pet. III. 9: "The Lord is not willing that any should perish."

Summa, 3ª, 89, 3, c.: "Man can by repentance return to the principal dignity which he had lost by sinning; therefore, there is greater joy over Him in heaven, as a general in battle would rather love that soldier who, having turned back, returned and strongly pressed the enemy; than one who never having turned back, had equally never performed any brave action."

Prelude 1. *Pet. de Blois. Ep.* 50: "God more readily accepts the repentance of a humble and contrite sinner, than the innocence of the lukewarm and careless righteous." *Haymo Bp. in loco*: "The angels of God have greater joy over those sinners who bitterly afflict themselves with fastings and vigils, than over those remaining just who, since they have not committed the heavier sins, trouble themselves but little about them."

—— 2. The joy is "over" but not in the penitent; sorrow and thankfulness are within him.

—— 3. An abiding sense of humiliation remains ever after pardoned sin. This joy over the penitent must be,

I. COMPARATIVE; founded upon a comparison of his two states.

II. COMPASSIONATE; not of exultation, but of pitying gladness.

III. UNEXPECTED, and therefore the more welcome.

IV. MINGLED with many a fear, lest a relapse take place.

Epil.—Repentance is glorious; much more glorious never to have fallen.

Fourth Sunday after Trinity.
SERMON 129.
LIBERALITY.
(*Holy Gospel, Ser.* 1).

(1). S. Luke VI. 38 :" Give and it shall be given unto you."
(2). Isai. XXXII. 8 : " The liberal deviseth liberal things and by liberal things," etc.

Summa, 22^c, 117, 3, 2^m. : " As it pertains to the fortitude of the soldier not only to use the sword against the enemy, but also to sharpen it and to preserve it in its sheath ; so does it pertain to liberality, not only to use money, but also to prepare and preserve it for use. The special act of liberality is the good use of money." *id. art.* 4, 3^m. : " Liberality is the foundation of giving, and it does not pertain to the liberal to be prompt in receiving and to be much less so in asking."

Prelude 1. *John Sarisber. de Nugis Curtal c.* 15 : " Liberality is the most grateful of all graces since it is profitable to many; and when the means of giving is wanting, it pours out compassion ; that is, it bestows its proper effect."

—— 2. *Si quis in hoc mundo vult multis gratus haberi, Det :—Capiat quærat, plurima, pauca, nihil.*

—— 3. Liberality demands receiving, gaining, preserving, as well as giving. Liberality includes,

I. JUSTICE ; the being just before being generous ; the giving only of one's own.

II. GENEROSITY ; it admits of no stint, it delights in giving above measure.

III. UNSELFISHNESS ; not giving out of superfluity, but by a personal sacrifice.

IV. KINDNESS, which prompts the giving to relieve the wants of others.

Epil.—If we close our hearts and hands, our riches, etc. will perish with us ; but by liberality we lay up in store for ourselves a good foundation against the time to come.

Fourth Sunday after Trinity.
SERMON 130.
MONEY.
(Holy Gospel, Ser. 2).

(1). S. Luke VI. 38 : " Give and it shall be given unto you."

(2). Acts XX. 35 : " It is more blessed to give than to receive."

Summa, 22', 117, 5, 3^m. : " The giving of liberality arises because he who gives, is in a certain way affected as it regards money, since he neither longs for it nor loves it ; whence he gives, not only to friends, but to unknown persons, when it is right so to do."

Prelude 1. *Fr. David de August:* " Three kinds of love of money. (1) Anxious desire of possession. (2) Tenacity of preserving it, which, without grief of mind, will not allow it to be expended either for pious or necessary uses. (3) The gaining an increase to it by any means, lawful or unlawful."

—— 2. Proverb. " To the wise, money is a kind of God," *i. e.* to help, etc.

—— 3. Avarice, the over love of money, turns the blessing of it into a curse.

—— 4. Money is a servant ; when loved and hoarded, it becomes a master.

—— 5. Money is a gift of God and in itself is a blessing.

—— 6. Money, like all else in this world, can be turned into a curse. Money is a,

I. NEED in this present life : a common need to support our common life.

II. POWER, which its possessor can use for or against the glory of God.

III. GOOD, by means of which pain is alleviated ; education etc. is procured.

IV. MEANS, if well used, of laying up a good foundation for the time to came.

Epil.—If riches increase, set not your heart upon them. If little wealth, be content with that little. Strive by grace to use much or little well.

Fourth Sunday after Trinity.
SERMON 131.
LOST POWER.
(*Holy Gospel, Ser.* 3).

(1). S. Luke VI. 41: "Why beholdest thou the mote?" etc.
(2). Rom. II, 21 : " Thou which teachest another, teachest thou not thyself ? "

Summa, 22ᵉ, 33, 5, c. : "The sinner," from preceding sin, is rendered unworthy to correct another, and especially if he has committed a greater sin himself, he is not worthy to correct another, who has committed a lesser sin. S. Jerome says: "He speaks of those who, being under the condemnation of mortal sin, are not allowed to reprove the lesser sins of their brethren."

Prelude 1. *S. T. Aq. ad Rom. c, ii. &c.*, 1, 4, *vv.* 21-24 : "Theft is a defect towards one's neighbour; adultery, a defect towards the person; sacrilege, a defect towards God. *S. Cyril Alex. in Luke, Ser.* 33: "If thou art sick with maladies more severe than those of others, why, neglecting thy own, dost thou find fault with them ? By what boldness doest thou do this ? First deliver thyself from thy rebellious passions, and then thou mayest correct him who is guilty of but trifling faults."

—— 2. Fable of the two wallets; one in front, other's sins; one behind, our own, *Bab. F.* 66.

—— 3. No sinner is wholly vile ; he has the knowledge to rightly reprove.

—— 4. Retaining the needful judgment and knowledge he has forfeited the power to reprove

—— 5. Sinner bears a twofold burden—his own and another's uncorrected sin. For his words of reproof are wanting in,

I. FORCE or moral power, without which words are vain.
II. VALUE, as coming from a corrupted source ; untrustworthy.
III. AUTHORITY, very feeble. "Do as I say, not as I do," example before precept.
IV. ACCEPTANCE ; the reproved will naturally turn round and recriminate.

Epil.—Avoid, by personal holiness, this loss of power to correct others.

Fourth Sunday after Trinity.
SERMON 132.
THE GROUNDS OF MERCY.
(*Holy Gospel, Ser.* 4).

(1). S. Luke vi. 36 : " Be ye therefore merciful."

(2). Jam. ii. 13 : " Mercy rejoiceth against judgment."

Summa, 22ᵉ, 30, 2 c. : " Inasmuch as anyone is saddened by the miseries of another, by so much does he apprehend this misery as his own ; either by union of the affection, as by love ; or by the real union of relationship ; or as being old and wise, for such consider that they may fall into a like evil ; so that the weak and timid are more merciful than they are who feel themselves to be happy and strong, and who deem that they themselves will not suffer any ills."

Prelude 1. *S. Greg. Nyssa, Orat. v.*: " Mercy is the voluntary sadness which arises from the grief of others ; is a stretching of the affectionate disposition, mingled with the affection in grief ; it is the mother of benevolence ; the pledge of love ; the bond of all friendly affection."

—— 2. Mercy is utterly opposed to every form of selfishness.

—— 3. Mercy implies forgiveness and pity, in respect to wrong doing. The grounds of mercy are,

I. AFFECTION or sympathy ; God shows mercy as feeling for us.

II. TIES, whether of kindred or of association, by which a union is established.

III. EXPERIENCE of past suffering, and of the welcome need received from others.

IV. FORETASTE of the infinite mercy which, sooner or later, we shall require at God's hands.

Epil.—Be merciful ; enlarge your sphere of love and sympathy, so that you may receive mercy alike at the hands of God and man.

Fifth Sunday after Trinity.
SERMON 133.
REVERENCE.
(*Holy Gospel, Ser.* 1).

(1). S. Luke v. 8 : " Depart from me, for I am a sinful man, O Lord."
(2). Heb. xii. 28 : " Serve God with reverence."

Summa, 3ª, 80, 10, 3ᵐ. : Reverence has fear combined with love, since the fear of reverence to God is called filial fear. Zacchæus and the centurion both honoured the Saviour though not in the same way : the one " joyfully received" Him ; the other said, " Lord, I am not worthy," etc., yet the love and hope to which the scriptures ever move us are to be preferred to fear ; hence, when Peter said " Depart from me," Jesus answered " Fear not."

Prelude 1. *S. Pet. Cælest. Opusc.* 1, *pt.* 5, *c.* 2 : " Reverence is the virtue by which we express the worship of honour to the highest and sublimest things." *S. Pe. Doroth. Abb. de. div. Tim. c.* 4 : " No one worships God without reverence nor clings to His least precept. Presumption leads mutual reverence, and the fear of God from us." *Sedulius Hyber. in Heb. c.* 5 : " There is in reverence a fear mingled with love."

—— 2. On earth reverence contains fear as being imperfect.
—— 3. In heaven, where perfect love casteth out fear, is perfect reverence.
—— 4. It was S. Peter's fearful reverence that made him bid the Lord depart. The reverence due to Jesus, to His church and worship should be

I. OUTWARD, or bodily, as a sign of devotion, attention, and respect.
II. INWARD and spiritual, the soul prostrating itself with the body.
III. SINCERE, offered upon the abiding conviction of the majesty, etc., of God.
IV. HUMBLE AND PROFOUND, as standing in the presence of a higher power.

Epil.—Render reverence to whom it may be due, hearty and humble.

Fifth Sunday after Trinity.
SERMON 134.
THE SEAT OF FAITH.
(*Holy Gospel, Ser. 2*).

(1). S. Luke v. 5 : "At Thy word I will let down the net."
(2). Rom. x. 10 : "With the heart man believeth unto righteousness."

Summa, 22^c, 6, 1, *c.* and 3^m : "The things of faith exceed the human reason, hence they do not come under the knowledge of man except God may reveal them. To believe, consists or stands in the will of the believing, which must be prepared by God through grace, that it may be lifted up to those things which are above nature."

Prelude 1. *Estius on Rom.* x. 10 : "'With the heart,' that is, by the mind and the will; although faith is an act of the intellect; but on account of its want of evil and the difficulty of the act of believing, a concurrence and command of a pious will is necessary; which will can control the intellect so that it may believe things difficult and obscure."

—— 2. Faith is an act of the will which, by God's grace, surpasses the reason.

—— 3. Faith teaches us to believe things taken upon trust; things never seen and supernatural.

—— 4. Two great claimants for faith—Holy Scripture and the Church, as to her divine powers. God prepares the will, the seat of faith, for the exercise of faith, by grace, which

I. PURIFIES it from the darkness of sin and unbelief, bringing into the light of grace and love.

II. EMPTIES it of the pride of reason (II. Cor. x. 5), moulding it into humble submission.

III. DIRECTS it to heavenly things, that it may attain to, and find, its rest in them.

IV. RESTRAINS it from journeying further from its heavenly home (Isai. xxvi. 3)

Epil.—See that the will, the charioteer of thy soul, directs and guides aright thy heart, that it may truly believe and pass onwards and upwards along the narrow way of eternal life.

Fifth Sunday after Trinity.
SERMON 135.
INDUSTRY.
(*Holy Gospel, Ser.* 3).

(1). S. Luke v. 2 : "The fishermen were washing their nets."

(2). 1. Thess. IV. 11 : "Study to work with your own hands."

Summa, 22^c, 47, 14, 1^m. : " There is a twofold industry; the one which is sufficient for the things necessary for salvation, which is given to all having grace (1 John ii. 20) ; the other is a more abounding industry, by which anyone can provide for himself and others ; including not only those things which are necessary to salvation, but also those which pertain to human life. Industry of this kind does not exist in all having grace."

Prelude 1. *Guarric. Abb., Ser. in Eph. Dom.* : " Industry distils that myrrh which prevents the fermentation of heart and body, which kills the worm of idleness, which enters the soul by allurement ; bites with laughter ; which changes by pleasing, and which kills by voluntary consent." *S. Nilus ad Mag. c.* 25 : "Although many whirlwinds, tempests, and violent gales threaten the soul with shipwreck, it remains firm, clinging to industry as to an anchor."

—— 2. The fishermen, afterwards apostles, had "toiled all night," yet now were washing their nets.

—— 3. Industry is the key to all progress, both in this life and the next. It makes life,

I. PLEASANT, from inward satisfaction and the rapid passage of time.

II. PROGRESSIVE, as enlarging its sphere of action and its capacities for good.

III. PROFITABLE, to the worker himself, as well as for those for whom he works.

IV. PROSPEROUS, in its ends and issues, for this and the eternal life.

Epil.—Be industrious ; industry and prayer will carry the day against talent and idleness ; against many advantages when combined with sloth.

Fifth Sunday after Trinity.
SERMON 136.
AFFECTED IGNORANCE.
(*Holy Gospel, Ser.* 4).

(1). S. Luke v. 1 : " The people pressed upon him to hear," etc.

(2). Rom. i. 21 : " Their foolish heart was darkened."

Summa, 3ª, 47 5, c. and 3ᵐ. : " The ignorance of the Jews did not excuse them from their crime ; since to a certain extent they affected ignorance, for when they saw the evident signs of His divinity, out of envy and hatred to Christ, they perverted them and refused to believe in His words in which He confessed Himself to be the Son of God. Hence He said of them (S. John xv. 22-24). Affected ignorance is no excuse for sin, but it rather aggravates the guilt, for it shows that a man is strongly attached to sin when he is ready to incur ignorance rather than to avoid it."

Prelude 1. *S. P. Marcus Eremit de leg. Spirit.*, S. 4, *n.* 97 : " Ignorance is the leader of all evil, and the second after it is incredulity. *S. Odo Clun.*: " The horrid depth of ignorance is to be dreaded which engenders the love of many evils."

———— 2. The people " pressed," etc. ; the Jews affected ignorance to continue in unbelief.

———— 3. Real ignorance is not sinful. Affected ignorance merits punishment, since it,

I. Excuses sin (S. John ix. 41) ; a cloak of sin. It will add to the punishment of it.

II. Defiles the conscience, as choosing darkness rather than light.

III. Shuts out mercy, as being a sign of impenitence and pride.

IV. Merits a punishment the most severe ; as leaving the light and cleaving to darkness

Epil.—Learn everything possible that is good, rest not in twilight, seek for the perfect day ; the darkness of ignorance will pass, and the true day of knowledge at length shine to rejoice and sanctify thy life.

Sixth Sunday after Trinity.
SERMON 137.
UNHOLY ANGER.
(Holy Gospel, Ser. 1).

(1). S. Matt. v. 22 : "Everyone that is angry with his brother," etc.
(2). Eph. IV. 3. : "Let all anger be put away from you."

Summa, 22^e, 158, 3, 2^m. : "The Lord said this 'Everyone', etc., as if He had added, 'he that would kill his brother, shall be in danger of the judgment,' speaking of the emotion of anger by which anyone desires to slay his brother, or that some harm may befal him. If to this desire, the consent of the reason may arise; then, without doubt, this anger, by which anyone desires an unjust revenge, will be a deadly sin."

Prelude 1. *Greek poet uncert.*: "Anger is a harvest of dangers." "Undisciplined anger is the mother of many ills." *Alvian. Massill. de Guber. dei lib*, 3 : "Anger is the mother of hatred, and therefore the Saviour willed to exclude it, lest of anger, hatred should be born."

—— 2. The Lord here speaks of unholy anger; unjust anger; "without a cause."

—— 3. There is a righteous and praiseworthy anger which is the enemy of sin.

—— 4. Anger is a mental affection, and the intention is to be punished, if it fails in action.

—— 5. We often say in a fit of unholy anger that which we do not mean. Unholy anger can be subdued by

I. WATCHFULNESS, lest under a sudden provocation we give way to anger.
II. SELF DISCIPLINE, which enables us to control and regulate the feelings.
III. DELAY, by which the first impulse to anger is gradually cooled down.
IV. PRAYER, inward, yet fervent, that the temper may be restrained.

Epil.—The kindest and sweetest dispositions, the most forgiving are subject to the emotion of anger. Seek to gain that meek and quiet spirit, which is of great price, for anger is a sure token of the want of sound mindedness, the condition of the purified soul.

Sixth Sunday after Trinity.
SERMON 138.
TO DO GOOD.
(*Holy Gospel, Ser.* 2).

(1). S. Matt. v. 20 : " Except your righteousness," etc.
(2). Heb. XIII. 16 : " To do good forget not."

Summa, 22^e, 79, 1, 3^m. : "' To do good ' is the complete act of righteousness, and is truly the principal part of it; ' To depart from evil ' is an imperfect act, and secondary part of righteousness, whilst ' To do good ' is the material part, without which the formal part cannot be complete."

Prelude 1. *S. Clem. ad* 1. *Cor. c.* 2 : The reward of humility was "an unsatiable desire for doing good and an unchanging desire toward every form of doing good." *Id. c.* 3 : " Shall we be slothful in doing good ? " *Evag. ad Anat. :* " Man approaches by nothing nearer to the likeness of God than by doing good to others." *Arnolphus Bp. :* " Hatreds are calmed by doing good and by a wonderful revolution are changed into the contrary affections, so that you love whom you hated."

—— 2. To do good the positive side of the Christian life consists of helping, speaking well of, etc.

—— 3. From a good and holy heart flow good thoughts, words, and deeds.

—— 4. The pure fountain gives pure water.

—— 5. To do good is Christlike (" He went about doing good "), is holiness in action. We must do good,

I. UP TO OUR POWER and means : not be " weary in well doing."

II. AT ANY COST, putting self wholly aside; denying self to help others.

III. BECAUSE IT IS GOOD in itself so to do, as a token of our faith and love.

IV. DISINTERESTEDLY, not looking for any reward, but because it is right so to do.

Epil.—The Scribes and Pharisees did no good, therefore their righteousness was of no avail for their own consciences, for God and for others ; the foundation on which it was built was rotten and unsound.

Sixth Sunday after Trinity.
SERMON 139.
DECLINING FROM EVIL.
(Holy Gospel, Ser. 3).

(1). S. Matt. v. 20: "Except your righteousness," etc.
(2). II. Tim. II. 19: "Let every one that nameth the name of Christ depart from iniquity."

Summa, 22^c, 79, 1, 2^m. "To depart from evil and to do good belongs to righteousness as being parts of it. But to decline from evil does not imply a mere negation only; which is, not to do evil; which in itself does not merit a palm, but only avoids punishment; but it rather implies a motion of the will of him repudiating evil. This action is in itself meritorious especially when anyone is hard pressed to do evil and resists," the pressure or temptation to do it.

Prelude 1 *S. Chrysost. Hom. v. in* II. *Tim.* "How can anyone be of God Who is just, if he does iniquity; if by his words he opposes Him; if he insults Him by his misdeeds." "If they were held by constraint [to sin] and not by love they would soon depart" from it.

—— 2. S. August. in Ps. xxxiv. 14. "So decline from evil that you may do good."

—— 3. No easy task to fulfil, this part of righteousness.

—— 4. Passive resistance at times becomes real action.

—— 5. A really meritorious act to decline from evil since it involves a

I. PRINCIPAL which is well grounded upon the faith and united with the moral sense.

II. MOTION of the will to move onwards and outwards into a purer and holier life.

III. STRUGGLE and resistance to evil; against inclination, habit and temptation.

IV. VICTORY: a victory over self, hardly won after many a previous defeat.

Epil.—Depart from, decline from iniquity; touch not the unclean thing any longer. Time past sufficed for that; walk heavenwards in newness of life, putting the old life and sins out of remembrance.

Sixth Sunday after Trinity.
SERMON 140.
THE NEW LAW.
(*Holy Gospel, Ser.* 4).

(1) S. Matt. v. 20: "Except your righteousness shall exceed," etc.

(2) Gal. III. 24: "The law was our schoolmaster (pædagogue) to bring us unto Christ."

Summa, 12^e, 91, 5, C. "The state of the old law represents that of a child (Gal. III. 24); of the new law, that of the perfect man; the former promised sensible and earthly good (Ex. III. 3, 17); the latter intelligible and heavenly good, *i.e.*, the kingdom of heaven. To the former, it pertained to direct human actions according to the order of justice; to the latter, the ordering of the interior actions of the mind; the former enforced obedience through fear of punishment; the latter by love shed abroad in our hearts by the grace of Christ (Rom. v. 5). Brief, said Augustine, is the difference between the law and the gospel; fear and love."

Prelude 1. *Tsych. in Levit. lib.* 7: "The letter of the law is like a leaf, by which the fruit of the tree is hidden; but under the letter of the law is concealed the spirit. Let us strip off the leaves of the letter [the old law] that we may find the fruit of the spirit," the new law.

—— 2. Scribes and Pharisees represented the letter of the old law.

—— 3. The Lord substituted the new law, of the spirit which giveth life, for the old letter that killeth. The new law is,

  I. SPIRITUAL, acting, regulating man's spiritual nature, &c., is of spiritual things.

 II. LOVING, in expression, in purpose, in reward.

III. SEARCHING, reaching to the thoughts and intentions of the heart.

 IV. BINDING, by the sweetest and gentlest yet strongest of bonds.

Epil.—By this law may we live, as preparing ourselves by submission and obedience to attain to the perfect will of God, in the perfect state of renewed life.

Seventh Sunday after Trinity.
SERMON 141.
OBEDIENCE.
(Holy Gospel, Ser. 1).

(1). S. Mark VIII. 6: "He commanded the people to sit down on the ground."
(2). II. Cor. X. 5: "Bringing every thought into captivity to the obedience of Christ."

Summa, 3ᵃ, 47, 2, 2ᵐ.: "Obedience although it implies necessity in respect to that which is commanded, implies likewise a ready will for the fulfilment of the command. Such was the obedience of Christ. His passion and death in themselves were repugnant to His will, yet He willed to fulfil the will of God (Ps. XL. 8, S. Matt. XXVI. 42.)"

Prelude 1. *Will. of Auvergne T.* II. *p.* 89. "It is of obedience not to judge what is commanded, but humbly to fulfil it. The voice of the devil was 'yea, hath God said.'" (Gen. III. 1.) S. John Climac. Scala Parad. grad. 4. "Obedience is the perfect abdication of the individual soul manifested by the offices of the body; it is the security of the soul in death; the burial of the will; the wakening of humility."

Fr. Humb. de Rom. Spec. Relig. 5, *c.* 14. The seven grades of obedience are to obey,

I. WILLINGLY, removing obstacles, from the will, as the branch is cut off to insert the graft.
II. SIMPLY, asking no questions; which lead to murmurs and excuses.
III. CHEERFULLY, they who obey with a murmur, wish to feed God with false things.
IV. QUICKLY, the will wishing to leave its own imperfections like Zacchæus (Luke XIX).
V. MANFULLY, neither opposition nor harshness causing the regal path to be left.
VI. HUMBLY, as obeying the direction of a superior power.
VII. CONSTANTLY, by perseverance which is the singular daughter of the great king.

Epil.—So be ye obedient to Him, whose commands are not grievous; that so in soul, life and death, you may be found in Him who was "obedient unto death."

Seventh Sunday after Trinity.

SERMON 142.
ABSTINENCE.
(*Holy Gospel, Ser.* 2).

(1). S. Mark VIII. 2: "They have now been with me three days and have nothing to eat."

(2). 1. Cor. VIII. 8: "Neither if we eat, are we the better, neither if we eat not are we the worse."

Summa, 22^e, 146, 1, 1 and 1^m.: "The Apostle says Rom. XIV. 17) that 'the Kingdom of God is not meat and drink'; which the Gloss explains 'neither in eating, nor in abstaining, is there righteousness.' The Apostle says again, 'meat commendeth us not to God' (1. Cor. VIII. 8); but both of these acts if done reasonably from faith, and from the love of God, pertain to the Kingdom of God. Such an abstinence as is governed by reason, obtains the name and the dignity of virtue."

Prelude 1. *S. Pet. Chry. Ser.* 41: "Abstinence is chief medicine of man; it shuts out the diseases of vices; it cuts off the passions of the flesh; it expels the causes of crimes; yet without the ointment of mercy; without the stream of piety; without the cost of almsgiving; it does not restore perfect safety to minds."

—— 2. "As pertaining to the Kingdom of God;" as a means and help, abstinence is valuable.

—— 3. It is not so much for faith, as for morals.

——4. The Church, from the beginning, had Her seasons of abstinence, which mark the

I. BREAK, in the continuity of our daily life.

II. DEDICATION of holy days and seasons to special commemorations.

III. FOLLOWING of the order and practice of the Church in every age.

IV. IMITATION and a following of the example of the Lord, who fasted oft.

Epil.—Poor is the spiritual life of such as keep neither fast nor festival, who make their days one unvaried round, one sad monotony of sin or toil.

Seventh Sunday after Trinity.
SERMON 143.
FORTITUDE.
(*Holy Gospel, Ser.* 3).

(1). S. Mark VIII. 3 : " They have now been with me three days," etc.
(2). Eph. VI. 10 : "Be strong in the Lord and in the power of His might.
Summa, 22', 123, 2 c. : " Fortitude implies a certain firmness of mind, and as such, is a general virtue; but when it is applied to cases in which it is very difficult to have this firmness, as in the case of certain grave dangers, it becomes a special virtue. Cicero says : *Rhet.* I. 116, that fortitude is the undertaking of dangers well considered and the endurance of labours."
Prelude 1. *S. Julian, Archb.* : " The four parts of fortitude are high-mindedness, (magnificentia)—*i.e.*, the administration of great things with a comprehensive mind; confidence which brings hope to the soul in trying circumstances; patience, and the voluntary and daily endurance of arduous and difficult things; and perseverance."
—— 2. The fortitude of the multitude sustained them fasting for three days.
—— 3. Note the fortitude displayed by the martyrs of the Church and confessors of the faith.
—— 4. An axiom of fortitude 'when I am weak, then am I strong.' Fortitude leads on to victory through
  I. ENDURANCE and suffering well sustained, nay borne with cheerfulness.
 II. OPPOSITION firmly resisted at any cost, in spite of great disadvantages.
III. DANGERS from which cowardice would involuntarily shrink.
IV. THREATS apalling to the weak-hearted, but harmless to the brave.
Epil.—The Lord charges all His servants to be "strong and very courageous."

Seventh Sunday after Trinity.
SERMON 144.
THE NEEDS OF THE BODY.
(Holy Gospel, Ser. 4).

(1) S. Mark VIII. 3 : "They have nothing to eat."
(2) Philip IV. 19 : "My God shall supply all your need .. by Christ Jesus."

Summa, 1^a, 91, 3, c. 3^m; "It is rightly said that the human body was formed by God, its artificer, according to the best arrangement, and one which agrees with the rational soul and its operations. Since it behoves man to take food with his mouth, so has he an oblong mouth and hard and flat lips, and a hard tongue lest it be hurt by external things."

Prelude 1. *S. Aug. De Civ. Dei, xiii.* 23 : Of the first man, "His body had need of food and drink, lest he should be afflicted with thirst, and the other ailments outside paradise were not denied to him." The sinless man had his bodily needs.

—— 2. The body a wonderful creation of adaptation and design.

—— 3. God fashioned the body adapted to its earthly life and condition.

—— 4. He formed it and its surroundings after a pattern in the Divine mind.

—— 5. He ordained that certain needs should be inherent in the body.

—— 6. Artificial needs are not natural, but acquired. The genuine needs of the body are.

I. IMPLANTED by God at man's creation ; hence a paradise for him.

II. IMPERATIVE and involuntary ; death intervenes without sleep and rest.

III. PROVIDED for by God's good providence ; hence fruitful seasons, rain, etc.

IV. PLEASURABLE to the body to be fulfilled, as eating, etc., and rest after toil.

Epil.—The Lord condescended to supply many of man's bodily needs. He did not ignore nor despise the body. These needs are to be supplied sparingly and thankfully, etc., but they are to be supplied, for the body is a temple of the Holy Ghost.

Eighth Sunday after Trinity.
SERMON 145.
ORDINATION.
(*Holy Gospel, Ser.* 1).

(1). S. Matt. VII. 15 : " Beware of false prophets."
(2). I. Tim. V. 22 : " Lay hands suddenly on no man."
Summa, 22^c, 172, 4, 3^m. : " Because prophecy is ordained for the utility of others it is manifest that such are false prophets because they are not sent by God."
Prelude 1. *S. Jerom. lib. xvi. in Ezek.* : " The laying on of hands is the ordination of the clergy which is completed not only the imprecation, but by the imposition of the hand." S. Clem. i. ad Cor. c. 40 : "We ought to do all things in order, whatsoever the Master hath commanded. To the chief priest is given his own offices, and the proper place is assigned to the priests."
S. Ig. ad Mag. c. 13 : "Study to be confirmed in the doctrine of our Lord and of the Apostles, together with your Bishop and the well-wrought spiritual crown of your Presbytery, and your Deacons according to God."

—— 2. Prophets are preachers, and preachers are the ordained ministry of the church.

—— 3. Apostolical succession is the one and only true test of a church. It is no church when wanting orders.

—— 4. No one is allowed to preach, nor to dispense the sacraments of the church without orders. The three orders in the church from the beginning, of Bishop, Priest and Deacon, involve

I. COMMISSION as given by the Lord to His Apostles.
II. SUCCESSION, the channel of the grace of orders transmitting by the Apostles to the clergy.
III. SELECTION, carefully made and guarded by many safe-guards; examination, etc.
IV. ORDINATION, transmission of the grace of Holy Orders by Bishop to Priest.

Epil.—" Beware of " [turn your attention to] and mark with a steady scrutiny, such persons as are not canonically ordained, who are false teachers, who are wanting in the powers and graces of Holy Orders ; to note how feeble and poor is their teaching, and how the life contradicts the assumed ministerial functions.

L

Eighth Sunday after Trinity.
SERMON 146.
ASSOCIATION WITH NON-CONFORMISTS.
(*Holy Gospel, Ser.* 2).

(1). S. Matt. VII. 15: "Beware of false prophets."
(2). Titus III. 10: "An heretic after the second admonition reject."

Summa, 22ᵉ, 2, 9, c: "The church does not forbid communion or association of the faithful with unbelievers, who, have in no form received the faith of Christ, such as the heathen or the Jews; but the Church does forbid communion with such as err from the faith received; either by corrupting it as the heretics; or by departing wholly from it, as the Apostates."—

Prelude 1. *Etherius Bp.*: "The frog is a most chattering emptiness, unclean, it gives the sound of a voice with cackling and importunate clamours, it wallows in pools and dirty water. So heretics, not in the clearest living water which flows from the fountains of salvation, *i.e.* the doctrine of the Apostles; but amongst a people itself ignorant, and slippery with unworthy clamours, emit their voices from the mud, like the frog."

—— 2. As to unbelievers and Jews: as to marriage (1. Cor. vii. 12, 18): as to judgment (1. Cor. v. 12, 13).

—— 3. The heretic, the man who chooses his own religion, is to be rejected (Tit. iii. 10).

—— 4. Mark your disapproval of Nonconformists by withholding from them your

I. SYMPATHY, they have rejected your faith openly (II. Cor. vi. 15).

II. FRIENDSHIP, lest you become defiled by their pitch (Isai. lii. 11).

III. HELP, lest by their increased means and power you extend their influence.

IV. Notice of them as a body; as far as possible ignore their very existence.

Epil.—Pray for them as in second collect for Good Friday; sorrow over them; try if possible to win them back into the fold of Christ—but " be ye separate."

Eighth Sunday after Trinity.
SERMON 147.
FALSE PROPHETS ARE RAVENING WOLVES.
(Holy Gospel, Ser. 3).

(1). S. Matt. VII. 15: "Beware of false prophets, inwardly they are ravening wolves."

(2). Acts XX. 29: "Grievous wolves shall enter into you, not sparing the flock."

Summa, 22^c, 172, 4, 3^m.: "Not all evil or false prophets are ravening wolves, but only those who intend to harm others. For as Chrysostom Hom. 27 in Matt. says: That even if Catholic teachers are themselves sinners and are said to be the servants of the flesh, yet they are not to be called ravening wolves, because they have not the intention to destroy Christians."

Prelude 1. *Origen in Matt.*: "These wolves are the heretics who heavily oppress and pursue the Church, or frequent to molest her. By means of the Christian name they strive to seduce many, bringing in their stumbling-blocks with many sweet words, who 'by good words and fair speeches deceive the hearts of the simple.' (Rom. xvi. 15)." S. Eucherius Form. Spirit, c. 5: "The wolf is the heretic."

—— 2. Unworthy prophets and teachers; teaching the faith; are not "ravening wolves."

—— 3. Every form of heresy is soul destroying; more than an offence, as "ravening wolves" these heretical false prophets, devour the Church, despoiling her

I. AUTHORITY, both moral and spiritual, they destroy the true to set up the false.

II. TEACHING, by denying the faith at the beginning delivered to the saints.

III. CEREMONIES, for these substituting every form of irreverence and vulgarity.

IV. PROPERTY, as ravening wolves, if they can but lay hold of it.

Epil.—*Eph. v.* 6: "Let no man"—no heretic—"deceive you with vain words," hold fast to all that has been believed "everywhere, always and by all men"; walk in the old paths, scorning the profane novelties of heresiarchs.

Eighth Sunday after Trinity.
SERMON 148.
FALSE PROPHETS AND HOLY SCRIPTURE.
(Holy Gospel, Ser. 4).

(1). S. Matt. VII. 15: "Beware of false prophets."
(2). II. Cor. II. 17: "We are not as many, which corrupt the word of God."

Summa, 22^e, 11, 2, 2, 2^m.: "The materials of the faith are the things which are believed; but heresy is not only concerning things, but also concerning the words, and exposition of Holy Scripture. S. Jerome says; ad Gal. c. 5; whosoever understands Scripture otherwise than the sense of the Holy Spirit demands, though he may not have left the church; yet can he be called a heretic, since he so twists the exposition of Holy Scripture that it becomes the contrary to that which the Holy Spirit hath revealed. Ezekiel writes of such, c. xiii. 6, 7."

Prelude 1. *Vincent. of Lirin. c.* 25: "Man may behold them (the heretics) raging in every part of the sacred volume, in Moses, in the Kings, Psalms, Gospels, in the Apostles and the Prophets, where the fraudulent bringing in of wicked error is intended that there the authority of the word of God should be pretended."

—— 2. The heretic attacks the Church first, and Holy Scripture afterwards.

—— 3. The heretic handles the word of God deceitfully, "huckstering" it.

—— 4. The Church determined the Canon of Scripture, of which the heretic attacks the

  I. Books, Luther denied S. James' Epistle, Colenso the Pentateuch.

  II. Facts, as the grace and value of the holy sacraments; orders of the ministry, etc.

  III. Words altered, united, interpolated as by the unitarians.

  IV. Expositions and interpretations current in the church for nearly two thousand years.

Epil.—The consent of interpretation by the Fathers, both Apostolic and of the Fourth Century, establishes what the Holy Spirit signified by the words of the inspired Canon of Scripture; the same consent which also formed and confirmed the Canon itself of Holy Scripture.

Ninth Sunday after Trinity.
SERMON 149.
WORLDLY PRUDENCE.
(*Holy Gospel, Ser.* 1).

(1). S. Luke xvi. 8 : " The children of this world are in their generation wiser," etc.

(2). I. Cor. i. 19 : " I will bring to nothing the understanding of the prudent."

Summa, 22ᶜ, 47, 13, c. and 1ᵐ. : " There is a false prudence which belongs to the wicked only ; also an imperfect prudence which is common alike to the good and bad ; and a perfect prudence which belongs to the righteous. This word of the Lord is to be understood of the first kind of prudence [the false prudence of the wicked], whence it is not merely said 'are wiser' (*i.e.* more prudent), but 'in their generation' is added. This is the prudence of the flesh of which S. Paul speaks, Rom. viii. 6."

Prelude 1. *S. T. Aq. in* 1. *Cor. I.* 19 : " Because they who deem themselves to be prudent in worldly things, regard prudence, as only the means whereby they may cling to the things of this world."

—— 2. *Euseb. Gallic in nat. Apost. in S. Matt.* ix. 16 : Evil spirits and wicked men are called serpents. See that you do not deceive yourselves by your cunning, ' for the children ' etc. Be ye prudent, but so prudent as not to lose your simplicity.

—— 3. This worldly prudence, so cultivated and admired is

I. Short-sighted, looking only to present gain, and not to the future and eternal reward.

II. Evil-purposed, aiming at overreaching others and securing self.

III. Feeble, it gains its end for a time ; it grasps the shadow, it loses the substance.

IV. Dangerous, as being often detected by men, and punished by God.

Epil.—Worldly prudence destroys principle, independence, all nobility of thought and action ; it eats out the very life of Christian nobleness and simplicity ; it is essentially of the world worldly ; its guiding principles being expediency and profit.

Ninth Sunday after Trinity.
SERMON 150.
POSSESSIONS.
(Holy Gospel, Ser. 2).

(1). S. Luke XVI. 1 : " There was a certain rich man."

(2). 1. Tim. v. 8 : " If any provide not for his own, he hath denied the faith."

Summa, 22ᵉ, 66, 1, c. : " There is to man a certain natural possession of external things by means of which he can use them through his reason and will to his profit and advantage. God, who holds the dominion over all things, ordained by His providence certain things for the bodily support of man, who thereby holds a natural dominion over certain things for his own use."

Prelude 1, *Lucr*. III. 984 : " Vitaque mancipio nulli datur, omnibus usu ; " add, et alia. Pet. de Blois. Ep. 161 : " David on the royal throne said that he was poor and needy (Ps. lxxxvi. 1). I believe riches to be commendable if sought in an honest way ; if spent without luxury, as moderate necessity may demand. Abraham held riches for his proper use, and many of the Holy Fathers largely endowed with possessions laid up for themselves treasure in heaven."

——— 2. All have the desire of possession, more or less implanted in them by God.

——— 3. This desire stimulates a man to the acquisition of possessions.

——— 4. Possessions give their possessor a great means of, and influence for good, when the use made of them is

I. GOOD, they not being prostituted to the service of sin, luxury or oppression.

II. NATURAL, used for the due and proper support of those dependent upon the then possessor of them.

III. PRODUCTIVE of many blessings, spreading relief of suffering, education, &c.

IV. HOLY, a portion of them being consecrated to God, to His Church, to Missions.

Epil.—Use all your means well and God will commit to your keeping the true riches.

Ninth Sunday after Trinity.
SERMON 151.
HOLDING ONE'S OWN.
(*Holy Gospel, Ser.* 3).

(1). S. Luke XVI. 5: "How much owest thou unto my Lord."

(2). 1. Thess. v. 21: "Hold fast that which is good."

Summa, 22ᵉ, 66, 2, c: "That each man should possess his own is necessary for human life for three reasons. Firstly, because each one is more anxious to procure something that belongs to himself alone, rather than what is common to all or many. Secondly, because human affairs are handled more orderly, if to each one belongs the special care of something to be procured. There would be confusion, if anyone indiscriminately could procure whatsoever he wished. Thirdly, because by this, a more peaceful state of man is preserved, whilst each one is contented with his own."

Prelude 1. Communion of gods subverts all rights human and divine; is a type of hell.

—— 2. The desire of possession, implanted by God, leads to honest industry.

—— 3. What is stated of material possessions applies equally to mental and spiritual gifts; to the Christian graces, to learning, and to accomplishments.

—— 4. For this world and the next, all ought to hold their own,

I. FIRMLY, so as not to be defrauded of it by the devil and wicked men.

II. CAREFULLY, so as not to fritter it away; to lose it without any return.

III. AS A POSSESSION, earned at the cost of repentance, toil and self-denial.

IV. IN TRUST, for use and profit, for both worlds, for self and others.

Epil.—God will never dispute our lawful gains for body or soul. That the debts were owing to the rich man, the unjust steward did not attempt to deny.

Ninth Sunday after Trinity.
SERMON 152
WHY ONE BEGS AND ANOTHER ABOUNDS.
(Holy Gospel, Ser. 4).

(1). S. Luke XVI. 1 : " There was a certain rich man which had a steward."

(2). S. Matt. XIII. 12 : " Whosoever hath, to him shall be given," &c.

Summa, 22^c, 66, 2, 2 and 2^m. : S. Basil said, the man who, if going before to the games, would prohibit those coming after him, appropriating to himself that which was ordained for the common use, is like the rich who having preoccupied common things, consider them to be their own. But if he going before to the games, prepares the way for others, he does not do wrongly unless he prohibits others. So the rich man does not act unlawfully if preoccupying the possession of a thing which was common at the beginning, he communicates it to others, but he sins indiscretely if he prohibits others from the use of it."

Prelude 1. *Theophy. in Matt. xiii.* 12 : " To him showing diligence knowledge is given, but from him not having diligence that which he seems to have shall be taken away."

—— 2. What is true of knowledge is true of riches, station, &c.

—— 3. The idle and thoughtless beg; the diligent and thoughtful abound. The man who preoccupies and therefore abounds is,

I. WATCHFUL, as to ways and means; so as to seize the occasion.

II. ENERGETIC, striving with all his powers after that which he seeks.

III. INDUSTRIOUS, industry is energy rightly directed to a special object.

IV. THRIFTY, wasting power neither of grace, nor of body nor of soul.

Epil.—If spiritual grace and means and material wealth were equalized to-day, to-morrow would be found, one that begs and another that abounds.

Tenth Sunday after Trinity.
SERMON 153.
THE TEACHING OF JESUS.
(*Holy Gospel*, Ser. 1).

(1). S. Luke XIX. 47 : " He taught daily in the Temple."
(2). 1. Tim. IV. 6 : " Nourished up in words of faith and doctrine."

Summa, 3^a, 42, 3, c : " The teaching of Jesus was not secret, neither on account of envy of Him teaching, nor from the fewness of those to whom it was propounded. Secret teaching springs from the intention of the teacher; the fewness of those to whom it is propounded; the manner of teaching. It is not secret teaching, when parables were used to express spiritual mysteries to such as were neither fit, nor worthy to otherwise receive them ; especially as the open and naked meaning of the parables was explained by the Lord to His disciples."

Prelude 1. *Theophy. in Matt. vii.* 29 : " The simple people were astonished and they wondered not at the eloquence of His words, but at His boldness or freedom of speech."

—— 2. Spiritual teaching cannot be made too plain and simple.

—— 3. This was the great charm of the Lord's teaching, it was simple, loving and practical.

—— 4. Hence large multitudes followed Him in spite of toil and hunger, to,

I. HEAR, with attention, delight and a sincere desire to profit by the hearing.

II. UNDERSTAND, as much as they possibly could; to gain all that was possible.

III. APPLY, words spoken generally to their own particular case.

IV. PRACTICE, or to test the truth of the Lord's teaching in their daily lives.

Epil.—May we all profit by the teaching of the Lord delivered by Holy Scripture and the Church to all nations to the end of time : teaching, as fresh now as it was at the first.

Tenth Sunday after Trinity.
SERMON 154.
THE POWER OF CEREMONY.
(*Holy Gospel*, Ser. 2).

(1). S. Luke XIX. 45: "He went into the temple, and began to cast out them that sold therein."

(2). I. Cor. XIV. 40: "Let all things be done decently," *i.e.* with grace.

Summa, $3^a, 44, 3, 1^m$.: "It behoved Christ, in order that He might show Himself to be the Man-God and Saviour, to work miracles in respect of man. And, says S. Jerome, amongst the mighty miracles which the Lord wrought, this seems to me the most wonderful, that one man, and He of that time of no account, should be able by the stripes of one scourge to cast out of the Temple so great a multitude of men; surely a certain glittering light was shining from His eyes, and the majesty of divinity was beaming in His countenance."

Prelude 1. S. August. *Ep*. 86: "The custom of the people of God and the decrees of our forefathers are to be kept."

—— 2. Jesus was almost unknown. He never spoke. He was alone and weak.

—— 3. Men saw Him and were awe-stricken; they resisted not, so He cleared the Temple.

—— 4. So is there a power in the outward worship, in the ceremonies of the Church, which is His spiritual body. This appeal to the eye has a force which is,

I. IMPRESSIVE, striking the beholder at a glance: the size of Church; the phase of worship.

II. QUICK, to arrest the attention; a presence is felt and recognized.

III. POWERFUL, to act on the feelings, and to excite emotions of holiness.

IV. LASTING, as a scene of "the beauty of holiness stamped on the soul for ever."

Epil.—So may the ceremonial spectacle of an august worship, drive the wordly thoughts, the buying and the selling, out of the temple of the soul.

Tenth Sunday after Trinity.
SERMON 155.
THE DESOLATION OF THE LOST.
(Holy Gospel, Ser. 3).

(1). S. Luke xix. 41 : "He beheld the city and wept over it."

(2). Rom. ii. 2 : "I have great heaviness and continual sorrow of heart."

Summa, 22^e, 30, 1, 1^m. : "From the consideration of sin that it is voluntary, it has no ground for commiseration, but rather ground for punishment ; but since guilt can in some way become a punishment, inasmuch as it has a something joined to it which is contrary to the will of him sinning, it is able to have from this circumstance a certain ground of compassion."

Prelude 1. *S. Cyril. Alex. in loco :* "We could not have known that He pitied them [the Jews], had He not made manifest that sorrow which we could not see. For the tear which drops from the eye is a symbol of grief."

—— 2. Jesus wept as Son of Man not yet glorified ; there are no tears in heaven.

—— 3. Jerusalem was doomed, therefore He shed tears : it was not long to be wept over.

—— 4. The marvellous power of sympathy to relieve sorrow and suffering.

—— 5. Lazarus in Abraham's bosom did not sympathise with Dives in torments. The desolation of the Lost will be,

I. COMPLETE, a loving eye never seen ; a loving voice never heard

II. RETRIBUTIVE, once the soul turned away from love and goodness, now they are turned away from it.

III. AGONIZING, in its torturing memories of former affections and yearnings.

IV. ETERNAL, never more will the tear be shed over the lost soul.

Epil.—Join yourself now to every form of loving affection and goodness: so that when sorrow comes the house of the soul cannot be left destitute.

Tenth Sunday after Trinity.
SERMON 156.
THE HOUSE OF PRAYER.
(Holy Gospel, Ser. 4).

(1). S. Luke XIX. 46: "My house is the house of prayer."
(2). I. Tim. III. 15: "The house of God which is the Church of God."

Summa, 22ᵉ, 84, 3, 2ᵐ.: "It would seem that adoration does not require a determinate place. It is said 'The hour cometh,' &c. (S. John iv. 21). In these words the Lord fortells the cessation of adoration after the manner of the rights of the Jews at Jerusalem, and of the Samaritans at Gerizim. A chosen place is determined upon for adoration, not because God can be shut up in any place (1. Kings viii. 27), but for the sake of those worshipping."

Prelude 1. *Angel. del Pas.*: "My house" where God dwells under an oath, and assists by a certain covenant in virtue of consecration and dedication, and aids with particular benevolence those praying there, and communicates His blessings, and supplies those who are needy; more readily hearing prayer there.

—— 2. *S. Jerome Isai. lvi. 7*: "'My house of prayer' is the Church which is divided throughout the whole world."

—— 3. "My house" is God's house, built for Him and dedicated to His use.

—— 4. God's house is the house of prayer and sacrament, not of preaching. Churches, as special places of worship and adoration are valued on account of

  I. CONSECRATION, by which the worshippers gain a special devotion and presence.
 II. CONTENTS, the sacred mysteries and symbols which are celebrated in them.
III. CONCOURSE, by worshippers demanding a special building for their use.
 IV. ASSOCIATION, of the place which naturally excites pious feelings.

Epil.—Like David, let us love, the habitation of the Lord and the place in which His honour dwelleth; use it daily; support it with all our means.

Eleventh Sunday after Trinity.
SERMON 157.
PRESUMING UPON GOD.
(Holy Gospel, Ser. 1).

(1). S. Luke XVIII. 4: "God I thank Thee," etc.
(2). II. S. Pet. II. 10: "Presumptuous are they."

Summa, 22^e, 21, 1, 1^m.: "The presumption by which anyone inordinately leans upon God, is a heavier sin than the presumption by which anyone leans upon his own strength. For as far as anyone leans upon the divine power for the purpose of carrying out something which does not befit God, so to do is to lessen the divine power. But it is manifest that he sins more grievously who diminishes the divine power, than he who over extols his own strength."

Prelude 1. *Haymo in loco*: "The Pharisee prayed truly not as the humble, with a bowed head, but with a neck erect and proud." *S. Cyril. Alex. in loco.*: "Moderate thyself, O Pharisee. Await the decree of the Judge; presumption is both accursed and hated by God."

—— 2. So do they who "continue in sin that grace may abound" (Rom. VI, 1).

—— 3. So did the Jews of Old (Rom. II. 4-5), presuming upon God's goodness, forbearance, etc.

—— 4. So did the men before the flood, till God would strive with them no longer (Gen. VI, 3).

—— 5. To presume upon man shows a bad heart; how much more to presume upon God? This presumption presumes upon God's,

I. LOVE, in creating and giving life, giving no love to Him in return.
II. PROVIDENCE, guiding and providing; by living in carelessness and extravagance.
III. PARDON, continuing in sin without any earnest repentance.
IV. GRACE, trusting vainly to gain glory hereafter without present holiness.

Epil.—Let us walk humbly before our God, feeling ourselves wholly unworthy of the least of all the many mercies with which He so bountifully enricheth us.

Eleventh Sunday after Trinity.
SERMON 158.
PRESUMPTUOUS SPEECH.
(*Holy Gospel, Ser.* 2).

(1). S. Luke XVIII. 11 : "God, I thank Thee that I am not as other men are."

(2). S. Jude v. 16: "Their mouth speaking great swelling words."

Summa, 22^e, 130, I. 3 and 3^m : "The Apostle said (II. Cor. III. 5) not that we are sufficient, etc. If presumption strives to do what it is not sufficient to accomplish, it is a sin, it would seem then that man is not able rightly to think any good thing, which is not fitting. Therefore presumption is not a sin. But what we can do by others, to a certain extent we can do by ourselves, and we who are able to think and to do good, by the divine help, this good does not wholly exceed our natural power. It is not presumption if anyone applies himself to do a virtuous work, provided he does not do so without a trust in the divine help."

Prelude 1. *Pet. de Blois :* "Presumption is the ascribing of the gifts which came from God, not to God, but to oneself; the philosophers of the heathen saying (Ps. XII. 4), 'Our lips are our own, who is Lord over us.'"

—— 2. *S. August. de Verb. Dom.* : "He would say at least 'as many men.' Who are the 'other men,' unless all save himself? 'I am just, the others are sinners.'"

—— 3. The Pharisee spoke as if for and by himself. It was 'I,' 'I' not even 'God and I.'

—— 4. He was right in doing what he did, fasting, etc. It was true what he said.

—— 5. His presumptuous speech was wrong—utterly wrong. Such presumptuous speech is a sign of

I. SELF-CONCEIT, of a false assumption and pride which was founded upon undue confidence.

II. IGNORANCE of his own shortcomings and of the humility of soul which God requires.

III. FOOLISHNESS, as if God did not know the thoughts and intents of the heart.

IV. WANT OF DIVINE GRACE to enable to subdue his natural pride of heart.

Epil.—Your prayer "Keep thy servant also from presumptuous sins." Ps. XIX. 13.

Eleventh Sunday after Trinity.
SERMON 159.
SELF PRESUMPTION.
(Holy Gospel, Ser. 3).

(1). S. Luke XVIII. 11 : "God I thank Thee," etc.
(2). Gal. vi. 3 : "If a man think himself to be something when he is nothing," etc.

Summa, 22^c, 21, 4, 0 : "Presumption which leans upon its own power is born of vain glory, it arises from pride of life ; it attempts, as if possible to itself, something that is beyond its own power. Such a presumption as this manifestly proceeds from vain glory, leading him to attempt that which he is unable to do, reaching after something, as possible, which is impossible, and wholly excluding fear."

Prelude 1. *Titus Bost.* : "There are four kinds of self presumption ; when we think that we can gain what is good by ourselves ; or if we believe that it cometh down from above we think that we have received it for our merits ; or when we boast that we have that which we do not possess ; lastly when others being despised individually we seem to desire to have what they have."

—— 2. It is a poor and wretched thing for weak, sinful man to presume upon himself.

—— 3. Note S. Paul, 2 Cor. III. 5 : "Not that we are sufficient of ourselves," &c.

—— 4. To trust in and presume upon self is to lean upon a broken reed. Also! How often do we presume upon our,

I. POWERS, whether of mind or body.
II. HEALTH AND STRENGTH, trying them beyond their legitimate powers of endurance.
III. RICHES, as if they rendered us more worthy of honour, respect and love.
IV. STATION AND POSITION, life to do that which would put humbler persons to shame.

Epil.—We want sufficiency, we crave for it, but the lesson to be learned is that "our sufficiency is of God." May the Lord make us to abound more and more.

Eleventh Sunday after Trinity.
SERMON 160.
THE HIGHER RULE.
(*Holy Gospel*, Ser. 4).

(1). S. Luke XVIII. 12 : "I Fast Twice in the week."

(2). I. Cor. VIII. 8 : "Meat commendeth us not to God," etc.

Summa, 3", 40, 2, 2'" : "As other men by abstinence acquire the virtue of continency, so also Christ used to restrain the flesh in Himself and His disciples by the virtue of His divinity. Whence as S. Matthew says (IX. 14), The disciples of John and the Pharisees used to fast, but not the disciples of Christ. Bede explains this on the ground that John did not drink wine and strong drink, since from abstinence his reward or merit was increased, to whom no [divine] power was inherent in his nature. But the Lord to whom it naturally appertained to remit sins, why should he withdraw from those [the publicans and sinners, S. Matt. IX. 10] whom He was enabled to make more pure than the abstainers themselves?"

Prelude 1. *S. T. Aq. on Heb.* XVIII. 9: "The kingdom of God is not meat and drink." Rom. XIV. 17. There is no stabiliment of heart in the moderate or superfluous taking of food but rather in the grace of God. Ps. CXII. 8."

—— 2. It is proper to observe the fasts of the Church sanctioned by the example of the holy in all ages.

—— 3. No one is exempt from the rule of God and His Church, but there is a higher fasting than that of the bodily abstinence of the letter; the spiritual fasting of the soul which gives to the life a greater,

  I. PURITY, weaning it from all impure thoughts and conceptions.

  II. STRENGTH to resist successfully all the assaults of the devil.

  III. OBEDIENCE to the law of the love of Jesus; discipling it to His will.

  IV. REWARD for its victories in many a hard contest with the flesh.

Epil.—To scorn the rule of the Pharisee, and to neglect the rule of Jesus leaves the soul utterly undone.

Twelfth Sunday after Trinity.

SERMON 161.
THE CHURCH A WITNESS TO THE TRUTH.
(Holy Gospel, Ser. 1).

(1). S. Mark VII. 31 : "Departing from the coasts of Tyre and Sidon."

(2). 1. Tim. III. 15 : "The Church the pillar and ground of the Truth."

Summa, 3ª, 40, 1, c. : "He came into the world to make manifest the truth as He said (S. John XVIII. 37): 'For this cause came I into the world,' etc. Therefore it did not behove Him to hide Himself by leading a solitary life, but to go forth into public, publicly preaching. He said to those desirous of detaining Him, 'I must preach the Kingdom of God to other cities also' (S. Luke IV. 42, 43)."

Prelude 1. S. *Chrysost. Hom.* 36 *in* 1. *Cor.*: "The Church is the place of angels, of archangels, is the Kingdom of God." S. *August. De Civ. Dei*, xx. c. 9: "For neither are the souls of the pious dead separated from the Church which is now the Kingdom of Christ."

—— 2. The Kingdom of God is the Church; to preach this Kingdom is to preach the Church.

—— 3. The office of the Church is to witness to the truth.

—— 4. The Church bears this witness, universally through all times and places.

—— 5. She bears it steadily, boldly, successfully, by means of her,

I. DOCTRINE, boldly proclaimed, the faith once delivered to the saints.

II. DISCIPLINE, of fast, festival, worship, and communion.

III. RITUAL, which is the outward form and signification of her faith.

IV. POWER, which has changed the face of the whole world.

Epil.— Follow the example of Jesus, carry about the teaching of the Church by purity of life; by confession of her faith, by steadfastly walking in the "old paths."

Twelfth Sunday after Trinity.

SERMON 162.
SACRAMENTS, THE MEDIATION OF THE BODY.
(Holy Gospel, Ser. 2).

(1). S. Mark VII. 33 : "He put His finger into his ears and he spit and touched his tongue."

(2). Heb. VI. 2 : "The doctrine of baptisms and of laying on of hands."

Summa, 3ª, 44, 3, 2ᵐ. : "Christ came to save the world not only by divine power, but also by the mystery of the Incarnation itself; therefore frequently in the healing of the infirm, He not only used His divine power for curing, by the way of command, but also by applying something pertaining to his humanity (S. Luke IV. 40). He laid His hands on every one of them, showing thereby His own flesh to be efficacious as a remedy (S. Mark VII. 38—VIII. 23 ; S. John IX. 6)."

Prelude 1. S. August. *Tract* 54 *in Joan* says : "The Lord used spittal for 'the Word was made flesh,' and He formed man out of the clay of earth. He washed his eyes in the pool; he was baptized into Christ and then he saw. The depth of so great a sacrament can be explained and treated of one way and another. You have heard the great mystery."

—— 2. The Lord's material body wrought miracles by the mediation of the body.

—— 3. His material flesh, being sanctified, had spiritual and miraculous power.

—— 4. The Church "His body" partakes of this power through sacramental grace. The sacraments must be,

I. STUDIED, explained, thought over, prayed over.
II. BELIEVED IN, unbelief hindered the Lord's miraculous power (S. Matt. XIII. 58).
III. USED, diligently, that we may draw water out of these wells of salvation.
IV. HONOURED, not for their blessings alone, but from the source whence they are derived.

Epil.—From the holy Body of Jesus incarnate flow all the sacramental channels of grace. Succession and sacrament, are the true notes of the Church.

(163)
Twelfth Sunday after Trinity.
SERMON 163.
MODESTY.
(*Holy Gospel, Ser.* 3).

(1). S. Mark VII. 36 : " He charged them that they should tell no man," etc.
(2). I. S. Pet. III. 4 : " A meek and quiet spirit which is in the sight of God of great price."

Summa, 22^e, 104, 4, 1^m.: "Not as if intending to bind them by the power of the divine precept; but He gave to His servants following Him, an example, that they indeed should desire to hide their graces, but that others might profit by their example, they unwillingly disclosed the miracle."

Prelude 1. *Euseb. Emiss. in loco.*: "These words have respect to us, they strike at our boasting, who, if we have at anytime done anything worthy of praise should not extol and proclaim it to the favour of the common people, but rather humbly hide it."

—— 2. *Remig. Bp.*: "Modesty is meekness and softness of mind." "By which (*F. Humb.*) the shyness of honesty acquires a pure and firm authority."

—— 3. Moses a singular example of Modesty; kept Jethro's flocks; doubted his own ability to speak.

—— 4. It is an unconscious sign of great spiritual and mental power.

—— 5. Over modesty unmixed with manliness is apt to lead to undue inaction and diffidence (*Plato Stat.* 310, D.)

—— 6. We ought to hide our gifts and graces; but by no means to omit to use them. Modesty should be seen in,

I. SPEECH, avoiding all boasting and mention of self.
II. MANNER, " in honour preferring one another ; " being gentle and subdued.
III. DRESS, quiet and unassuming ; avoiding any extravagant and vain ornamentation.
IV. ACTION, doing things great and noble without any attempt at effect or for show.

Epil.—Let the modest never forget that the Father who seeth in secret one day will reward openly.

Twelfth Sunday after Trinity.
SERMON 164.
THE RECOMPENSE OF GRATITUDE.
(Holy Gospel, Ser. 4).

(1). S. Mark VII. 37: "He hath done all things well."
(2). Eph. v. 20: "Giving thanks always for all things unto God."

Summa, 22^e, 106, 6, 1^m.: "In the recompense of a benefit, the disposition (*affectus*) is rather to be considered than the effect (*effectus*). In effect, a son can give no equal recompense to his parents; but if we consider the will of him giving, and recompensing, the son can recompense something to his father: for Seneca says, De Benefic. 3: If he can return nothing, the will shall suffice for the gratitude of him recompensing."

Prelude 1. This act of praise "He hath done," etc. expressed the gratitude of the people recompensing the Lord in words.

—— 2. S. T. A'Kemp. II. c. 10: "Grace ever attendeth him that is truly thankful."

—— 3. The recompense of gratitude is (S. August. Epist. ad Rom.) "to give thanks unto God is to feel that all things are given by Him; to believe in Him by word and deed."

—— 4. God and our parents will guide us not by what we can, but by what we desire to repay.

—— 5. Heavenly or earthly parent can never be repaid. To God and our parents is due a gratitude which will be

I. DEEP, no mere surface feeling, but a sincere desire of the heart.
II. ACCEPTED by God and man as being the all of that we have to give.
III. SWEET for us to give; the fulness of our outpoured love: sweet to its recipient.
IV. SUFFICIENT, to satisfy to the full the demands alike of God and man.

Epil.—As S. August. says: "We are able to give thanks to God; we are not able to repay Him"; let us do all that we can, and then trust ourselves to His infinite mercy.

Thirteenth Sunday after Trinity.
SERMON 165.
LOVE IS EXPANSIVE.
(Holy Gospel, Ser. 1).

(1). S. Luke, x. 27 : "Thou shalt love the Lord thy God with all thy heart."

(2). Rom. v. 5 : "The love of God is shed abroad in our hearts."

Summa, 22^{e}, 27, 7, c. : "A friend is loved for his own sake, an enemy for the sake of God; for the love of God stretches the mind of man to remoter objects, even to the love of enemies, as the virtue of fire by so much is shown to be stronger, as by how much it diffuses its heat to remoter places."

Prelude 1. *Theophyl.*; "With all the parts and powers of the soul to cleave to Him." S. Basil. in loco : "If any-one asks how we can obtain divine love, I may say that it is not to be taught; for we have never been taught by anyone to rejoice in the presence of light, or to cling to life, to love parents, etc., but a certain seminal reason is placed within us, having intrinsic causes that man should cling to God."

—— 2. A very hard thing to love God, but the exercise of love expands the affections.

—— 3. The love of the unseen God ; the great Lover; embraces all love's lower forms.

—— 4. Like fire, the stronger love becomes, the greater is its diffusing power. The striving and effort needful to love God, expands the heart's

  I. CONCEPTIONS, lifting it beyond the ties of earth to those who are the Lord's, and dwellers in heaven.

  II. DESIRES, "Like as the hart desireth the water-brooks, so longeth my soul," etc.

  III. SYMPATHIES, stretching them over and above the things of time and sense; yearning for the divine.

  IV. AFFECTIONS, once stretched, fix themselves on Him in Whom is the fulness of love.

Epil.—The spent soul, like the fledgling in the nest, sinks at the feet of Jesus—places all its love there ; He is my own, my very, my true and only love for eternity as also for time.

Thirteenth Sunday after Trinity.
SERMON 166.
THE PASSIONS OF THE SINLESS MAN.
(Holy Gospel, Ser. 2).

(1). S. Luke x. 30: "A certain man went down from Jerusalem to Jericho."

(2). S. James v. 17: "Elias was a man subject to like passions as we are."

Summa, 12ᵉ, 95, 2, c.: "In the first man there were passions of the mind, of present good, such as joy, love, etc.; so those which bring future good as desire, and hope which does not grieve. All those passions which imply the presence of evil existed not in Adam."

Prelude 1. *S. August. De Civ. Dei*, XIV. 10: "There were not in him, Adam, any passions of the mind save those which followed from the evidence of reason. Undisturbed love was in Adam and Eve, and certain other passions of the mind."

—— 2. A passionless nature implies a low condition of organization and development.

—— 3. Souls the most sensitive, are most strongly influenced by their passions.

—— 4. In a holy soul, the passions and emotions all tend to goodness and happiness.

—— 5. Sinful nature is the receptacle of evil passions.

—— 6. Our nature being a mingled one, we are subject to joy and grief; to love and hate, etc. Our passions, or emotions, which imply capacities must be when good

I. RESTRAINED from running into any undue excess; into evil from what is good.

II. CHERISHED and nurtured lest the heart become dry and hard.

III. AWAKENED, new hopes, desires, a new love for the true, good, and beautiful.

IV. SANCTIFIED by the Holy Ghost, centred and concentrated around the Lord.

Epil.—Through Jesus the second Adam, try to regain the condition of the first, the sinless man; cherish every holy emotion and rejoice in the fact that where sin abounds, there in the soul doth grace much more abound.

Thirteenth Sunday after Trinity.
SERMON 167.
THE SIN OF THE FIRST MAN.
(*Holy Gospel, Ser.* 3).

(1). S. Luke x. 30: "A certain man went down from Jerusalem to Jericho."

(2). I. Tim. II. 14: "Adam was not deceived, but the woman being deceived," etc.

Summa, 22ᵉ, 163, 1, c. : "In the state of pure innocency there was no rebellion of the flesh against the spirit; hence the first disorder of the human appetite did not arise from the desire of sensible good, through the lust of the flesh, but from the longing for some spiritual good which was above Adam's measure and for which he sought; and this pertained to pride."

Prelude 1. *S. August. De Civ. Dei*, XIV. *c.* 13 : "He, Adam, could not have come to an evil work unless an evil will had preceded it. What could be the beginning of an evil will except pride? Pride is the beginning of all sin. What is pride but the appetite for a perverse excellency or highness? This perverse excellency is, He being forsaken to Whom the mind ought to cling as to head, then the mind becomes a head or chief to itself."

—— 2. It was not a sensual temptation, to desire to become wise.

—— 3. The desire springing from pride, and ending in disobedience became the sin.

—— 4. Perversion of the good is the worst perversion of all—Adam fell by an aspiration in itself.

I. High, desiring a deeper knowledge, and a higher range of thought.

II. Pure, longing to know more clearly the distinction between good and evil.

III. Useful, as being under certain circumstances a sure guide of life.

IV. Godlike, "Ye shall be as God's" (Gen. iii. 5): a tempting promise to be fulfilled (1. S. John iii. 2).

Epil.—Evil must never be wrought in the hope that good may come of it.

Thirteenth Sunday after Trinity.
SERMON 168.
THE WOUNDS OF SIN.
(Holy Gospel, Ser. 4).

(1). S. Luke x. 34; "And bound up his wounds."

(2). Isaiah i. 5: "The whole head is sick and the whole heart is faint."

Summa, 12ᵉ, 85, 3, 0: "The sin of the first parent inflicted four wounds upon human nature, namely, ignorance upon the understanding; evil on the will; weakness in the irascible part, and lust in the desiring part of it. By evil is to be understood a proneness to sin. The effect of one sin may become the cause of another; so that the soul already disordered by a former sin is the more easily inclined to sin again."

Prelude 1. *S. August. De Civ. Dei*, XIV. c. 11: "Adam was unwilling to grieve Eve whom he thought would waste away without his comfort, if she were alienated from his heart, and that the disunion would kill her."

―― 2. It is sad to mutilate a beautiful building or work of art.

―― 3. Sadder still to destroy the soul, beautiful as being God's image and masterpiece.

―― 4. Sin converted Adam's true affection into a curse.

―― 5. Sin is the great destroyer. In Adam, by his sin the

I. UNDERSTANDING became darkened; and the promises of a serpent a deadly parody of good.

II. WILL, once so obedient, true and good, led into rebellion and disobedience.

III. IRASCIBLE or courageous power of the soul reduced to craven weakness.

IV. APPETITE depraved and sensual; desiring bodily rather than spiritual delights.

Epil.—Wounds of sin are deep, deadly, and many: fly for healing to the Great Physician of all souls.

Fourteenth Sunday after Trinity.
SERMON 169.
JESUS, A NAME OLD AND NEW.
(Holy Gospel, Ser. 1).

(1). S. Luke XVII. 13 : "Jesus, Master, have mercy on us."
(2). Philipp. II. 10 : "At the name of Jesus every knee should bow."

Summa, 3ª, 37, 2, 1 and 2ᵐ.: "The prophet Isaiah, (VII. 4,) gave him another name, Immanuel, Wonderful, Counsellor, Prince of peace (*Id.* IX. 6) 'a new name' (*Id.* LXII. 2), but the name of Jesus is used many times in the Old Testament as implying some particular and temporal salvation. But both by spiritual reason and universal salvation it became a 'new name' rightly bestowed upon Him by the angel that he might become the Saviour of all."

Prelude 1. *S. Eph. Ryth.* VI. *De Fide* : "Jesus, Thou glorious name, Thou hidden bridge that carrieth over from death to life; at Thee have I arrived and stand still." I. Clem. Alex. Pædag. III. 12. "O Jesus who is healing body and soul, the whole (or particular) man!" etc. Strom. VI. § 145. "The blessed name Jesus." "Saviour indeed, since Son and Word of God." S. Iren. iii. 11.

—— 2. The name of Jesus is both old and new, uniting the Old and New Testament in one stream of tradition.

—— 3. The new name sanctifies the old and carries on the blessed work.

—— 4. It is more glorious in the Lord by contrast with its former possessors.

—— 5. It epitomizes the whole course of redemption from the fall to final glory. Jesus, Saviour saves from

I. OURSELVES, in this our lost, fallen, corrupt and helpless state.

II. SIN, with all its vast powers, its place in our nature; its manifold forms.

III. DEATH, in the soul, dead in sins, and from a lasting death in the body.

IV. HELL, from eternal loss, pain, separation of God; from the undying worm and fire.

Epil.—"Jesus, Master," etc. This your prayer ; this your life ; for eternity as well as time He will be your Jesus, your Saviour.

Fourteenth Sunday after Trinity.
SERMON 170.
BODILY ADORATION.
(Holy Gospel, Ser. 2).

(1). S. Luke XVII. 16: "He fell down on his face at His feet."
(2). I. Tim. ii. 8: "I will therefore that men pray everywhere lifting up holy hands."

Summa, 22^c, 84, 2, o and 2^m.: "Because we are composed of a two-fold nature, the Divine Majesty is to be adored by us, not only with spiritual but also with bodily adoration; with spiritual adoration, which consists in the devotion of the interior mind; with bodily adoration which consists in the humiliation of the exterior body. It seems from S. John, IV. 24, that true and spiritual worship is not an act of the body, but it is so, inasmuch as it proceeds from spiritual devotion and is ordained to this end. So also is it with prayer (I. Cor. XIV. 15), primordially it is in the mind, and then it is expressed in words."

Prelude 1. *S. T. Aq. on* I. *Tim.* II. 8: "August. that which we do outwardly in praying, we do that our interior affection may be excited; for genuflections and things of this kind are not in themselves acceptable to God, but because by these, as if by a sign of humility, the interior man is humbled, as the elevation of the hand signifies the lifting up of the heart."

—— 2. Adoration is a custom in every age, country and religion.

—— 3. Adoration consists of standing, kneeling, crossing, and prostration on receiving the Holy Communion. The Adoration of the body is spiritual in its

I. ORIGIN, which arises from the devotion, pure and simple of a loving heart.
II. EFFECT, which is to raise the soul to a higher pitch of devotion and fervour.
III. ACT, which implies either supplication or thanksgiving, or confession of sin.
IV. TEACHING, genuflection indicating our infirmity; prostration, our nothingness.

Epil.—Preserving the outward forms of adoration, its inward power will react upon the soul; to man's salvation and to God's greater glory.

Fourteenth Sunday after Trinity.
SERMON 171.
PRIESTLY ABSOLUTION.
(Holy Gospel, Ser. 3).

(1). S. Luke XVII. 14: "Go show yourselves unto the priests."
(2). Rom. VIII. 10: "The body is dead because of sin; but the spirit is life because of righteousness."

Summa 12^c, 102, 5, 7^m.: "By the rites of the law the leper was not cleansed from his spots; but when cleansed he was shown to the priest (Levit. XIV. 3), who commanded him to be purified. Now the leper was cleansed, but God commanded him to be purified, inasmuch as by the sentence of the priest he was restored to his association with men and to divine worship."

Prelude 1. *S. Cyp. Ep. Jubian:* "S. John XX. 21-23: Whence we learn, that they only who are set over the Church may lawfully give remission of sins; but, without nothing can be bound or loosed, where there is no one who can either bind or loose. Nor do we propound this without the authority of Divine Scripture."

——— 2. The priest, and he alone was authorized to pronounce the word of healing.

——— 3. Leprosy, a type of sin; so pardon and absolution are spoken by the priest only.

——— 4. This, not by virtue of an inherent power, but of a power deligated to him by God.

———, 5. The priest pronounces in God's name a sentence ratified by God.

——— 6. Note the weight of only one sin on the soul. Priestly absolution is,

I. NEEDFUL, that men's hearts and consciences may be mercifully lightened.
II. TRUE, as being a personal application of the precious Blood of Jesus. 1. John I. 7.
III. PERFECT, in its action, remitted is the sin, entirely and for ever.
IV. ORDAINED OF GOD, by the Commission given by the Risen Lord Himself.

Epil.—Avail yourselves of this sacrament of repentance.

Fourteenth Sunday after Trinity.
SERMON 172.
BAPTISM INTO DEATH.
(Holy Gospel, Ser. 4).

(1). S. Luke XVII. 14: "Go show yourselves unto the priests."
(2). Rom. VI. 4: "We are buried with Him by baptism into death."

Summa, 12ᵃ, 102, 5, 7: "By the two birds of Leviticus (IV. 4), are signified the divinity and the humanity of Christ. The one of these signifying His humanity is slain over running water; hence the waters of baptism are consecrated by the passion of Christ. Man washes by the baptism of water and tears his garments and hair (Lev. XIV. 8), *i. e.* his thoughts and deeds." It is the priest, who looking at the leprosy, orders the birds to be taken.

Prelude 1. *S. T. Aq. in Rom.* vi. 4: " Burial is only for the dead (S. Matt. VIII. 22). Men are buried by baptism, they are conformed to the burial of Christ Himself; for as he who is buried is placed beneath the earth, so he who is baptized, is immersed under the water." *S. Chrysost. in Rom. vi.*: "We die as He did. Baptism is a cross. He died in flesh and was entombed, we die to sin."

——— 2. Holy Baptism is a death unto the world and sin, and a new life to holiness and to God.

——— 3. The slain bird signifies the death; the living bird purified with blood the new baptismal life.

——— 4. Life is one long baptism; one long dying to sin and carrying of the cross; one continued new life through the spirit rising from the death of sin to the life of righteous. This baptism into death is one of

I. SORROW, or contrition for sins of the will, of the flesh, of infirmity, or carelessness.

II. CONFESSION, *S. T. Aq. in Rom.* X. 10: The three-fold confession of sin; of God's goodness, and of divine truth.

III. PARDON, or absolution by which the past is blotted out and all things become new.

IV. AMENDMENT, or satisfaction which is the only reparation possible for the past.

Epil.—Partake of this spiritual death and of that new life which from it flows.

Fifteenth Sunday after Trinity.
SERMON 173.
HATRED OF GOD.
(Holy Gospel, Ser. 1*).*

(1.) S. Matt. VI. 24: "He will hate the one and love the other."

(2.) Rom. I. 30: "Haters of God."

Summa, 22ᶜ, 34, 1, 0: "It is impossible that anyone seeing God in His essence can hate Him; but there are certain effects of God which oppose an inordinate will; such as the infliction of punishment, and the restraint of sinners by the divine law. On these grounds therefore can God be hated by some as being the restrainer of sinners and the inflictor of punishments."

Prelude 1. *S. Johan. Clem. Parad. Grad. iii.* 10: "Hatred is a hidden affection of the mind by which it is angered by anything that offends it; a turning away of the mind from what displeases it." *S. Bruno in Ps. cxl.* 20: "The haters of God are justly horrible, and to be condemned by a proper and religious execration."

—— 2. It is an awful fact, deadly in its results, that man can hate the good God.

—— 3. God is love, is perfection, all-wise, all-powerful, omniscient, omnipresent.

—— 4. God is our maker, redeemer, preserver, sanctifier, father and judge.

—— 5. When a man serves the devil, God's enemy, then he turns round and hates God.

—— 6. Horrible nature of sin; it sets man against God; it turns blessings into curses. The hatred of God implies a,

I. REBELLION, the most wicked and ungrateful possible against god's infinite love and goodness.

II. PROSTITUTION, complete of grace, of life, of being and of all God's gifts.

III. DEGRADATION, by wilful sin growing therein, more devilish instead of Christ-like.

IV. PREPARATION, for hell, into which, in torments are gathered God's haters.

Epil.—Learn to love, and obey God. May the thoughts of hate be but a vision of Satan.

Fifteenth Sunday after Trinity.
SERMON 174.
OUR MASTER AN ULTIMATE END.
(Holy Gospel, Ser. 2).

(1.) S. Matt. vi. 24 : " No man can serve two masters."
(2.) Eph. vi. 9 : "Your master also is in heaven."
Summa, 12^e, 1, 5, c. : " When anyone desires anything as an ultimate end, he desires it as being a perfect good, and the completion of himself; so that there cannot be, at the same time, many ultimate ends of one man. 'We say,' says Augustine (*De Civ. Dei*, xix. 1), 'that the end of man is not that which is consumed and is not; but that which is to be perfected.' Each one desires a something for himself, as an ultimate end and as being to him a perfect and complete good."—This ultimate end becomes a master. "Philipp. iii. 19: 'Whose God is their belly.' For the delights of the belly constitute their ultimate end." S. Matt. vi. 24: "No man," etc. Therefore it is impossible that there are many ultimate ends in one man, which are not ordained in respect to each other.

Prelude 1. *S. Greg. Naz. T.* ii. p. 200, c.: "That to which all other things tend, I call an end."
—— 2. No one is free from such a master as an ultimate end.
—— 3. This may be a person, a desire, an expectation, an ultimate good.
—— 4. This ultimate end, this master ever directs and regulates thought, word and deed. It is ever,

I. REMEMBERED, is before the eye of the mind at all times.
II. OBEYED, being the master who rules thought and action with an iron rule.
III. UNITED, to its pupil, becoming a part of his being and life.
IV. IN THE FUTURE, looking onwards and upwards to a perfect development.

Epil.—Choose the best possible master, the best ultimate end; for time and for eternity—even Jesus in whom all are complete.

Fifteenth Sunday after Trinity.
SERMON 175.
SOLICITUDE.
(*Holy Gospel*, Ser. 3).

(1). S. Matt. VI. 34 : "Take no thought for the morrow."
(2). 1. Tim. V. 8 : "If any man provide not for his own, he is worse than an infidel."

Summa, 22^c, 108, 3, 5^m and 5. : " The Lord did not prohibit necessary, but undue solicitude. It is naturally imprinted upon man to be solicitous about the things which are necessary for life, in which respect the animals resemble man—'Go to the ant,' etc. (Prov. vi. 6-9). Every precept which is opposed to the inclination of nature is opposed to natural law. There is a four-fold undue solicitude concerning temporal things which is to be avoided.

Prelude 1. *Remigius Bp.* : "Solicitude is superfluous care." *Pet. of Antioch, Hom.* 119 : "It is plainly a sign of want of faith and faint-heartedness." *Paschas. Rath.* 6 : "It chokes the word and renders the Christian unfruitful."

—— 2. Utter carelessness and recklessness is worse than undue solicitude.

—— 3. Both the one and the other are contrary to the law of God, and imply distrust in Him.

—— 4. The immeasurable importance of spiritual as compared with temporal concerns.

—— 5. Temporal things have an earnest claim upon us, but it is a secondary one. The four reasons which S. Thomas gives why undue solicitude is to be avoided are lest men should,

I. REST, in temporal things as the end of life; serving God for gain only (S. Matt. VI. 19).

II. DESPAIR, of divine help in time of need. "Your heavenly Father," etc. (S. Matt. VI. 32).

III. PRESUME, as being able to gain these things without God's help. "Which of you," etc. (*id*. 27).

IV. LABOUR, only for the present, the morrow of this life, not of eternity.

Epil.—Undue solicitude divides the heart, leaving it no rest, preventing all progress in the outward as well as in the spiritual life.

Fifteenth Sunday after Trinity.

SERMON 176.
THE NEED OF PRAYER.
(*Holy Gospel, Ser.* 4).

(1). S. Matt. vi. 32 : "Your heavenly Father knoweth that ye have need of all these things."

(2). Philipp. iv. 6 : "By prayer and supplication let your requests be made known unto God."

Summa, 22^e, 83, 2, c. and 1^m. : "To pray is not idle but necessary; not indeed that the divine disposition can be changed, but that we may obtain that, which God through the prayers of the Saints is disposed to grant. It is not needful for us to lengthen out our prayers to God, for us to manifest to Him our needs and desires, but that we ourselves may be led to consider, how in our prayers, recourse is had to the divine help."

Prelude 1. *S. Ephrem. T.* ii. p. 330 : "When prayer goeth up in love, then the gates of heaven are opened, and there is none that preventeth it from entering. Let each man be in love with prayer. Let him that prayeth, never faint; it raised Jonah ; it rescued Daniel ; it preserved Ananias and his company. Prayer bringeth forth and giveth its gifts to him that loveth dealings with it."

S. Greg. Naz. T. ii. p. 200 : "Prayer looks at higher things than supplication for the relief of need."

—— 2. If 'your heavenly Father knoweth,' why pray ? for your own sakes but not for his.

—— 3. It is not needful to God to tell Him our wants, which He already knows. (S. Matt. vi. 8).

—— 4. Prayer is needful to dispose God's heart. Prayer is needful for us in order to,

I. LEAD, us to God, as bringing us into His holy sight and presence ; it is a communion with God.

II. TEACH, us our entire dependence upon God ; to refer all our blessings to Him.

III. SHOW, us our own needs more clearly and especially our spiritual wants (Rev. iii. 17-18).

IV. RAISE UP, in us a spirit of love, thankfulness and of obedience to God.

Epil.—The prayerless life is hard, unloving, cold, worldly, and unfit for heaven.

Sixteenth Sunday after Trinity.
SERMON 177.
GOD'S PUNISHMENT.
(Holy Gospel, Ser. 1).

(1). S. Luke VII. 12 : " There was a dead man carried out."
(2). Rom. v. 12 : " By one man sin entered into the world, and death by sin."

Summa, 22^c, 164, 1, c : " Death and bodily defects are the consequent punishments of the sin of our first parents. 5^m. : " Death is a certain evil of human nature and so it is not of God, but is a certain defect incident to the sin of man. 8 : If death had been the punishment of sin it would have immediately followed after the sin (Gen. ii. 17), but our first parents lived long after their sin (Gen. iv). 8^m. : Yet Augustine says (Gen. et Lit.) Although they lived many years afterwards, yet they began to die on that day in which they received the law of death by which they grew into old age."

Prelude 1. *S. Greg. Naz. T.* 11. *p.* 298, D : " Death is the separation of the bond of body and soul." *S. Cyril. Jerusa. Cat. Lect. xiii.* 2 : " One man's sin, even Adam's, had power to bring death to the world. The first man formed out of the earth, brought in universal death." *Sedul. Hyber :* " Sin is the sting or arrow of death."

—— 2. Wrongly thought because punishment is delayed that it will never come.

—— 3. Adam and Eve felt, in secret awe and dread, the slow working out of God's sentence.

—— 4. Fear ever follows sin. The general order of God's punishment is,

I. SLOW, sometimes it is quick ; as a rule darkness, perplexity and sorrow go before it.

II. SURE, sooner or later the black cloud of God's anger will discharge itself.

III. INCREASING, as sin increases, and the heart grows harder, and the hope of repentance grows dim.

IV. FATAL, for at last the unrepentant soul that sinned will surely die

Epil.—Thank God, a door of repentance and pardon is opened by Jesus through whom death, the punishment of sin, can be turned into life.

Sixteenth Sunday after Trinity.
SERMON 178.
SYMPATHY.
(*Holy Gospel, Ser.* 2).

(1). S. Luke VII. 12: "Much people of the city were with her."
(2). Rom. XII. 15: "Rejoice with them that do rejoice, and weep with them that weep."

Summa, 12ᵃ, 38, 3, 0 and 2ᵐ.: "By the compassion of friends, grief and sadness are naturally lightened. The grief itself of a friend by itself would make the sufferer the more sorry, but the consideration of its cause, which is love, brings a delight with it which is greater" than the superadded grief of the friend.

Prelude 1. S. Chrysost. T. IX. 680, E.: "Nothing so unites love as when we share with one another joy and sorrow. Partake of tears, that you may lighten the despondency; partake of joy, that you may plant cheerfulness; that you may fix love." S. Thomas in Rom. xii.: "The compassion itself of a friend condoling brings a two-fold consolation to the afflicted, as being a strong argument of friendship, and because the friend seems to offer himself at the same time to bear the burden of adversity, which causes the sorrow, and which being divided appears to become lighter."

——— 2. Rejoicing with those who joy we increase their joy.
——— 3. Grieving with those who are sorrowful we lighten their burden.
——— 4. Either joy or grief joins heart to heart and becomes a source of love. The law of sympathy

I. JOINS heart to heart and hand to hand; bearing each other's burdens.
II. EXPANDS and developes the best and least selfish of our feelings.
III. GENERATES a new love and a holier bond of union.
IV. BLESSES, increasing joy and lessening grief; its action is all for good.

Epil.—A great lesson, none of us liveth to himself; we are all members of the one great family of God.

Sixteenth Sunday after Trinity.
SERMON 179.
THE SOUL AFTER DEATH.
(Holy Gospel, Ser. 3).

(1). S. Luke VII. 12 : " There was a dead man carried out."
(2). II. Cor. v. 8 : " Willing rather to be absent from the body, and to be present with the Lord."

Summa, 1ª, 89, 2, c. : " The separated soul sees other separated souls and has perfect knowledge of them. Dives saw Lazarus and Abraham. It understands, by turning to those things which are intelligible to itself; it understands itself by itself." *Id.* 1ᵐ. : " In a certain way it is more free to understand inasmuch as it was [before death] hindered by the weight and occupation of the body from purity of understanding." *Id.* 89, 7, c. : " It understands by an influx of forms from the divine light which equally enlightens things near and distant. Distance of place in no way hinders the knowledge of separated souls." *Id.* 89, 8, 1ᵐ. : " The souls of the dead have a care for the things of the living ; they know them, not by themselves but by the souls who go hence to them, or by the angels." *Id.* 89, 4, c. : " Separated souls know only those things to which they are limited by preceding knowledge, or by some affection ; or by natural habit ; or by divine ordination." *Id.* 89, 5, c. : " The habit of knowledge here acquired, being in the intellect, remains in the separated soul, nor can it be lost by itself, or by any contingency." These thoughts teach us,

I. THE CONTINUATION, of this life to the soul after death ; as to habit, etc.
II. THE NEARNESS, and connection of our dead with us now ; as knowing us still.
III. THE VALUE, of this life, as to holiness, knowledge, etc., as a preparation for the life to come.
IV. THE CONTRAST, between the body which has yet to die, and the infinite and immortal soul.

Epil.—Learn the glory, dignity, and how great ought to be the holiness of this life, it being but the beginning of the life to come.

Sixteenth Sunday after Trinity.
SERMON 180.
PERFECTION.
(*Holy Gospel, Ser.* 4).

(1). S. Luke VII. 15: "He that was dead sat up and began to speak."
(2). 2. Cor. XIII. 9: "This also we wish, even your perfection."
Summa, 3ᵃ, 53, 3, 1 and 2, c: "Some were raised by Elijah and Elisha. Heb. XI. 35. 'Women received their dead,' etc. The Lord raised three persons. At the Crucifixion bodies of saints arose. S. Matt. XXVII. 52, 53. Christ risen 'became the first fruits,' etc. I. Cor. XV. 20. That resurrection by which anyone is snatched from death [to die again] is an imperfect one, but He became the first fruits by rising to the perfect immortality of life. He dieth no more. Rom. VI. 9."

Prelude 1. The Widow's son was an imperfect resurrection since he had again to die.

—— 2. *Sum.* 1ᵃ, 103, 1, c: Since it is of the best to produce the best; it would not agree with the highest goodness of God that He should not lead the things He produced to perfection. But the ultimate perfection of each thing consists in the attainment of its end; whence it pertains to the divine goodness, that as He produced so He should lead them to their end."

—— 3. *Id.* 1ᵃ, 73, 1, c: "Perfection is according to an end; the end of the harpist is to play the harp; or it is something arrived at by an operation, as the end of the builder is the house which he builds by his building."

—— 4. *Id. Id.*: "Perfection implies consummation; of nature, on the seventh day; Gen. II. 3, of Grace, at the Incarnation; S. John I. 17, of glory, at the end of the world. Perfection implies a state not subject to

I. CHANGE, which is either for the better or the worse, which is a manifest sign of imperfection.
II. PROGRESS, the fact of being able to progress, implies an imperfection not yet overcome.
III. FAILING in any way; for any failing implies weakness, etc., which is alien to the perfect state.
IV. BEING SURPASSED, according to its own kind and order. Jesus was perfect man and perfect God.

Epil.—Look onwards and upwards towards the perfect life in a perfect condition of being.

Seventeenth Sunday after Trinity.
SERMON 181.
THE OUTWARD CHRISTIAN LIFE.
(*Holy Gospel, Ser.* 1).

(1). S. Luke XIV. 1 : He went into the house of one of the chief Pharisees to eat bread."
(2). Philipp. I. 27 : " Let your conversation be as it becometh the Gospel of Christ."

Summa, 3ª, 40, 2, c. and 1ᵐ : " It was most suitable that Christ should commonly carry Himself as others since in His conversation He gave us in all things an example of perfection, in what pertains to salvation. But abstinence from food and drink do not do this ; 'for the Kingdom of God is not meat,' etc. Rom. XIV. 17. In all such things, it is not the use but the sensuality in the using of them which is sin. He walked in a contrary way to John, going to the table of Publicans eating and drinking."

Prelude 1. *Tertull. Apol. c.* 42 : " We [Christians] put not away from us any enjoyment of His works ; certainly we refrain from using them immoderately or wrongfully."

—— 2. *S. Cyp. Ep.* XIII. 2 : " Meekness, humility, and the even tenor of a good life are suitable to all Christians. *S. T. Aq. on Eph.* IV. 1. " If anyone was called to a noble kingdom it would be unworthy of him to do rustic works ; but you are called," etc. (*Id. c.* II. 19, 20.)

—— 3. What is said of eating and drinking, applies equally to manners, dress and expenditure. The outward Christian life is to be

I. SIMPLE, natural and suitable to each one's position and station in life.
II. MODEST, I Tim. II. 9 : In speech and manner, as well as in apparel.
III. UNAFFECTED, any studied peculiarity like Quaker's dress, etc., is proud as well as silly.
IV. UNOSTENTATIOUS, I S. Pet. III. 3, 4 : All real, and with nothing for effect or vain show.

Epil.—So live your Christian life, that men may take knowledge that you have been and are still with Jesus (Acts IV. 13), following in the steps of His most holy life.

Seventeenth Sunday after Trinity.
SERMON 182.
FOUR FRUITS OF PRIDE.
(*Holy Gospel, Ser.* 2).

(1.) S. Luke xiv. 3 : " Sit not down in the highest room."
(2.) S. James iv. 6 : " God resisteth the proud."
Summa, 12^e, 162, 4. c. and 4^m : " Pride implies an undue desire for excellence, which is not according to right reason. Anselm says that the lifting up of pride shows itself in the will, in speech and in act. The four forms of pride are to regard blessings, as if from ourselves, or if given from above, to be due to our merits; or the boasting of having what we do not possess; or others being despised, they desire to seem to have in a particular way that which they have." *Id.* 22^e, 162, v. c. :
" Pride is opposed to humility which looks at the subjection of man to God, whilst pride looking at the defect of this subjection makes him a rebel."

Prelude 1. *S. Greg. Nazian. T. ii.* 199 *c.* : " The proud is he who desires to be seen by all."

—— 2. Pride like all sin is many sided, hidden, open, clothed in humility.

—— 3. It corrupts all that it touches, strength and beauty, wealth, honour and learning.

—— 4. It is the origin of all sin; and it ever carries the devil's mark with it.

—— 5. It is the snare of the devil (*S. T. Aq. in* 1 *Tim. iii.* 6). Pride renders a man,

I. BLIND, What can be greater blindness than to attribute God's gifts to self.

II. ARROGANT, as despising others above whom he wishes to appear.

III. CONCEITED, acknowledging God's gifts and yet attributing them to his own merits.

IV. BOASTFUL, as assuming to have that in which he has no portion.

Epil.—The lowest, the very lowest place let it be thy portion here in humble clinging to the cross—hereafter will thine exultation come. " Before honour is humility."

Seventeenth Sunday after Trinity.
SERMON 183.
AMBITION.
(Holy Gospel, Ser. 3).

(1.) S. Luke xiv. 8: "Sit not down in the highest room."
(2.) Rom. xii. 16: "Mind not high things."
Summa, 22ᶜ, 131, 1, c.: "Ambition is the sin through which anyone inordinately desires honour; and this inordinate desire for honour is seen, when anyone desires a testimonial for excellence which he has not, which is to desire honour above his proportion; also when he desires it for himself, but not to render it to God; lastly, when this appetite rests in the honour itself and is not referred to the benefit of others." *Id*. 3ᵐ.: "This inordinate desire is the occasion of many ills being done, as when a man does not care by what means so ever he can gain honour. Whence Salust said that the good and the base equally desire for themselves glory, honour and rule." *Id*. 131, 2, 3ᵐ.: "It seems to pertain to exterior equipage as shown in 'the great pomp' of Agrippa" (Acts xxv. 23). *Id*. 131, 1, 1 and 1ᵐ.: "Honour is the reward of virtue; sought for beyond reason, it becomes a sin."

Prelude 1. *S. Isid. Pelus. Ep. iii.* 34: "The love of ambition is something terrible and audacious."

—— 2. *S. Greg. Naz. T. ii.* 189, D.: "Ambition is the moderate desire of honour."

—— 3. *S. Pet. de Blois Ep.* 14: "Ambition is the ape of charity, the latter suffers for things eternal; the former for windfalls; charity is kind to the poor, ambition to the rich; charity never faileth, ambition never raises up; it is the iniquity upon the talent of lead" (Zech. v. 7). Ambition is the parent of,

I. WORLDLINESS, this world and its theatre is the scene of its operations.
II. PRIDE, as such the cause of the fall of the angels.
III. DECEIT, the really great are really humble; such have no desire to appear great.
IV. DISCONTENT, desiring things higher, greater, etc., breeds discontent of the present.

Epil.—Note the Lord's condemnation of ambition (S. Matt. xx. 25-26, xxiii. 2).

Seventeenth Sunday after Trinity.

SERMON 184.
THE WAY OF HUMILITY.
(*Holy Gospel*, Ser. 4).

(1.) S. Luke xiv. 11: "He that humbleth himself shall be exalted."

(2.) 1. Pet. v. 6: "Humble yourselves under the mighty hand of God that He may exalt you."

Summa, 22ᵉ, 161, 5, 4ᵐ.: "Christ chiefly commended humility to us because the impediment to human salvation is greatly removed by it. It is needful for salvation that man may tend to things spiritual and heavenly, from which he is hindered whilst he studies to be magnified as to earthly things. So the Lord, that He might remove this hinderance to salvation, pointed out by the example of humility, that exterior loftiness is to be condemned. So humility is, as if a certain disposition for the free approach of man to spiritual and divine blessings."

Prelude 1. *S. August. Ser.* 2, *de Ascen.*: "Behold a great miracle! God is high. Lift up yourself, He flies from you. Humble yourself, He descends to you."

—— 2. *S. August. Ser.* 218: "The heights of heaven are mounted by the steps of humility."

—— 3. *S. August. in Joan*: "The country is high, the way is humble. How can he who seeks the country, refuse the way?" Humility removes the hinderances to salvation by causing the soul to be,

I. WEANED from earthly things by its lonely walking in this time and life.

II. DIRECTED to things spiritual, as the end of faith, hope and waiting.

III. SOFTENED to receive the impressions of grace and the teachings of the Spirit.

IV. DEPENDENT upon God, as feeling its own weakness and imperfection.

Epil.—*S. Bern. de* 12 *Grad. Humil.*: "Humiliation is the way to humility. If you desire the grace of humility you must not refuse the way."

Eighteenth Sunday after Trinity.

SERMON 185.
CONTROVERSY.
(Holy Gospel, Ser. 1).

(1). S. Matt. XXII. 3 : " He had put the Pharisees to silence."
(2). Acts IX. 22 : " Saul confounded the Jews which dwelt at Damascus."

Summa, 22^e, 10, 7, 1^m, and 3^m : " The Apostle (II. Tim. II. 14), did not wholly prohibit disputation, but an undue use of it, which was rather for the contention of words, than for the strengthening of the faith. Those things which are of faith ought not to be disputed about, as if there was any doubt about them ; but for the confirmation of the truth and for the confutation of errors. It is needful sometimes to dispute with unbelievers for the confirmation of the faith: sometimes indeed in defence of the faith (I. S. Pet. III. 14) ; for the purpose also of convincing those who are in error (Tit. I. 9). To dispute with unbelievers, as if doubting of the faith before simple and illiterate believers, is a sin."

Prelude 1. *S. Isid. Pet.* IV. *Ep.* 162 : It is the wisdom of the uncultivated, only to hold a controversy concerning things indifferent; to repress fierce and heated controversies;" (*Id.* IV. 92.) which are " not to be held with shadows, nor concerning vain things."

—— 2. The truth cannot be too thoroughly thrashed out by prayerful temperate controversy which

I. CLEARS UP misconceptions, false and distorted views.
II. DISSOLVES doubts, meeting every possible objection.
III. OPENS OUT the truth, plainly, minutely and forcibly.
IV. CONFIRMS the faith, by manifesting its foundations.

Epil.—" Be ready always to give an answer," etc. (I. S. Pet. III. 15.)

Eighteenth Sunday after Trinity.
SERMON 186.
LOVE THE FIRST AND GREAT COMMANDMENT.
(Holy Gospel, Ser. 2).

(1). S. Matt. xxii. 38: "This is the first and great Commandment."

(2). 1. Tim. 1. 5: "The end of the commandment is charity out of a pure heart."

Summa, 22^e, 44, 1, c: "The end of the spiritual life is that man may be united to God. This union is effected by love. 1. Tim. 1. 5. All the graces concerning the acts for which precepts are given; either for the purification of the heart from the whirlwinds of passions; or for the obtaining 'a good conscience and faith unfeigned.' 'All these three are required for loving God. The impure heart is drawn away from the love of God by passions which incline it to earthly things. The evil conscience makes a horror of divine justice by the fear of punishment. Feigned faith separates the affections from the truth of love: so love is the first and great commandment.'"

Prelude 1. *S. Eph. Syr.*: "Love is the treasurer of thy heavenly treasure." So keeping this first commandment the treasures of grace are opened to the soul.

—— 2. *Auct. Imperf.*: "Fear is the beginning of worship, etc., its perfection is love." 1. S. John iv. 18.

—— 3. Love acts upon man's whole life and being for time and eternity; it

I. PURIFIES the heart from all that is mean, low and selfish; it burns it out.

II. QUIETS the conscience as bringing the will into subjection to the loved One's will.

III. CONFIRMS the faith; for it centres reason and affection on the love of God.

IV. UNITES the soul to God: Who is not only loving, but God in sympathy.

Epil.—*S. Greg. Mag. on Ezek.*: "The love of God is never idle; if present in the heart it works great things, if it refuses to work it is not love."

Eighteenth Sunday after Trinity.
SERMON 187.
THE LOVE OF GOD.
(Holy Gospel, Ser. 3).

(1). S. Matt. XXII, 37: "Thou shalt love the Lord thy God with all thy heart."

(2). Rom. v, 5: "The love of God is shed abroad in our hearts."

Summa, 22^e, 44, 2, c.: "The love of God is the end to which the love of the neighbour is ordained. Therefore the precept concerning the love of God ought not alone to be given; but that also of the love of the neighbour is added on account of such as are apt; of those who could not understand one of the precepts to be contained in the other." *Id.* 184, 3, c.: "By itself and essentially the perfection of the Christian life consists of love." *Id.* 184, 2, c.: "Although no one in this life is able to arrive at the absolute perfection of divine love, yet man is able to attain to so great a perfection of love, that he repudiates and detests all those things which are contrary to love."

Prelude 1. *S. Tho. Aq. in Rom. v.* 5: "The love of God signifies His love to us (Jer. xxxii. 3); also our love to Him (Rom. viii. 38-39). The Holy Spirit leads us to the participation of that love by which we become the lovers of God."

—— 2. "Thou shalt." No impossible command. Man can love God if he wills so to do.

—— 3. The love of God includes all other loves. The love of God

I. GLORIFIES the whole spiritual nature, for it kindles the light and fire of God.

II. RULES, the one directing, powerful moving passion of the soul.

III. QUICKENS, awakening a new energizing strong life within the soul.

IV. SATISFIES the soul's every longing; leaves no void or want within.

Epil.—*S. August. Medit.*: "O fire of love, which ever burns and never is to be quenched! O love! inflame and may I burn and love, but only Thee!"

Eighteenth Sunday after Trinity.

SERMON 188.
DISSIMULATION.
(*Holy Gospel*, Ser. 4).

(1). S. Matt. XXII. 35 : " Tempting Him."
(2). Rom. XII. 9 : " Let love be without dissimulation."

Summa, 22ᶜ, III, I, c. : "All dissimulation is sin; since it is a lie which is expressed in signs of outward actions; a lie, by which one thing is indicated in deed, or outward sign, whilst another or contrary feeing lies hidden in the secret recesses of the mind. Outward signs consist not only in words, but in deeds which are opposed to the truth. That which is opposed to the truth, whether spoken in words or signified by signs, is properly dissimulation, and as such is a lie and a sin."

Prelude 1. *S. Zeno Veron.* : " The double tongue and mind is born of envy, it incites hatred in the depth of the heart; it professes apparent sweetness from the surface of the lips, as rocks covered by waves lead the ignorant and incautious to unforeseen shipwreck."

—— 2. The lawyer asked a good and proper question, tempting the Lord with a smiling face.

—— 3. Every form of dissimulation or insincerity is hateful to God.

—— 4. *Cassiodorus:* " Dissimulation is a virulent pest." We can dissimulate or lie by

I. SILENCE, appearing to assent to that which we know and feel to be false.

II. WORD, using words to conceal thought; saying what we do not mean.

III. LOOK, the expression of surprise at something we knew before.

IV. GESTURE or motion of the body, implying satisfaction or contempt.

Epil.—*Primasius.* " The fraud is great when gold is adulterated with baser metals; how much greater the evil, if the heavenly good in the heart be corrupted by dissimulation."

Nineteenth Sunday after Trinity.

SERMON 189.

THE LESSONS OF BODY.
(Holy Gospel, Ser. 1).

(1). S. Matt. IX. 1 : "He entered into a ship."
(2). 1. Cor. VI. 13 : "The body is for the Lord; and the Lord for the body."

Summa, 3ª, 5, 2, c. : As Christ assumed a true body, so, it is to be believed that the body which He assumed was an earthly and not a heavenly one, which is impassible and uncorruptible. If the Son of God had assumed a heavenly body, He would not really have fasted, nor thirsted, nor have sustained His passion and death, and had He showed Himself to men as having an earthly and fleshly body, it would have been a false demonstration had his body been a heavenly one."

Prelude 1. *S. Ephr. Ryth.* XIV. : "Meet it is for the highest angels to worship Thy humanity."

—— 2. *S. Isidor Peter, lib. iv. Ep.* 384 : "A chariot ought to be driven with skill, the driver rides badly when carried away by the horses; the body therefore is to be guided by the mind.

—— 3. The Incarnation hallowed our human body for evermore.

—— 4. The Incarnation showed us how our bodies ought to be used. It was in His human body that the Lord taught us the lessons of,

 I. ENDURANCE, by His suffering, privation and death.
 II. CONTENTMENT, He never murmured at His hard earthly lot.
 III. PURITY, by the chastity of His holy life.
 IV. DISCIPLINE, His whole life was one long course of discipline of the flesh.

Epil.—S. Pet. Chrysos. in Rom. xii. 1 : "Is not the soul from heaven, the body from earth." This is governed, but that rules; the body lives, the soul gives it life; the soul remains, the body dies.

Nineteenth Sunday after Trinity.
SERMON 190.
WHAT WE CAN DO FOR GOD.
(Holy Gospel, Ser. 2).

(1.) S. Matt. IX. 2: "They brought to Him a man sick of the palsy."

(2.) II. Cor. VIII. 12: "It is accepted according to that a man hath."

Summa, 22ᵉ, 31, 1, 1ᵐ.: "S. Dionysius says, that love changes all things ordained to a mutual condition; that it converts things inferior, into things superior so that by the superior things the inferior things may be perfected, and that moreover it changes things superior into a provision for the inferior. In like manner it is not of us to do good to God, but we can honour Him by subjecting ourselves to Him."

Prelude 1. *Theodor. on* II. *Cor.* VIII, 12: "The God of all, is wont to measure what is offered to Him according to our power. He looks not at the work but at the intention."

—— 2. The Lord healed the palsied man not for his worth, but for his need.

—— 3. God is ever doing good to us; can we make Him no return?

—— 4. Yes! in a sense. Since He changes our unworthy offerings into such as He can receive.

—— 5. God can consecrate ourselves and all that we have to His blessed and accepted use. God by His grace enables us, all unworthy to,

I. HONOUR HIM in our worship; sacraments and ceremonial.

II. OBEY HIM in thought, word and deed, in our daily life, in body, soul and spirit.

III. PLEASE HIM by poor, feeble and imperfect attempts to fulfil His will

IV. LOVE HIM for Himself alone with a love which is strong, unselfish and pure.

Epil.—Intention and power can consecrate and make acceptable to God our humble efforts. To a God, so willing to accept can we strive to offer too much?

Nineteenth Sunday after Trinity.

SERMON 191.
WHAT JESUS KNOWS.
(Holy Gospel, Ser. 3).

(1). S. Matt. IX. 4 : " Jesus knowing their thoughts," etc.
(2). S. John II. 25 : " He knew what was in man."
Summa, 3^a, 10, 2, c. : " Certain things truly are not only in the divine power, but are also in the power of the creature ; and the mind of Christ in the Word knows all things of this kind ; for He comprehends in the Word the essence of every creature, and consequently also the power and virtue of all things which are in the power of the creature. The mind of Christ knows all the things which God knows in Himself by the knowledge of vision."

Prelude 1. *S. August. in Joan.* II. 25: " The Artificer knew more what was in His work than did the work itself what was in itself."

—— 2. *S. Chrysost. Hom.* 23 *in Matt.*: " The knowledge of human hearts belongs alone to God who formed them. There was no need of Jesus for witnesses of what He had formed."

—— 3. *Theophyl. in Joan.*: " The Searcher of hearts, He knew the thoughts in each heart."

—— 4. Knowing our thoughts He knows us altogether; hence our confidence in Him.

—— 5. His knowledge of us is intuitive as well as experimental. He knows our,

I. STRUGGLES after a higher, better and holier life, and our defeats too.
II. HOPES, some to be realized, others to end in darkness.
III. FEARS, flowing from the want of a deeper love and a firmer faith.
IV. VICTORIES over sin, such as they may be are blessed by Him.

Epil.—We knowing that He knows us, can throw ourselves unreservedly upon His infinite mercy and love.

Nineteenth Sunday after Trinity.

SERMON 192.
CONTRITION.
(*Holy Gospel, Ser.* 4).

(1). S. Matt. IX. 2 : " Thy sins be forgiven thee."
(2). 1. Pet. v. 6 : " Humble yourselves under the mighty hand of God."

Summa, 12^e, 113, 5, 3^m. : " Man ought to detest each single sin which he commits, of which he has the recollection, and from such a preceding consideration there follows in the soul a certain notion of detesting all sins that have been committed, amongst which also are included the sins that have been given over to oblivion, for a man in this state is so disposed that he becomes contrite if they become present to his memory." *Id.* 3^a, 84, 9, c. : " It is impossible that the act of contrition be continuous, as being interrupted by sleep and other needs of the body, but as a habit; it ought to be perpetual. Waiting and tears pertain to the outward acts of contrition or penitence."

Prelude 1. *Pet. Cælest. Opusc.* 8, *c.* 7 : " Four things are demanded for true contrition : bitterness of heart ; detestation of sin ; hope of pardon ; resolution of amendment."

—— 2. " Spiritual confession, that of the soul to God implies contrition, griefs, fears," etc.

—— 3. Contrition, the sign of repentence, signifies a breaking up, pounding, etc.

—— 4. Sin hardens the heart, contrition breaks up and softens its hard,

I. IMPENITENCE sitting itself against, the truth, the providence, and the laws of God.

II. UNBELIEF, refusing to accept alike revelation and faith.

III. COLDNESS by which all holy love and its tenderer emotions are congealed.

IV. UNFRUITFULNESS, causing it to produce fruit " meet," etc. (S. Matt. III. 8.)

Epil.—"A broken and contrite heart, O God, thou wilt not despise."

Twentieth Sunday after Trinity.
SERMON 193.
THE GLORIFICATION OF LIFE.
(*Holy Gospel, Ser.* 1).

(1) S. Matt. XXII. 2: "A certain king made a marriage for his son."

(2) 1. Cor. XV. 22: "As in Adam all die, even so in Christ shall all be made alive."

Summa, 3^a, 8, 2, c. and 3 and 3^m.: "Christ drew His body from other men as is plain from the genealogies of Matt. I. and Luke III.; but though He did this, all men draw the immortal life of the body from Himself, according to I. Cor. XV. 22. The whole humanity of Christ flowed into all men, and as much as to the soul, so much so to the body; to that indeed principally, but to this secondarily. He received from the soul life and the other proprieties agreeable to the human body according to his species. Whence the whole humanity of Christ, that is according to soul, and body, flowed into men."

Prelude 1. S. *Eph. Ryth.* 24: "He clad on a body which was from Adam, and from David, that, in that body which the wicked one had made guilty, He might be brought low."

—— 2. Stones or bricks arranged by the skilful architect show mind, power and beauty. As the painter does with his brush, and the musician by his instrument.

—— 3. The spirit of man flows into stone, brush or instrument.

—— 4. Jesus, by this marriage; for He is the king's son, flows into us.

—— 5. Partakers of His divine nature, power and grace, we can make our lives,

I. Noble, free from anything mean and sordid; a life of aspiration.

II. Heavenly, so that here on earth our better life may begin.

III. Pure, as far as is possible in this imperfect estate; free from mortal sin.

IV. Strong, by the power of His might to bear and forbear. "I can do all things," etc.

Epil.—Not I live but Christ liveth in me. He glorifies alike my life and nature.

Twentieth Sunday after Trinity.

SERMON 194.
THE ACT OF CONSCIENCE.
(*Holy Gospel*, Ser. 2).

(1). S. Matt. XXII. 12 : " He was speechless."
(2). Rom. II. 15 : " Their conscience also bearing witness."
Summa, 1ª, 79, 13, c. and 1 : "Conscience, if properly taken, is not a power, but an act, by which we apply our knowledge to those things which we do, which application, a binding or excusing follows. But the application of knowledge to something is by some act. That conscience is such an act of application, appears from those actions which are attributed to it, since it said to bind, instigates to excuse, to gnaw, or to reprove. All these result from the application of some of our cognisance or knowledge to the things which we do. It is applied in three ways, as we recollect something which we have done or not done to which it witnesses; or it indicates that something should be done or not; or lastly it indicates whether that which is done is bad or good."

Prelude 1. *Pet. de Blois. Ser.* 56 : " Conscience is an inscrutable abyss." *Pet. of Cluny*: "Conscience and God are two witnesses which cannot be deceived."

—— 2. "What is freedom? Periander replied, 'a good conscience.'" The Act of Conscience is,

I. QUICK as the thought, word or deed to which it is applied.
II. INVOLUNTARY, by it the soul often betrays itself. The voice must be heard.
III. TRUE, the testimony that it bears, can be stifled, but not gainsaid.
IV. SEARCHING, it strips off all pretence, and applies itself to motive.

Epil.—Let conscience have fair play; tamper not with its judgments, quench not its pleadings.

Twentieth Sunday after Trinity.

SERMON 195.
THE FREEDOM OF THE WILL.
(Holy Gospel, Ser. 3).

(1) S. Matt. xx. 3 : "They would not come."
(2) 1. Cor. ix. 17 : "If I do this thing willingly I have a reward."

Summa, 12^c, 6, 4, 1 and 1^m.: "It seems that violence can be placed upon the will, since everything can be forced by that which is stronger than itself. Since God is stronger than the human will He is able to move it. Prov. xxi. 1: 'He turneth it,' the king's heart, 'whithersoever he will.' But if this is done by violence, it is no longer an act of the will; nor is the will itself moved thereby, but something which is contrary to the will. As a stone can be thrown by violence so man can be dragged by violence but his will strives against the violence of the action."

Prelude 1. *S. Aug. De Civ. Dei*, v.: "If anything is voluntary it is not of necessity, but everything forced is of necessity; therefore that which is of the will cannot be forced; therefore the will cannot be forced to action."

—— 2. *S. Chrysost. Hom.* v. *in Thess.* ii. *cites S. Matt.* xxviii. 20: "This takes place when we are willing. He will not be altogether with us, if we place ourselves at a distance."

—— 3. Really no such thing as absolute "free will." Will implies a,

I. POWER to act upon thought, word and deed; upon every circumstance of life,

II. JUDGMENT, approving that which it accepts and disapproving and rejecting what displeases it.

III. PUNISHMENT, accepted by the sinning will.

IV. REWARD, as of a will subjecting itself to God.

Epil.—Use the freedom of the will to resist sin; and to gain grace, power and goodness.

Twentieth Sunday after Trinity.
SERMON 196.
INGRATITUDE.
(*Holy Gospel, Ser.* 4).

(1). S. Matt. XXII. 6: "The remnant took his servants and entreated them spitefully."

(2). II. Tim. III. 2: "Men shall be unthankful." *Vulg. ingrati.*

Summa, 22^c, 107, 1, 2^m.: "No one on account of any inability to repay is excused for ingratitude, since the will itself is sufficent to repay the debt. Forgetfulness of a favour through negligence implies ingratitude. Anyone is ungrateful who not only omits to fulfil the debt of gratitude, but also does what is contrary to it."

Prelude 1. *Pet. de Blois. Ep.* 66: "Nothing so provokes the indignation of the Most Highest as ingratitude; it is the provocation of evils; it is the emptying of benefits, and the extermination of merits." *Nicol. Notar.*: "It is a wind raging and burning; it dries up the fount of mercy; it wipes off the dew of piety; stopping up the streams of grace."

—— 2. Worst form of ingratitude, to injure the benefactor's is a deadly sin.

—— 3. This form of ingratitude the king's servant committed.

—— 4. S. Paul places the ungrateful (II. Tim. III. 2) or unthankful, with the unholy.

—— 5. Ingratitude is present in that expression of the will which owns no,

I. REMEMBRANCE of the favour bestowed. It is received, used and forgotten.

II. DESIRE to make some return for it, however little or unworthy.

III. THANKFULNESS for the favour itself; as being an act of undeserved grace.

IV. LOVE to the person who grants the favour for his expression of kind feeling.

Epil.—*S. Leo. Mag. Ser. in Oct. SS. Pet. and Paul*: "Let the expression of the Saviour (S. Luke, XVII. 17) touch your hearts, I beseech you. Consider that though the nine had obtained health of body, yet they were not wanting in impiety of soul."

Twenty-first Sunday after Trinity.

SERMON 197.
ACTUAL SIN.
(*Holy Gospel, Ser.* 1).

(1). S. John iv. 46: "There was a certain nobleman whose son was sick."

(2). 1. S. John v. 17: "All unrighteousness is sin."

Summa, 12ᵉ, 85, 5, 3 and 3ᵐ.: "Actual sin involves more of blame from the reason, than original sin, but it does not change the nature of the body, as to any defect. In it two things are to be considered, the substance of the act, and the reason of the fault; by the former bodily defect can be produced, as when excess of food renders people weak and they die; but by the reason of the fault, it deprives man of the grace which is given to him to amend the acts of the mind, but it does not prohibit bodily defects as did original righteousness." *Id.* 3ᵃ, 8, 5, 1ᵐ.: "Original sin in Adam, which is the sin of nature, was derived from his actual sin, which is personal, since it corrupts the nature in that person."

Prelude 1. S. Cyr. Jer. *on actual sin, Lect.* ii. 1. iv. 20: "It is the sorest ailment of the soul; a shoot of evil taking its increase from thyself; one order only of souls; good and bad act alike from choice; the essence of the soul being alike in all.

—— 2. The natural defects of original sin are common alike to the righteous and the holy. Actual sin is,

I. VOLUNTARY, we have the means to refrain from sin.

II. DEPRIVATIVE, depriving the soul of the means of grace.

III. CORRUPTIVE, like an evil disease corrupting the body.

IV. PERSONAL, it belongs to the sinner and cannot be charged to another's account.

Epil.—Let not sin have dominion over you—tread it under foot.

Twenty-first Sunday after Trinity.
SERMON 198.
GOD'S ORDERING.
(*Holy Gospel, Ser.* 2).

(1). S. John IV. 47: "He was at the point of death."
(2). S. Jam. IV. 15: "If the Lord will we shall do this or that."
Summa, 12^c, 85, 5, 1^m.: "Equality of cause produces by itself equality of effect; so increased or diminished cause by itself produces increased or diminished effect, but not when it is applied to different objects; so when original righteousness was taken away, the nature of the human body was left to itself. It is from the diversity of natural constitution (complexions) that the bodies of some are subject to more; and those of others to fewer defects, though equally being under original sin."

Prelude 1. *S. Chrysost. Hom. xiv. ad Philipp.*: "God orders all things for our profit although we know it not, and this is a proof that it greatly profiteth, that we know it not."

—— 2. *Theodor. in Ezek.* 38: "Nothing is without the divine will which orders for good or permit calamities on account of sins which were formerly committed.

—— 3. The nobleman's son was at the point of death whilst others were in the fulness of life.

—— 4. This 'diversity of natural constitution' is wonderfully ordered, no two lives being alike.

—— 5. From this diversity of constitution arises the diversity of God's ordering, which is,

I. WISE, knowing in His infinite wisdom what is best for each single life.

II. MINUTE, God orders the smallest as well as the greatest things

III. UNCEASING, never for a single moment are we void of God's ordering.

IV. LOVING, yes! if we love Him. All things will work together for our good.

Epil.—Accept with loving hearts whatsoever things are given to us by God—Sorrows as well as joys; sickness as well as health; life as well as death.

Twenty-first Sunday after Trinity.
SERMON 199.
MIRACLES.
(*Holy Gospel, Ser.* 3).

(1). S. John IV. 48 : "Except ye see signs and wonders, ye will not believe."
(2). 1. Cor. I. 22 : "The Jews require a sign."
Summa, 22^c, 178, 1, c. and 3^m : "Supernatural effects are called miracles. A miracle exceeds the faculty of nature; it is a supernatural manifestation, and as such is called a 'sign,' and on account of its excellence a portent or 'wonder' as if showing something." *Id.* 5 : "The working of miracles followed faith, either of the worker (1. Cor. XIII. 2) or of those on account of whom the miracle was wrought (S. Matt. XIII. 58)." *Id.* 3^a, 43, 3, 3 and 3^m.: "The disciples were chiefly attached to the Lord by His miracles (S. Luke IV. 36), but they followed Him when they had not seen him work any miracle. 'His disciples believed on Him' (S. John II. 11), not as if for the first time, but because henceforth they believed more diligently and perfectly." *Id.* 3^a, 43, 4, o.: "The miracles of Christ proved sufficiently that He was God."

Prelude 1. When the reign of grace was fully developed, miracles generally ceased.

―― 2. The higher spiritual miracles are ever continued, *i.e.* the new birth at the font; the real Presence in the Sacrament of the altar, etc.

―― 3. Our very selves are standing miracles of God's grace and mercy. These spiritual miracles are,

I. REAL in their nature, as real as if they could be tested by the sense.
II. DIVINE in origin, miraculous effects of a miraculous love and power.
III. ACTIVE in operation, as in the conversion of a sinner.
IV. BLESSED in effect, all tending to God's glory and to man's salvation.

Epil.—Recognize God's miracles in creation, providence and grace, for "Blessed are they that have not seen and yet have believed."

Twenty-first Sunday after Trinity.

SERMON 200.
FAITH IN THE INCARNATION.
(*Holy Gospel, Ser.* 4).

(1). S. John IV. 53: "Himself believed and his whole house."
(2). Acts XVI. 31: "Believe on the Lord Jesus Christ and thou shalt be saved."

Summa, 22ᶜ, 2, 7, c.: "The mystery of the Incarnation and passion of Christ is the way for man to come to blessedness (Acts IV. 12). Therefore is the mystery of the Incarnation of Christ in some way to be believed in for all time; and by all men; and in different ways according to the diversity of times and persons. Before the state of sin, man had an explicit faith in the Incarnation of Christ; that it was ordained for the consummation of glory; but not for liberation from sin by the Passion and the Resurrection. Man's prescience of this faith is expressed in Gen. II. 24; as explained by the Apostle, Eph. V. 32."

Prelude 1. *S. Ephrem. Rythm.* 80: "Faith is a second soul; as the body standeth by the soul, so the life of the soul hangeth on faith; and if it deny it, it becometh a corpse."

—— 2. To believe in or on Jesus Christ implies a belief in His Sonship—in His Incarnation, Passion, Resurrection; in His work and Church as part of Himself.

—— 3. Faith in the Incarnation implies faith in the sacraments, in redemption, etc., which faith must be,

I. LIVING, bringing forth the fruits of holiness; using diligently all the means of grace appointed.

II. FIRM, not to be moved or shaken by every wind of false doctrine.

III. FULL and complete, embracing every portion of the work of Jesus.

IV. OPEN, held before all the world, in evil as well as in good report.

Epil.—"Lord increase our faith" (S. Luke XVII. 5); that its end may bring everlasting life.

Twenty-second Sunday after Trinity.
SERMON 201.
THE LIABILITY OF ETERNAL DEATH.
(Holy Gospel, Ser. 1).

(1.) S. Matt. XVIII. 24: "One was brought unto him which owed him ten thousand talents."

(2). Rom. III. 8: "Whose damnation is just."

Summa, 12^c, 88, 1, c.: "Sin is a certain infirmity of the mind which is called mortal after the similitude of a disease which is mortal when it produces an irreparable defect [death]. Mortal sin engenders the liability of eternal condemnation."

Prelude 1. *Remig.*: "Those called 'tormentors' in the Gospel are the demons who are ever prepared to receive the souls of the lost, and who torture them in the punishment of eternal damnation."

—— 2. "It remains," says S. Chrysost. "that he who cannot be made better by benefits, should be tortured by punishment."

—— 3. *Christ. Druth.*: "We are debtors to Him for ten thousand talents, *i.e.* the heavier sins which each one feels and acknowledges that he has committed."

—— 4. The servant could never pay the ten thousand talents, but was liable for them.

—— 5. These talents represent mortal sin, which renders the soul liable to eternal death.

—— 6. All unrepented sin is more or less a sword of Damocles, hanging over the sinner's head. This liability of eternal condemnation or death is,

I. UNCERTAIN in its issue as to the time when its punishment will be exacted.

II. CONTINUOUS, never leaves the soul; is ever resting upon the unpenitent sinner.

III. HEAVY to bear, carrying with it a certain sense of fear and dread.

IV. DANGEROUS, for by it the soul is liable at any time to be plunged into hell.

Epil.—Seek for pardon and remission, by means of repentance, through the Precious Blood which cleanseth us from all sin.

Twenty-second Sunday after Trinity.
SERMON 202.
THE COMPASSION OF GOD.
(Holy Gospel, Ser. 2).

(1). S. Matt. XVIII. 27 : "The Lord of that servant was moved with compassion."

(2). S. James v. 11: "The Lord is very pitiful and of tender mercy."

Summa, 1ª, 21, 4, 0: "It is of justice to repay the debt; it is of compassion to lighten the misery. Justice and compassion are found in every work of God. God cannot do anything which does not agree with His wisdom and His goodness; but the work of divine justice ever presupposes the work of compassion. That which suffices to preserve the order of justice is less than that which the divine goodness confers, which excels all the proportion of the creature." In a sense, God swallows up justice in compassion and mercy.

Prelude 1. *S. Greg. Nyssen. T.* 1. *p.* 802: "Compassion is the voluntary sadness which arises from the ills of others." *Id. p.* 804: "Compassion is the father of benevolence, the pledge of love, the bond of all friendly affection." In God, compassion becomes pity.

—— 2. God makes no compromise with sin; the unrepentant sinner finds only justice.

—— 3. The object of God's compassion must have some claim to it; by sorrow or repentance. To obtain God's infinite compassion and mercy we must throw ourselves upon it,

I. REPENTANTLY, resolving by divine grace to amend the past life.

II. HUMBLY, as being wholly unworthy, yet hoping for mercy in spite of all.

III. SORROWFULLY, with true contrition for the unholy and unworthy past.

IV. WHOLLY, as having, and being, nothing in ourselves; as casting self upon God.

Epil.—All that man can do is to repent, and through the sacrament of penitence, seek for mercy, the outcome of God's compassion. 'Have patience with me' Lord.

Twenty-second Sunday after Trinity.

SERMON 203.
THE BURDEN OF SIN.
(Holy Gospel, Ser. 3).

(1). S. Matt. XVIII. 34: "His Lord delivered him to the tormentors."

(2). Heb. VI. 6: "They crucify to themselves the Son of God afresh."

Summa, 3^a, 88, 2, 2^m.: " Sins which have been forgiven by penitence, by subsequent sin are said to return on account of their ingratitude, since the assured guilt of them is virtually contained in the subsequent fault. *Rabanus; De Pœnit diff.* c. 4 ; says that not only will the sin which a man commits after baptism will be reckoned up against him for punishment, but also the original sin which was remitted to him in baptism."

Prelude 1. *Haymo Bp. in loco*: "'Until,' it, the sin, will ever return ; the sinner will receive punishment for all former sins, both original and actual." *Alcuin:* " Of what avail a man to have healed over his wound if he taints the scar and opens the wound anew?"

—— 2. To carry any weight, even a light one, for a long distance is a burden.

—— 3. The burdens of the mind, sin; sorrow, etc., are harder to bear than weight is to the body.

—— 4. The sinner because he adds sin to sin, adds weight to weight till he is pressed down to hell. The burden of sin,

I. OPPRESSES, its weight being felt, the elasticity of the soul is destroyed.

II. HARDENS, continual pressure hardens the soul to all impressions for good.

III. NUMBS it, so that it cannot rise and shake off the lethargy of sin.

IV. SADDENS, as a constant pain eating out all joy and hope in life.

Epil.—Cast thy burden of sin upon the Lord and He will remove it and sustain thee. Ps. lxxxix. 8 : " O remember not against us former iniquities."

Twenty-second Sunday after Trinity.

SERMON 204.
THE SINNER SUFFERS ALONE.
(Holy Gospel, Ser. 4).

(1). S. Matt. xviii. 31: "His fellow servants were very sorry."
(2). 1. Cor. xiii. 6: "Rejoiceth not in iniquity."

Summa, 1ª, 113, 7, c: "The angels do not grieve over the sins, nor over the punishments of men. They are perfectly blessed, since with them there is neither death nor grief (Rev. xxi. 4). Nothing happens in the world which is contrary to the will of the angels and other blessed spirits, since their will wholly cleaves wholly to the order of divine justice which governs the world. Even in the sin of men, there remains one cause of joy to the angels, the fulfilment of the order of divine providence."

Prelude 1. *Theophy. in loco:* "These 'fellow servants' are the angels, the haters of evil, the lovers of the good; who do not say these things as to an ignorant Lord, but that you may learn how angry they are with the unmerciful and inhuman."

—— 2. The angels are sorry both for sinners and for sin; yet their own real happiness is not affected thereby; for angels and blessed spirits cannot grieve.

—— 3. We pity a fallen friend, go on our way, and straightway forget him.

—— 4. Sin separates man from God, the angels, and the blessed spirits. The sinner bears his own,

I. CONSCIENCE, as God's deputy ever accusing and humbling him.
II. CONSEQUENCES, of sin ever leading to remorse, disgrace and ruin.
III. PUNISHMENTS, in their deeper and acuter forms, unshared in by others.
IV. Loss, great and certain for this world; infinite and eternal for the life to come.

Epil.—Give no ground for others to sorrow over sin wrought by you.

Twenty-third Sunday after Trinity.

SERMON 205.
TRUTH IN LIFE.
(Holy Gospel, Ser. 1).

(1). S. Matt. xxii. 16: "Master we know that Thou art true, and teachest," etc.

(2). ii. Cor. iv. 2: "By manifestation of the truth commending ourselves."

Summa, 22^c, 109, 2, c. and 3^m.: "Truth is a certain special virtue by which man orders its outward things, words, or deeds or signs in their due order, and man is perfected to do this by the virtue of truth. Truth in life, is truth according as something is true; it is not truth, because anyone may say that it is true. Truth in life is that by which anyone lives rightly, of which Isaiah speaks (xxxviii. 3) 'Remember O Lord,' etc., calling it that true life which reaches its rule and measure, that is to say, the divine law, by conformity to which it gains its rectitude."

Prelude 1. *B. Bruno*: "Many speak the truth with their lips, but not in the heart. Christ had no guile, because what He spake by the mouth He fulfilled in work or life."

—— 2. Truth in life is truth in action, in thought, word and deed.

—— 3. The Herodians expressed unwittingly the truth and harmony of the Lord's life.

—— 4. Truth in life, the concord of thought, word and deed makes the harmony of life.

—— 5. The truth in life, as seen in the Lord for our imitation, was,

I. SINGLE, lived with a single eye to God's glory and man's salvation.

II. SIMPLE, devoid of outward or false show; sublime because simple.

III. SINCERE, in purpose, expression and action; real in all things.

IV. SANCTIFIED, by the very holiness of its truth; as well as of its end.

Epil.—Strive in life to be true to God, to His Church, to others, to your own souls.

Twenty-third Sunday after Trinity.
SERMON 206.
HYPOCRISY.
(*Holy Gospel*, Ser. 2).

(1). S. Matt. XXII. 18 : "Why tempt ye me, ye hypocrites?"
(2). 1. S. Pet. II. 1 : "Laying aside all hypocrisies desire the sincere milk of the word."

Summa, 22ᶜ, 111, 2 and 1ᵐ : "Hypocrisy since it a feigning by which anyone feigns that he has a character which he has not, by itself opposes the truth directly, for all simulation is a kind of lie. Yet after all, the truth reveals him such as he is in life and conversation. The hypocrite feigns to have some virtue to end, not of really wishing to possess it but only to appear to have it, so that he does not oppose the virtue itself but only the truth, inasmuch as he desires to deceive men concerning that virtue. Gain or glory is the remote end of the hypocrite as also of the lie."

Prelude 1. *Theophyl. in Matt.* : "Hypocrites are those who indeed are one thing, and who appear, in truth, to be another." *S. Cyril. Alex. de Adorat. l. vii.*: "Hypocrites have a fleeting, easy and feigned benevolence; they cover the form of the wolf in the skin of the sheep."

—— 2. Hypocrites acknowledge the value of truth in itself.

—— 3. Under the power of sin, the hypocrite wishes to appear holy.

—— 4. All shams are hateful alike to God, and to all true men. The hypocrite is,

I. Craven, cowardly, he is ashamed to appear in his true colours.

II. Vain, *S. Greg. Mag. Mor.* 31 : "Hypocrisy is born of vain-glory."

III. Feeble, wanting in all inward strength, grace and principle.

IV. Worthless, to himself, his "hope shall perish;" and a living lie to others.

Epil.—Let sincerity and truth be the guiding principle of life, in thought, word and deed. The Lord denounced the hypocrites. "Woe unto you hypocrites."

Twenty-third Sunday after Trinity.
SERMON 207.
RELIGION.
(*Holy Gospel*, Ser. 3).

(1). S. Matt. XXII. 21 : "Render unto God the things that are God's."

(2). 1. Tim. I. 17 : "To the only wise God be honour and glory."

Summa, 22^e, 81, 7, c : "We show reverence and honour to God, not on account of Himself, for of Himself, He is full of glory, to which no created being can add anything; but on account of ourselves, since by this means our mind becomes subjected to Him ; and in this subjugation our own perfection consists. Not only by inward acts is the power of religion itself perfected, but also by outward acts, not indeed principally, but as if in a secondary way and as of that which is ordained for what is inward. The end of religion, is to show honour and reverence to God. The human mind needs that it should be joined to God by the leading of outward things, as 'the invisible things of God are understood by the things that are made' (Rom. i. 20)."

Prelude 1. S. *Cyril. Jeru. Lect. xvi.* 4 : "The faith is indivisible ; religious worship is undistracted."

—— 2. 'Render,' give back; since being, and the power to worship come from God.

—— 3. Religion, binding back or fast to God, and doing this is blessed ; binding us to God in,

I. THOUGHT, so that God, His being and worship, is in all our thoughts.

II. SERVICE, He becomes the Lord our God, and Him only will we serve.

III. HONOUR, so that we are constrained to honour Him in word or deed.

IV. LOVE, as being the sweetest and dearest as well as the highest object of veneration.

Epil.—May love, faith, worship, go hand in hand ; our true religion being manifested, in life and in reverend and ceremonial worship.

Twenty-third Sunday after Trinity.

SERMON 208.
OBEDIENCE TO RULERS.
(*Holy Gospel, Ser.* 4).

(1). S. Matt. XXII. 21 : "Render unto Cæsar the things which are Cæsar's."

(2). Heb. XIII. 17 : "Obey them that have the rule over you."

Summa, 22^e, 104, 6, c. : "The faith of Christ is the beginning and cause of justice [or righteousness] (Rom. III. 22); therefore the order of justice is not taken away by Him, but rather comfirmed; and it demands that inferiors should be subject to superiors; otherwise the condition of human affairs could not be maintained." *Id.* 1^m. : "This servitude or subjection pertains to the body, not to the soul, which is free, by the grace of Christ; in this state of life we are freed from the defects of the mind, but not those of the body (Rom. VII. 23-24). They, therefore, who are the sons of God by grace, are freed from the spiritual servitude of sin, but not from the servitude of the body, by which we are held bound to our masters in temporal things (I. Tim. VI. 1)."

Prelude 1. *S. John Clim. Scala. Parad.* 4 : "Obedience is the perfect abdication of the soul, shown by the offices of the body." This is not required in respect of our rulers.

—— 2. Obedience to rulers implies outward submission only; implying,

I. DEPENDENCE on them, as being necessary for safety and protection.

II. SUBMISSION to them, by subjection of the will to their commands.

III. SERVICE for them, either by means or by person; for mutual profit.

IV. HONOUR as to the office if not to the holder of it; to whom "honour is due."

Epil.—Fear God and honour the king. I. Pet. II. 13-14: "Submit yourselves," etc.

Twenty-fourth Sunday after Trinity.
SERMON 209.
KNOWLEDGE THE PARENT OF DESIRE.
(Holy Gospel, Ser. 1).

(1). S. Matt. ix. 18: "Come and lay Thy hand upon her."
(2). Philipp. i. 9: "I pray, that your love may abound yet more and more in knowledge."

Summa, 1^a, 2, 1, 1^m.: "To know that there is a God is naturally implanted in man, for God is the blessing of man, who naturally desires blessedness and that which is naturally desired by man, is naturally known by him."

Prelude 1. *Rupert de Trin.* 3: "The woman saw, that is she considered, she regarded it diligently, she curiously scanned it, and constituted herself to be the judge of those things which she had heard."

—— 2. The knowledge of Eve led her to an unholy longing.

—— 3. But the knowledge of what is true, good and beautiful leads to the desire of them.

—— 4. Had not Eve known of the apple she would not have desired it.

—— 5. There are thousands of things which we neither know of nor desire.

—— 6. Jairus knew of the power of the Lord, therefore he desired his presence.

—— 7. The more we know of God, the more we must desire the riches of His grace.

—— 8. Knowledge and desire go hand in hand; the one the parent of the other.

—— 9. It is because our knowledge is so limited that our desires are so,

I. NARROW and small in their range and extent.
II. FEEBLE and paltry, with nothing great and exalted in them.
III. SENSUAL, as bound up for the most part in the body.
IV. EARTHLY, centred in and revolving round this life and world.

Epil.—Seek to gain such a knowledge of things, the highest and the best as make you long to take hold of them for your own.

Twenty-fourth Sunday after Trinity.

SERMON 210.
THE FOURFOLD SALVATION.
(Holy Gospel, Ser. 2).

(1.) S. Matt. IX. 25: "He took her by the hand and the maid arose."
(2.) I. Thess. V. 9: "God hath appointed us to obtain salvation by our Lord Jesus Christ."

Summa, 3^a, 46, 3, c. and 2^m: "That Christ might show Himself to be the God, Man and Saviour, it behoved Him to work miracles on man, and therefore it was fitting that He specially should miraculously by healing man show Himself to be the universal and spiritual *Saviour* of men. As Christ came to heal the world not only by His divine power, but by the mystery of the Incarnation itself, He often in the healing of the infirm not only used His divine power in curing by means of a command, but also by applying something; as hand, spital, etc.; belonging to His humanity." *Id.* 61, 3: "After sin none could be sanctified save by Christ." *Id.* 68, 1, c.: "It is manifest that none can obtain salvation, save by Christ (Rom. v. 19)."

Prelude 1. S. Cyril. *Jerusal.* IV. 9: "If the Incarnation was a phantom our salvation was a phantom." XIII. 37: "Abhor those who say that Christ was crucified according to appearance only, for if so, and if salvation is thus from the cross, then is salvation in appearance only."

—— 2. S. J. Clim. i. ad Cor. c. 7: "May we behold with intent eyes the Blood of Christ and consider how precious it is, which was poured out for our salvation and brought us pardon. The salvation of Jesus is,

I. UNIVERSAL, for all humanity was summed up and represented in His human body.

II. SPIRITUAL, it saves men's souls from the power, guilt and punishment of sin.

III. BODILY, Jesus saved men's bodies when on earth; and he will save and restore them at the resurrection.

IV. SINGLE and alone, it stands as the one work in time, for all the past and the infinite future.

Epil.—S. T. Aq. *in Thess. v.* 9: "He shows how God works in us; by preordination; by the grace of Christ; to obtain salvation by the Lord Jesus Christ." By the diligent use of the means of grace, make this salvation your own.

Twenty-fourth Sunday after Trinity.
SERMON 211.
DEATH THE FRUIT OF REBELLION.
(Holy Gospel, Ser. 3).

(1). S. Matt. ix. 18 : " My daughter is even now dead."
(2). Rom. v. 12 : "' By one man sin entered into the world and death by sin."

Summa, 22ᵛ, 164, 1, c. : " So long as the mind of man was subject to God, the powers of the soul were subject to the reason ; the body then too was subject to the soul. Life and safety to the body followed this subjection. As the rebellion of the carnal appetite against the spirit, is that punishment for the sin committed by our first parents, so is it also the cause of the punishment of death." *Id.* 5ᵐ.: " Death has a certain ground of good since it is a just punishment, and so it is from God, Who is the author of death only, inasmuch as it is penal." *Id.* 12ᶜ, 85, 5, o. : " Death and every bodily defect and the rebellion of the flesh against the spirit, are punishments for the sins of our first parents following upon the taking away of original righteousness."

Prelude 1. The sin which brought in death, was degradation as well as disobedience.

—— 2. There are three distinct rebellions in sin ; of the mind against God ; of the soul against the mind ; and of the body against the soul. The punishment of death is,

I. Just, this three-fold rebellion could only be subdued by death.
II. Wise, for God willed that out of death a better and eternal life should spring.
III. Merciful, an eternity of bodily agony, a punishment of devils only, not of God.
IV. Final, as the last, the extremest punishment of all. Non being is a limit.

Epil.—Still, a life arises from death. *S. Cyril. Jeru.* xiii. 33.: " God had appointed the sinner to die. Christ took our sins (1. Pet. ii. 24); The transgression of sinners was not so great as the righteousness of Him Who died for them."

Twenty-fourth Sunday after Trinity.

SERMON 212.
THE LIGHT OF FAITH.
(*Holy Gospel, Ser.* 4).

(1). S. Matt. IX. 22 : " Thy faith hath made thee whole."
(2). II. Cor. v. 7 : " We walk by faith, not by sight."
Summa, 22^e, 1, 5, 1^m.: " Infidels are ignorant of the things which are of faith, since they neither see nor know these things in themselves, so that they are not able to perceive that they are worthy of belief, the faithful have knowledge of these things not by demonstration but inasmuch as they see by the light of faith that they are to be believed."

Prelude 1. *Theod. in loco.* : " Now we do not look (*blepomen*) on the things themselves that are expected but we see them (*horōmen*) by means of faith alone."

—— 2. Faith is the faculty of seeing by the mind, that which is not beheld by the bodily eye."

—— 3. *S. Chromas. Aquil. Conc.* 1 : " Faith is compared to a light, which if it be in us pure and bright the whole body will be full of light."

—— 4. *Drogo. Abb. Ser.* 1. : " A cheerful eye-ball clearly sees ; faith is the eye-ball of your eye."

—— 5. A time when S. Paul had not this light (II. Tim. I. 13), " ignorantly in unbelief."

—— 6. Holiness is the oil by which the light of faith is maintained. The light of faith is

I. CLEAR and even, save when over-clouded by some sin or doubt.

II. FAR-REACHING, lighting the path to heaven ; leaving reason far behind it.

III. GUIDING, so that the faithful walk by faith and not by sight.

IV. BRIGHT, strong enough to light up the valley of the shadow of death.

Epil.—Walk we then by the inward spiritual light of faith, by the faculty of mental vision, and not by the sight of the bodily eye and the senses of earth.

Twenty-fifth Sunday after Trinity.
SERMON 213.
INCREASE.
(*Holy Gospel, Ser.* 1).

(1). S. John vi. 13: "They filled twelve baskets with the fragments."

(2). Coloss. i. 10: "Increasing in the knowledge of God."

Summa, 1ª, 92, 3, 1 and 1ᵐ: "The greater cannot be formed from the less except by addition, and in no way can the multiplication of material be understood without addition. In this way, S. Augustine says, Christ from five loaves satisfied five thousand men, as from a few grains producing a multitude of crops. It is said that by five loaves He fed the crowds because addition was made to the pre-existing material of the loaves."

Prelude 1. S. T. Aq. on Coloss. i. 10: "The increase of knowledge follows to fructification; increasing, for anyone who desires to fulfil that which is commanded is disposed to knowledge (Ps. cxix. 100).

—— 2. Increase is a sign of growth; and growth is a sign of life.

—— 3. That which the Lord did with the loaves and fishes He can do with our hearts.

—— 4. He takes the germs of holiness within us, and multiplies our graces.

—— 5. The germs or material is there; He gives to it a new and quickened life.

—— 6. Progress is a law of God's kingdom; and progress involves increase. He increases, or multiplies in us, our,

I. THOUGHTS, earnest and sincere for the present and the future; leading us to ponder on our ways.

II. DESIRES and yearnings after a purer and higher life; making us dissatisfied with the present.

III. GRACES, be they few or many of the Holy Spirit; "perfecting holiness in the fear of God."

IV. KNOWLEDGE of divine things; feeding the soul with the food of immortality.

Epil.—Your prayer: Lord increase our faith, our aspiration, our endeavours.

Twenty-fifth Sunday after Trinity.

SERMON 214.
PRAYER A CONSECRATION.
(*Holy Gospel, Ser.* 2).

(1). S. John VI. 11 : "When he had given thanks."

(2). 1. Tim. IV. 5 : "Sanctified by prayer."

Summa, 3ª, 43, 2, 2ᵐ : "We must believe that Christ since He was from the Father was equal to Him. That He might exhibit both these truths He wrought miracles; now with power, and then with praying. Christ looked to heaven in the lesser miracles, but in the greater miracles He worked alone. At the raising of Lazarus, He raised His eyes on high not on account of any need of petition but for an example, because of the people which stand by (S. John XI. 42).

Prelude 1. *S. Cyril. Jeru.* XXIII. 7 : "We call upon the merciful God to send forth His Holy Spirit upon the gifts; that He may make the bread the Body of Christ," etc., "for whatsoever the Holy Ghost has touched is sanctified and changed."

—— 2. The Lord consecrated His miracles by outward or inward prayer.

—— 3. The Church by prayer consecrates the baptismal water; the Holy Eucharist; her clergy; her buildings and sacred vessels and vestments, etc.

—— 4. Prayer is a consecration as well as an intercession. It consecrates,

I. OURSELVES, body, soul, and spirit to God's service; that all may tend to His glory.

II. EACH DAY as the fresh beginning of life; a time of new struggles, hopes, etc.

III. OUR WORK that it may be blessed, being begun, continued and ended in God.

IV. OUR LIVES, that their events may prosper for eternity and time.

Epil.—Be ye sanctified, consecrated by frequent, daily, earnest prayer.

Twenty-fifth Sunday after Trinity.
SERMON 215.
THE HOLY EUCHARIST SPIRITUAL FOOD.
(Holy Gospel, Ser. 3).

(1). S. John VI. 11 : " He distributed."
(2). Rev. II. 17 : " To him that overcometh will I give to eat of the hidden manna."

Summa, 3ª, 73, 1, c. : "The sacraments were ordained to carry on the spiritual life in man, which is conformable to the bodily life, since material things bear a similitude to spiritual things. The bodily life demands nourishment for its preservation in life; so it is necessary for the spiritual life that there should be the sacrament of the Eucharist which is spiritual nourishment."

Prelude 1. *S. Greg. Mag.* : " Figuratively the manna is the bread of life which came down from heaven for our sakes."

—— 2. *S. Ephrem. Ryth. iii.* : " The bread that He break exceeded the world's needs, the more it was divided, the more it multiplied exceedingly. The wheat that was sown, on the third day came up and filled the garner of life."

—— 3. *S. Cyril. Jeru. xxii.* 5 : " In the New Testament there is the bread of heaven, and the cup of salvation sanctifying soul and body."

—— 4. Terrible contrast between life and death; yet the fleeting, sorrowful life of the body is of high value.

—— 5. Far higher is the value of the spiritual life. Eucharistic, spiritual food gives to the soul,

I. STRENGTH to resist sin; to fight against doubt; to endure to the end.
II. JOY from the fulness of its power of satisfying, beyond the honey tasted by Jonathan.
III. GROWTH to produce those fruits unto righteousness the end of which is eternal life.
IV. LIFE, lifting it on high, joining it to the heavenly life of saints and angels.

Epil.—Use well; use often, the food-supplying and life-giving sacraments of the altar.

Twenty-fifth Sunday after Trinity.
SERMON 216.
THE HOLY EUCHARIST, JESUS WHOLLY.
(Holy Gospel, Ser. 4).

(1). S. John VI. 12 : "They were filled."
(2). I. Cor. X. 16 : "The bread which we break, is it not the communion of the body of Christ?"

Summa, 3ᵃ, 73, 1, 3ᵐ : "There is this difference between the Eucharist and the other sacraments having a sensible material; namely that the Eucharist contains something absolutely sacred; that is to say, the Body itself of Christ, and therefore it is perfected by the consecration itself of the material; whilst the other sacraments are perfected by the application of the material to the man about to be sanctified. From this also another difference follows : for in the sacrament of the Eucharist that which is the 'res,' and 'the sacrament,' is in the material itself."

Prelude 1. S. Aug. Confess. xii. 10, 2 : "Thou art my God, as if I heard thy voice from on high; 'I am the meat of those that are grown up; grow thou up, and thou shalt feed upon me.'"

—— 2. S. Ignat. ad Philadelp. 4 : "Give diligence to use one Eucharist for one is the flesh of our Lord Jesus Christ and one cup in the union of His blood."

—— 3. The Resurrection body was real yet spiritualized : He was still the Son the Man.

—— 4. Jesus is fully and wholly in the sacrament of His sweet and tender love.

—— 5. No mutilated or half Jesus is here; but all of Him. He is present in His,

I. GLORIFIED HUMANITY; whilst on earth He could be in two places at once (S. John III. 13).

II. GODHEAD, He is everywhere present, specially in the sacrament of His Love.

III. CHURCH, the Body of Him which filleth all in all. (S. Matt. XVIII. 20). How could He be absent in the highest act of worship?

IV. POWER AND LOVE to pardon and preserve and then to join Himself to the souls of the faithful.

Epil.—He filleth the soul with the bread of heaven; He cures its dying life by the food of life and the medicine of immortality.

JOHN HODGES' LIST OF
New Books & Books in the Press.

By the Rev. Oswald J. Reichel, M.A., B.C.L., &c.

SOLEMN MASS AT ROME IN THE NINTH Century. Second Edition, with corrections and additions, and a sketch plan of a Basilica. Demy 8vo. *Nearly ready.*

THE ORIGIN OF ENGLISH LITURGICAL VESTments, prescribed for use in the Thirteenth Century. With Illustrations. A paper read before the Exeter Diocesan Society. 8vo. *In the Press.*

A COMPLETE MANUAL OF CANON LAW. Edited by Oswald J. Reichel, M.A., B.C.L., F.S.A., &c., sometime Vice-principal of Cuddesdon College. Vol. I. The Sacraments. Demy 8vo. *Nearly ready.* Vol. II. Liturgical Discipline. *Preparing.*

THE PATHWAY OF HEALTH AND HAPPINESS. in Six Letters to young men of all classes by a Clergyman of the Church of England. Royal 32mo, limp cloth, price 1s. *Nearly ready.*

BIBLE STORIES FOR CHILDREN AND Schools. Second thousand. Square 16mo, cloth. *In the Press.*

CHRISTIANITY VERSUS INFIDELITY. Notes on Ingersoll, by the Rev. L. A. Lambert, of Waterlow, N.Y. A new edition reprinted from the seventieth thousand American edition. *In the Press.*

JOHN HODGES, Publisher, Bedford Street, Strand, London.

John Hodges' List of New Books.

THE REFORMATION IN ENGLAND: A series of Essays, by the late Dr. MAITLAND, Keeper of the MSS. at Lambeth, Author of the "Dark Ages," etc.

This Vol. is being published at the special request of many readers of the "Dark Ages," to which work it is an admirable Supplement. *Preparing.*

EVANS (A. B.)—REFLECTIONS DELIVERED AT the Mid-Day Celebration of Holy Communion in the Church of S. Mary-le-Strand. By A. B. Evans, D.D., Rector. Crown 8vo. *Third Edition in the Press.*

"Let a man before preparing his own sermon, sit down and read through carefully and slowly one of these 'Reflections,' and he will certainly derive a lesson in method, and instruction how to reflect, from a true master of the science, which he could not easily learn elsewhere."—*Ecclesiastical Gazette.*

A HISTORY OF THE SOMERSET CARTHU-sians. By MARGARET E. THOMPSON.

This Vol. has 16 page Illustrations of Hinton Charter-House, Witham Friary, etc., by the author's sister Miss L. B. THOMPSON, and will prove an interesting work to antiquarians, especially of Somersetshire and the West of England generally. *In the Press.*

COGITATIONES CONCIONALES. Being 216 short Sermon Reflections on the Gospels for the Church's Year, founded upon Selected Readings from the "Summa Theologica" of S. THOMAS AQUINAS. By JOHN M. ASHLEY, B.C.L., Rector of Fewston, author of "The Promptuary for Preachers," &c. *Nearly ready.*

SIMPSON'S LIFE OF EDMUND CAMPION. This valuable Book having been out of print many years, has become very scarce, second hand copies when met with realising fancy prices, it is now reprinted from a corrected copy, made by the learned Author for a new edition before his death. *In the Press.*

Bedford Street, Strand, London.

LIST OF BOOKS
PUBLISHED AND SOLD BY JOHN HODGES.

Always the Same; a Love Story. By M. E. S. Crown 8vo. 2s. 6d.

Antrobus.—History of the Popes from the Close of the Middle Ages. Drawn from the Secret Archives of the Vatican and other Original Sources. By Dr. LOUIS PASTOR, Professor of History in the University of Innsbruck. Translated from the German. Edited by FREDERICK ANTROBUS, of the Oratory, with a Preface by His Eminence, Cardinal MANNING. Vols. I., II., III., and IV. Demy 8vo. 12s. each.

Avrillon.—A Guide to Advent, being a Guide to the Holy Observance of the Season of Advent; containing A Practice, A Meditation, Affections, Sentences from Holy Scripture and the Holy Fathers, and a point of the Incarnation. From the French of AVRILLON. Sewed, 6d.; Cloth 1s.

A Guide from Lent.—In the press.

Autobiography of an Alms-Bag, The; or, Sketches of Church and Social Life in a Watering-Place. By the Author of "John Brown, the Cordwainer," "Recreations of the People," etc. *Second Edition.* Crown 8vo. 2s. 6d.

"A clever book. Sketchy, anecdotic, chatty, humorous and suggestive. We read of many topics, all full of interest."—*Literary World.*

"The author is a kind of ecclesiastical Dickens and Thackeray combined, and the work has all the trace of Dr. Holmes' 'Autocrat.'"—*Oldham Chronicle.*

"Overflows with good stories effectively told, and most of them brought into good and useful purpose."—*Guardian.*

A Lapide.—The Great Commentary upon the Gospels
of Cornelius à Lapide. Translated and Edited by Rev. T. W. MOSSMAN, D.D., (B.A., Oxon.), assisted by various Scholars. 6 Vols. Demy 8vo. 12s. each.
    SS. MATTHEW AND MARK'S GOSPELS. 3 Vols. *Fourth Edition.*
    ST. JOHN'S GOSPEL AND THREE EPISTLES. 2 Vols. *Third Edition.*
    ST. LUKE'S GOSPEL. 1 Vol. *Third Edition.*

The Acts of the Apostles. *In the Press.—The whole of the New Testament is in hand, and will be issued at an early date.*

A Chronicle of the English Benedictine Monks, from
Renewing of their Congregation in the days of Queen Mary to the Death of James II.; being the Chronological Notes of Dom. Bennett Weldon, O.S.B., a Monk of Paris. Edited from a Manuscript in the Library of St. Gregory's Priory, Downside, by a Monk of the same Congregation. Demy 4to. Handsomely printed. Price 12s. 6d.

Benedictine Calendar, The. From the Latin by Dom
EGIDIOUS RANBECK, O.S.B., edited by JOHN A. MORRALL, O.S.B., Sub-Prior of Downside.
This remarkable work was first published in 1677, at the cost of the great Bavarian Monastery in Augsburg.
The Life of a Benedictine Saint is given for every day in the year. The great merit of the work, however, consists in the beautiful engravings which illustrate the lives.
In the new Edition these Engravings have been most effectively reproduced by the Meisenbach Process, and the accompanying Lives, which will be adaptations rather than translations of the originals.
The work will be issued in Twelve Parts, beautifully printed by the Messrs. Dalziel on fine plate paper.
    ** Part I., containing the Month of January, with Thirty-One illustrations, price 3s. 6d., post free. *Ready.*
Part II., February. *In the Press.*

Bernard, St. The Works of St. Bernard, Abbot of
Clairvaux. Translated into English from the Edition of DOM JOANNES MABILLON, of the Benedictine Congregation of St. Maur (Paris, 1690), and Edited by SAMUEL J.

EALES, D.C.L., Vicar of Stalisfield. Vols. I. and II., containing the Letters of St. Bernard. Demy 8vo. 12s. each. *Vol. III. in the Press.*

Beardsley, E. E.—The Life of the Right Rev. Samuel Seabury, D.D., First Bishop of Connecticut and of the American Church. By E. BEARDSLEY, D.D., President of the General Convention of the American Church. Crown 8vo, 5s.

"He has told in a calm and simple style, with much dignity and restraint of panegyric, the story of a great and good man whose deeds live after him to remote regenerations."—*The Literary World.*

"He was a man who was in advance of his age, to whom the Church must always look up with admiration and reverent thankfulness, and be grateful also to Dr. Beardsley for this tribute to his memory."—*The Guardian.*

Benedict, St.—A Sketch of the Life and Mission of St. Benedict. With an Appendix, containing a complete List of the Benedictine Churches and Monasteries in England, with the date of their foundation. By a Monk of St. Gregory's Priory, Downside. Third Thousand. 1s.

Biographies.—Price 2d. each ; 12s. per 100.
    THE REAL MARTIN LUTHER. *Twenty-fifth Thousand.*
    LUTHER'S REAL TEACHING ON CONFESSION, BAPTISM, AND THE SACRAMENT OF THE ALTAR. With his Preface. *Fifth Thousand.*
    THOMAS CRANMER, an English Reformer and sometime Archbishop of Canterbury.
    THOMAS CRANMER, Archbishop of Canterbury, an English Reformer. *Fifth Thousand.*
    THE TRUE JOHN WYCLIFFE. *Second Thousand.*
    THOMAS CROMWELL AND HIS OFFICER.
These biographies are very useful for Missions.

Bowden, C.—Life and Martyrdom of St. Cecilia and her Companions. Edited by FR. CHARLES BOWDEN, of the London Oratory. Limp cloth, 1s. ; wrapper, 6d.

Burke, S. H.—Historical Portraits of the Tudor Dynasty, and the Reformation Period. By S. HUBERT BURKE. Complete in 4 vols. Demy 8vo. 12s. each. "Time unveils all Truth."

Ireland Sixty Years Ago, being an Account of a Visit to Ireland by H.M. King George IV. in the year 1821. By S. HUBERT BURKE. Price 1s.

The Catholic Standard Library.

Under this title is now issuing a Series of Standard Works, consisting of Foreign Translations, Original Works and Reprints, printed in the best style of the typographic art, bound in cloth, in demy 8vo, of from 450 to 500 pages, and issued at short intervals, price 12s. each Volume, net ; *post free to any part of the world;* or twelve Vols. may be selected for £5 5s.

The Great Commentary on the Gospels of Cornelius à Lapide. Translated and Edited by the Rev. T. W. MOSSMAN, D.D. (B.A., Oxon), assisted by various Scholars.

SS. MATTHEW AND MARK'S GOSPELS. 3 Vols. *Fourth Edition.*

S. JOHN'S GOSPEL AND THREE EPISTLES. 2 Vols. *Third Edition.*

S. LUKE'S GOSPEL. 1 Vol. *Third Edition.*

"It would indeed be gilding the finest gold to bestow praise on the great Commentary of à Lapide. It is a work of unequalled—we should say unapproached —value. We specially entreat the clergy not to neglect obtaining so vast a treasure of saintly wisdom, even if, in so doing, they are obliged to sacrifice many volumes far inferior to it in real helpfulness."—*John Bull.*

"Mr. Mossman has done his part as an able and sympathetic scholar might be expected to do it, and the volume, both in translation and execution, is worthy of its author."—*Saturday Review.*

"It is the most erudite, the richest, and altogether the completest Commentary on the Holy Scriptures that has ever been written, and our best thanks are due to Mr. Mossman for having given us, in clear, terse, and vigorous English, the invaluable work of the Prince of Scripture Commentators."—*Dublin Review.*

"Really the Editor has succeeded in presenting the public with a charming book. We have been accustomed to regard à Lapide for consulation rather than to be read. But in the compressed form, clear and easy style, and excellent type in which it now appears, it is a book we can sit down to and enjoy."—*The Month.*

"We set a high store upon this Commentary. There is about it a clearness of thought, a many-sided method of looking at truth, an insight into the deeper meaning, and a fearless devotion which lend a peculiar charm to all that he writes. The great value which his commentaries have for Bible students is in the fact that nowhere else can they find so great a store of patristic and scholastic exegesis."—*Literary World.*

v.

Henry VIII. and the English Monasteries. An Attempt to illustrate the History of their Suppression, with an Appendix, and Maps showing the situation of the religious houses at the time of their dissolution. By FRANCIS AIDAN GASQUET, D.D., O.S.B. 2 Vols. *Fourth Edition.*

"We may say in brief, if what we have already said is not sufficient to show it, that a very important chapter of English history is here treated with a fulness, minuteness and lucidity which will not be found in previous accounts, and we sincerely congratulate Dr. Gasquet on having made such an important contribution to English historical literature."—*Athenæum.*

"The old scandals, universally discredited at the time, and believed in by a later generation, only through prejudice and ignorance, are now dispelled for ever."—*Academy.* Signed, JAMES GAIRDNER.

"A most valuable contribution to ecclesiastical history."—*Saturday Review.*

"A learned, careful and successful vindication of the personal character of the monks. . . . In Mr. Gasquet's skilful hands, the dissolution of the monasteries assumes the proportions of a Greek tragedy."—*Guardian.*

Historical Portraits of the Tudor Dynasty and the Reformation Period. By S. HUBERT BURKE. 4 Vols. *Second Edition.* "Time unveils all Truth.'

"I have read the work with great interest, and I subscribe without hesitation to the eulogy passed on it by the *Daily Chronicle*, as making, as far as I know, a distinct and valuable addition to our knowledge of a remarkable period."—*From a Letter by* MR. GLADSTONE.

"We do not hesitate to avow that, in his estimate of character and events, Mr. Burke is seldom wrong. . . . We heartily wish it a large sale and an extensive circulation."—*The Academy.* Signed, NICHOLAS POCOCK.

"They are full-length portraits, often so life-like, that when placed beside each other, we feel no difficulty in realizing the relations which Mr. Burke aims at establishing between them."—*Annual Register.*

"The author writes history as it should be written. The men and women that pass before us in these portraits are no hard lifeless outlines, but beings of flesh and blood, in whom, and in whose fate we feel a keen and absorbing interest."—*Tablet.*

"We attach great importance to Mr. Burke's work, as it is, we believe, the first attempt on any considerable scale, to collect and arrange in a living picture, the men and women who made the England of to-day. . . . This effort, seriously and conscientiously undertaken, and aided by a graphic and attractive style, must do immense good."—*Dublin Review.*

"No honest student of a most memorable period can afford to neglect the aid of Mr. Burke's long and laborious researches, while the general public will find in his pages all the interest of a romance, and all the charm of novelty about events more than three centuries old. He is also what is rare—an historian of absolute impartiality."—*Life.*

Piconio (Bernardine a). Exposition on St. Paul's Epistles. Translated and Edited by A. H. PRICHARD, B.A., Merton College, Oxford. 3 Vols.

"The learning, the piety, the spiritual-mindedness and loving charity of the author, which deservedly earned for him a high reputation in France, are everywhere conspicuous, and there is a freshness in the mode in which he presents much that is suggestive, hopeful and beautiful."—*National Church.*

"We desire to recommend this book to all. Of course to the priesthood any commendation of it is unnecessary; but among the laity there are many souls, one of whose greatest drawbacks in the spiritual life is unfamiliarity with the Word of God. Let them read the Scriptures daily, if only for a few minutes, let them bear along with them such guides as Piconio, and the Spirit of God will illumine their minds and inflame their hearts with a freshness and vigour of Divine life altogether peculiar."—*New York Catholic World.*

The Dark Ages: A Series of Essays illustrating the State of Religion and Literature in the Ninth, Tenth, Eleventh, and Twelfth Centuries. By the late Dr. MAITLAND, Keeper of the MSS. at Lambeth. Fifth Edition, with an Introduction by FREDERICK STOKES, M.A.

"The Essays as a whole are delightful; although they are full of learning, no one can find them dull or heavy; they abound in well-told stories, amusing quotations, and clever sarcasm. Whatever the previous knowledge of a reader may be, he will be stirred up by these essays to learn more of a subject they treat so pleasantly."—*Saturday Review.*

"No task could be more worthy of a scholar and divine so eminently distinguished as the author of this volume, than a vindication of institutions which had been misrepresented for centuries, and a defence of men who had been maligned by those to whom they had been generous benefactors. We have read this work both with pleasure and profit."—*Athenæum.*

The History of the Popes, from the Close of the Middle Ages. Drawn from the Secret Archives of the Vatican and other Original Sources. By Dr. L. PASTOR, Professor of History in the University of Innsbruck. Translated from the German and Edited by FREDERICK ANTROBUS, of the Oratory. Vols. I., II., III., and IV.

"It would be difficult to name any great historical work written with so obvious an anxiety to tell the truth and nothing but the truth, and should these volumes not meet with a favourable reception, we should regard the event as little short of a literary calamity."—*Daily Chronicle.*

"It is no exaggeration to say that this work is one of the most important historical studies of the present century."—*Tablet.*

The History and Fate of Sacrilege. By Sir HENRY SPELMAN, Kt. Edited, in part from two MSS., Revised and Corrected. With a Continuation, large Additions, and an Introductory Essay. By Two Priests of the Church of England. New Edition, with Corrections, and some Additional Notes by Rev. S. J. EALES, D.C.L.

"All who are interested in Church Endowments and property should get this work, which will be found to be a mine of information on the point with which it deals."—*Newbery House Magazine.*

A Commentary on the Holy Gospels. In 4 Vols. By JOHN MALDONATUS, S.J. Translated and Edited from the original Latin by GEORGE J. DAVIE, M.A., Exeter

College, Oxford, one of the Translators of the Library of the Fathers. *Vols. I. and II. (St. Matthew's Gospel).*

"I have often consulted Maldonatus in the original with advantage, and I am glad to see it in English."—*W. E. Gladstone.*

"Maldonatus is as yet but little known to English readers, yet he was a man of far more ability than à Lapide, and is by far more original in his remarks and explanations."—*Month.*

"To those who may not with facility be able to read the Latin, this English version will be a great boon. The Commentary is certainly one with which a Biblical student should make himself acquainted."—*Guardian.*

The Complete Works of St. Bernard, Abbot of Clairvaux. Translated into English from the edition of DOM JOANNES MABILLON, of the Benedictine Congregation of St. Maur (Paris, 1690), and Edited by SAMUEL J. EALES, D.C.L., Vicar of Stalisfield. Vols. I. and II., containing the Letter of St. Bernard. *Volume III. in the Press.*

"In his writings great natural powers shine forth resplendently, an intellect more than that of the subtle Abelard, an eloquence that was irresistible, an imagination like a poet, and a simplicity that wins the admiration of all. Priests will find it a most valuable book for spiritual reading and sermons. The printing and binding of the work are superb."—*Catholic World* (New York).

"We wish Dr. Eales and his publisher all success in what may be called a noble undertaking."—*Church Quarterly Review.*

"No writer of the Middle Ages is so fruitful of moral inspiration as St. Bernard, no character is more beautiful, and no man in any age whatever so faithfully represented all that was best in the impulses of his time, or exercised so powerful an influence upon it. . . . There is no man whose letters cover so many subjects of abiding interest, or whose influence was so widely spread."—*Athenæum.*

"It is not a little strange that a man of intellect so powerful, and character so noble and self-denying, should have had to wait seven centuries for his works to be rendered into English. . . . The letters are of great historic interest, and many of them most touching. The simple earnestness of the man, and his utter freedom from ambition, strike us on almost every page."—*Notes and Queries.*

"We congratulate both the publisher and the editor upon the issue of these volumes, which we predict will be warmly appreciated by English readers, and which we can thoroughly recommend."—*Literary Churchman.*

"The task which Mr. Eales has undertaken of bringing out an English edition of Bernard's works is one that is deserving of every praise, and we hope that it may be carried to completion by the appearance of the remaining volumes without undue delay."—*Literary World.*

"English readers of every class and creed owe a debt of gratitude to Dr. Eales for the great and useful work which he has undertaken. It is strange that now for the first time has such a task been even, as far as we are aware, approached. . . . In this, the earliest complete English edition of Bernard's works, a reparation, tardy indeed, but ample, is about to be made for the neglect or indifference of so many bygone generations of the English-speaking race. . . . We have, indeed, much to be grateful for to the first English translator of St. Bernard's works."—*The Month.*

Edward VI. and the Book of Common Prayer. Its Origin Illustrated by Hitherto Unpublished Documents. With Four Facsimile Pages of the MS. By FRANCIS AIDAN GASQUET, O.S.B., *(Author of "Henry VIII. and the English Monasteries,")* and EDMUND BISHOP.

"A more accurate history of the changes of Religion and the motives of the statesmen of the reign of Edward VI. than has ever before appeared ; and as regards the antecedents and the compilation of the Prayer Book, we have no hesitation in saying this volume is the most valuable contribution to its history that has appeared since the time of Dr. Cardwell."—*Athenæum.*

"We cannot refrain from expressing our admiration of the method in which the author has conducted his whole inquiry. It ought to have a large circulation, for it contains by far the best account we have ever seen of the changes introduced in Edward VI.'s reign."—*Guardian.*

"This book will occupy a place of special importance in the library of every liturgical student."—*Saturday Review.*

"We may say, without hesitation, that the second, third, and fourth appendices are the most valuable contributions to the early history of the Prayer Book that have yet appeared."—*Church Quarterly Review.*

"This volume is one of the most interesting and valuable contributions to the study of the Reformation in England that has appeared for many a day." —*Academy.*

"The book deserves great praise for its learning and fairness."—*Spectator.*

"We gladly acknowledge our gratitude to its authors, and willingly bespeak for their labour the earnest attention of every priest and layman."—*Church Times.*

"The publication of this book has done more for the elucidation of the history of the first Prayer Book than any writer since Proctor."—*English Churchman.*

"A volume of hardly less than national importance, and most opportune at this moment for the sake of all interested in the Lincoln judgment."—*The Month.*

The Hierurgia; or the Holy Sacrifice of the Mass.
With Notes and Dissertations elucidating its Doctrines and Ceremonies. By Dr. DANIEL ROCK. A New and thoroughly Revised Edition, with many new Illustrations. Edited, with a Preface, by W. H. JAMES WEALE. 2 Vols.

"We hope the 'Hierurgia' may find many readers and command a wide and extensive sale. It is very serviceable as a book of reference."—*Dublin Review.*

The Relations of the Church to Society: A Series of Essays by EDMUND J. O'REILLY, S.J. Edited, with a Biographical Notice, by the Rev. MATTHEW RUSSELL.

The Church of Our Fathers, as seen in St. Osmund's Rite for the Cathedral of Salisbury. By the Rev. Dr. ROCK. A new and Revised Edition. By the Benedictines of Downside. 4 Vols. *Preparing.*

Change in Faith or Development. A Critical Exposition of St. Vincent of Lerins. *Quod ubique quod semper quod ab omnibus.* Addressed to Anglicans. By C. TONDINI DE QUARENGHI, Barnabite. 8vo. 1s.

Central London: Ten Years' Experience of Church Mission Work by EMILE ISH-RWOOD, with a Preface by the REV. R. ISHERWOOD, Senior Curate of St. Martin-in-the-Fields. Price 6d.

Church Congress Reports. Swansea, Leicester, Newcastle-on-Tyne. Demy 8vo. Cloth. Each 10s. 6d.

Church Congress -Complete Set of Church Congress Reports. 32 Vols. in Half-Calf Antique. Red edges. Price £24 net.
This would make a handsome present to a Home or Colonial Library.
Gentlemen having incomplete sets of the Church Congress Reports, and being desirous of completing them, should apply to Mr. Hodges, who has several of the Volumes that are out of print. Sets can be uniformly bound in any style at moderate charges. Back Vols. purchased or exchanged for others.

Church and Cottage Tracts. A Series of Leaflets for General Distribution, Nos. 1 to 48. A Specimen Packet, 1s., post free.

Come to the Woods, and other Poems. By C. J. CORNISH, M.A., Prebendary of Exeter. Cheaper Edition, cloth, gilt edges, 1s. 6d.

Conscience, H. -The Popular Tales of Henry Conscience (the Walter Scott of Flanders). Translated from the Flemish. To be issued in Volumes. In Wrapper, 1s. each.

> Vol.   I.   THE HAPPINESS OF BEING RICH.
> Vol.   II.   THE IRON TOMB.
> Vol.   III. FISHERMAN'S DAUGHTER.
> Vol.   IV.   WOODEN CLARA AND RICKETICKETACK.
> Vol.   V.   THE LOST GLOVE.
> Vol.   VI.   THE PALE YOUNG MAIDEN.
> Vol.   VII. LUDOVIC AND GERTRUDE.
> Vol.   VIII. THE YOUNG DOCTOR.
> Vol.   IX.   THE BLUE HOUSE.
> Vol.   X.   THE FATAL DUEL, etc., etc., etc.

" In simplicity and purity of tone, it leaves nothing to be desired: and like all that Conscience wrote, there is nothing that ordinary people cannot understand. Should have a place in every parish library."—*Church Times.*

Copinger, A. E.—A Short and Easy Catechism on the Creed. For the Young. Price 4d.

Creedy.—Mr. Daniel Creedy, M.P. An Extravaganza. Price 6d. Post Free.

Devotional Readings.—Being selected passages from the Rev. H. E. Manning's Anglican Sermons. *Second Thousand.* Limp cloth, 1s. ; cloth, bevelled boards, 1s. 6d.

Divine Counsels ; or, the Young Christian's Guide to Wisdom. Translated from ARVISENET, by Rev. W. B. CAPARN, M.A., with a Preface by JOHN SHARP, M.A., Vicar of Horbury. Cloth. 1s.

"A welcome addition to devotional literature : it should be in the hands of all young persons of an age to be preparing for Confirmation and First Communion. The style of the work is suggestive of the *Imitatio Christi*, and the teaching it contains is thoroughly plain and practical, while full of religious earnestness and devotion."—*Church Times.*

Drexelius, J.—The Heliotropium ; or, Conformity of the Human Will to the Divine. By JEREMY DREXELIUS. Translated from the original Latin. With a Preface by the late Bishop FORBES. Second Edition. Crown 8vo. 5s. net.

"A rational and simple-minded piety runs through the whole work, which forms excellent material for devotional reading, especially for men."—*Guardian.*
"An excellent book, and one that deserves to be more used than it is."—*Literary Churchman.*

Edward VI. and the Book of Common Prayer. Its origin illustrated by hitherto unpublished documents. By FRANCIS AIDAN GASQUET, O.S.B. (author of "Henry VIII. and the English Monasteries"), and EDMUND BISHOP. Demy 8vo. 12s. *Third Thousand.*

Evans, A. B.—Reflections Delivered at the Mid-Day Celebration of Holy Communion in the Church of S. Mary-le-Strand. By A. B. EVANS, D.D., Rector. Crown 8vo. *Third Edition in the Press.*

"Let a man, before preparing his own sermon, sit down and read through carefully and slowly one of these 'Reflections,' and he will certainly derive a lesson in method, and instruction how to reflect, from a true master of the science, which he could not easily learn elsewhere."—*Ecclesiastical Gazette.*

Gasquet, F. A.—Henry VIII. and the English Monasteries. An Attempt to Illustrate the History of their Suppression, with an Appendix, and Maps showing the situation of the religious houses at the time of their dissolution. By FRANCIS AIDAN GASQUET, O.S.B. 2 Vols. Demy 8vo. 12s. each. *Fourth Edition.*

Good Friday—How shall I keep it? With picture of the Crucifixion. 5s. per 100.

Hancock, T. Christ and the People. Sermons on the Obligations of the Church to the State and to the People. By THOMAS HANCOCK, M.A., Lecturer at St. Nicholas Cole Abbey. Second edition. Crown 8vo. 6s.

"As compared with the general run of pious, feminine, hazy sermons, they are as a breeze on the hill-top to the close atmosphere of a sick-room, with its faint smell of medicines and perfumes."—*Church Times.*

Headlam, S. D.—Priestcraft and Progress. Lectures and Sermons, by STEWART D. HEADLAM, B.A. *Fourth thousand.* 1s.

Headlam, S. D.—The Service of Humanity, and other Sermons. Price 2s. 6d.

"Almost every page contains suggestive hints which all will do well to ponder, especially those brought into contact with secularism and infidelity.—*Ecclesiastical Gazette.*
"Our advice to the clergy and laity is to get this book, read it, and preach it, and live by it."—*Church Times.*

Headlam, S. D.—The Laws of Eternal Life, being Studies in the Church Catechism. Price 2s.

Headlam, S. D.—Lessons from the Cross, being Addresses given on Good Friday. 1s. 6d.

Headlam, S. D.—The Theory of Theatrical Dancing. Edited from CARLO BLASIS, with the Original Plates. 8vo. Cloth. 3s. 6d.

Headlam, S. D. The Function of the Stage: A Lecture. Sewed. 6d.

HEROES OF THE CROSS.

Under this title is now publishing a series of biographies of eminent Christians, who have lived in all ages of the Christian Church. The lives will aim to be historical rather than devotional, and controversy will be avoided. Each biography will be complete in one vol., crown 8vo, cloth, 3s. 6d.

St. Gregory the Great. By the Right Rev. ABBOT SNOW, O.S.B. (*Ready*).

Christopher Columbus. His Life, Labours and Discoveries. By MARIANO MONTEIRO. (*Ready*).

Hugh of Avalon, Bishop of Lincoln. By Rev. GEORGE G. PERRY, M.A., Rector of Waddington and Canon of Lincoln. *In the Press.*

St. Stephen Harding. Founder of the Cistercian Order. Reprinted from "Newman's Lives of the Saints." *In the Press.*

The Most Rev. Robert Grey, D.D., Bishop of Cape Town and Metropolitan, by S. J. EALES, D.C.L., Vicar of Stalisfield. *In the Press.*

Holy Communion, the Service for the Celebration of, Commonly called the Canon. According to the use of the Famous and Illustrious Church of Sarum in England, being the only office authorised for use at the Celebration of the Most Holy Eucharist. Price 6d.

Holy Men of Old. Being Short Lives of the Saints, with Meditations for Every Day in the Year, by R. W. LOWDER. To be issued in twelve monthly parts at 1s. each, October, November and December ready. Each part is complete in itself, and contains one Month of the Calendar. Admirably adapted for reading at Family Prayer.

Hours of the Passion, Including in full the Daily Office for Morning and Night, chiefly after the Ancient English Use of Salisbury, with other Devotional Forms, for private and household use. Compiled and Edited by a Priest of the Church of England. Second and Revised Edition. Cloth. Red edges. 2s. 6d.

Ignatius.—Father Ignatius in America. BY FATHER MICHAEL, O.S.B. Crown 8vo, with frontispiece. 6s.

In the Light of the Twentieth Century. By INNOMATUS. Crown 8vo. 2s. 6d.

"This book is undeniably clever, full of close and subtle reasoning, lighted up with keen epigrammatic wit."—*Literary World.*

Jones.—Dishonest Criticism. Being a Chapter of Theology on Equivocation, and Doing Evil for a good cause. An answer to Dr. RICHARD F. LITTLEDALE. By JAMES JONES, S.J., Professor to Moral Theology in St. Beuno's College. Crown 8vo. 3s. 6d.

"Nothing like it has appeared since Newman's reply to Kingsley."—*John Bull*

Justorium Semita (The Path of the Just), being the Lives of the Saints commemorated in the Calendar in the Book of Common Prayer, a new edition of a book which has been many years out of print. *In the Press.*

Lights and Shadows.—Stories of Every-day Life. One vol., containing Thirteen Stories. Cloth. 2s. 6d., or in 3 parts, 6d. each.

Maitland, S. R.—The Dark Ages : A Series of Essays illustrating the State of Religion and Literature in the Ninth, Tenth, Eleventh, and Twelfth Centuries. By the late DR. MAITLAND, Keeper of the MSS. at Lambeth. Fifth Edition, with an introduction by FREDERICK STOKES, M.A. Demy 8vo. 12s.

Mermillod, Cardinal.—Lectures to Ladies on the Supernatural Life. By Cardinal MERMILLOD, Bishop of Lausanne and Geneva. Translated from the French, with the Author's sanction, by a Lady. Crown 8vo. 3s. 6d.

"These addresses are fine specimens of compilation which seem to stand midway between that of a meditation and a sermon. The spiritual teaching is most direct and excellent."—*Literary Churchman.*

Maldonatus, J.—A Commentary on the Holy Gospels. In 4 vols. By JOHN MALDONATUS, S.J. Translated and Edited from the original Latin by GEORGE J. DAVIE, M.A., Exeter College, Oxford, one of the Translators of the Library of the Fathers. *Vols. I. and II. (St. Matthew's Gospel.).* Demy 8vo. 12s. each.

Manuals for the People. Nos. 1 to 21. A Specimen Set. 1s. 9d.

Montifeore, A.—Life of Christopher Columbus. By Miss MONTIFEORE. Crown 8vo. 3s. 6d.

Mossman, T. W.—Mr. Gray and His Neighbours. By T. W. MOSSMAN, D.D. Second Edition. 2 vols. Crown 8vo. 9s.

"Mr. Gunter, the very unspiritual Rector, who cares less for principle than for preferment, and who makes his Laodicean principles pay, is a clever caricature."—*Standard.*

"The entire absence of goodliness or sentimentality in the way the matter is handled, and the mode in which Mr. Gray and his daughter are depicted as dealing with it, deserve warm praise."—*Academy.*

"Bishop Stubblegrass is equal to Bishop Proudie himself, which is saying not a little."—*Nonconformist.*

"Alice Gray is a finely-drawn character with all the virtues of a sincere Christian and the heroism of a Grace Darling. The style of composition is that of an accomplished scholar." —*Stamford Mercury.*

By the same Author.

Latin Latter, A. (with an English Translation) to his Holiness Pope Leo XIII., Successor of St. Peter, and Primate of the Catholic Church. By THOMAS W. MOSSMAN, D.D., Rector of Torrington, Lincolnshire. 1s.

The Relations which at present Exist between Church and State in England. A letter to the Right Hon. W. E. GLADSTONE, M.P. 8vo. Price 1s.

New Musical Works. By HENRY F. HEMY. Author of "Hemy's Pianoforte Tutor."

The Children's Musical Longfellow, Containing about 400 Songs. The Words from Longfellow. To be published in Shilling Parts, each complete in itself, and sold everywhere. Part I., containing 25 Songs. Price 1s.

The Westminster Hymnal for Congregational Use. Part I. containing 52 Hymns for Advent and Christmas. Price 1s.

Notes on Ingersoll. By the Rev. L. A. LAMBERT, of Waterloo, New York. Revised and Reprinted from the 50th Thousand. American Edition, price 1s. 6d.

"By far the ablest antagonist infidelity has met with. Every possible objection brought by Ingersoll against Christianity is completely crushed by Lambert."—*Guardian.*

"We hail with gladness the appearance of this volume, and heartily wish it the extensive circulation in England it has had in America."—*Rock.*

Our Vicar's Stories. In Six Numbers, 6d. Each. Illustrated. Edited by Rev. H. C. SHUTTLEWORTH, M.A. Also the First and Second Series. Cloth, 1s. 6d. each. And the Six Numbers in 1 Volume, Cloth, gilt, 2s. 6d.

    No. 1.—RHODA ST. BARB.
    No. 2.—TRUE AS STEEL.
    No. 3.—SUNFLOWER COURT: A Christmas Story.
    No. 4.—THE PEARL MERCHANTS.
    No. 5.—IN THE NEW FOREST.
    No. 6.—JEM, A REAL REFORMER.

"Well adapted for lending libraries and school prizes, and very like our old favourite 'The Curate's Budget.'"—*Church Bells.*

Peacock, E.—**Narcissa Brendon, A Romance.** By EDWARD PEACOCK, F.S.A., etc. 2 vols. Crown 8vo. 12s.

Pathway, The. A Practical Guide to Instruction and Devotion in the Elements of Christian Religion. Demy 18mo. Limp Cloth, 1s. Cloth Boards, 1s. 6d. Limp Persian, 2s. 6d.

"It is truly a pathway to the practice of devotion on the lines of the teaching of the Church of England, and is just such a book as we should like to see in the hands of every boy and every girl in the kingdom."—*Church Times.*

Perry, G.—**Life of Hugh of Avelon, Bishop of Lincoln.** A new and revised edition by GEORGE PERRY, M.A., Canon of Lincoln. Crown 8vo. *In the Press.*

Piconio (Bernardine a). Exposition on St. Paul's Epistles. Translated and Edited by A. H. PRICHARD, B.A., Merton College, Oxford. 3 Vols., Demy 8vo., 12s. each.

Public Health.—**A Popular Guide to the Rights** and the Duties of the Inhabitants of the County of London. By W. ADDINGTON WILLIS, LL.B. (Lond.), of the Inner Temple, Barrister-at-Law. Price 1s.

Rock, D.—**The Church of our Fathers, as seen in** St. Osmund's Rite for the Cathedral of Salisbury. By the late Rev. DR. D. ROCK. A New and Revised Edition. By the Benedictines of Downside. 4 Vols. *Preparing.*

Rock, D.— **The Hierurgia; or, the Holy Sacrifice of** the Mass. With Notes and Dissertations elucidating its doctrines and ceremonies. By the late Dr. DANIEL ROCK. A New and thoroughly Revised Edition, with many new Illustrations. Edited, with a Preface, by W. H. JAMES WEALE. Demy 8vo, 12s.

A Large Paper Edition, limited to 250 copies, printed on fine laid paper, with red rubric lines, price £2 10s., to secure copies of which, immediate application is necessary.

Spelman, H.—**The History and Fate of Sacrilege.** By Sir HENRY SPELMAN, Kt. Edited in part from two MSS., revised and corrected. With a Continuation, large Additions, and an Introductory Essay. By two Priests of the Church of England. Fourth Edition, with Corrections, and some Additional Notes by Dr. EALES, Demy 8vo.

Snow, T. B.—St. Gregory the Great, His Work, and his Spirit. By the Right Rev. ABBOT SNOW, O.S.B. Crown 8vo. Wrapper 2s. 6d., cloth extra, top edge gilt, 3s. 6d.

Sacristy, The, A Review of Ecclesiastical Art and Literature. Two vols., handsomely bound in cloth, top edge gilt, 12s. 6d. each ; or, One Guinea the Two Vols. on direct application to the publisher. Only a few copies remain.

"Such a contribution to the folk lore of Europe cannot but be welcomed by all antiquarians. . . We do not know when we have experienced greater pleasure, or learned more from the perusal of any book. As in matter it is excellent, so in its get-up it reflects the greatest credit upon its publisher."—*Weekly Register.*

Salvation—How shall I gain it? By LESLIE MAXWELL. Price 4d.

Staniforth, T. W., Carols, Hymns and Noels for Christmastide. 20 Selected and Edited. By THOMAS WORLEY STANIFORTH. Price 1s. Already the book has been adopted for use in several Churches.

"Some of them are very beautiful, and certain to become popular."—*Morning Post.*

Thoughts for Those that Mourn. Eleventh Thousand. Cloth, 1s. Roan and Red Edges, 2s. 6d.

The Treatise of St. Catherine of Genoa on Purgatory. Newly translated, with an introduction of Hell and the Future State. Price 2s.

Thoughts and Suggestions for Sisters of Charity, and for those desirous of becoming Sisters, with Heads of Mental Prayer and Consideration. Second Edition. 2s. 6d.

Winter, A.—Problems of Life. By Alexander Winter. Crown 8vo. Limp Cloth. 2s.

Order in the Physical World and its First Cause according to Modern Science. From the French by T. J. SLEVIN. One Vol. 3s. 6d.

The Life of Pope Adrian IV. (Nicholas Brakespeare), *The Only English Pope.* By the Right Rev. EDWARD TROLLOPE, D.D., Bishop of Nottingham, Suffragan of Lincoln. One Vol. *In the Press.*

JOHN HODGES, 7, AGAR STREET, CHARING CROSS, W.C.

www.ingramcontent.com/pod-product-compliance
Lightning Source LLC
Chambersburg PA
CBHW021405230426
43666CB00006B/639